day trade online

Founded in 1807, John Wiley & Sons is the oldest independent publishing company in the United States. With offices in North America, Europe, Australia, and Asia, Wiley is globally committed to developing and marketing print and electronic products and services for our customers' professional and personal knowledge and understanding.

The Wiley Trading series features books by traders who have survived the market's ever changing temperament and have prospered—some by reinventing systems, others by getting back to basics. Whether a novice trader, professional, or somewhere in-between, these books will provide the advice and strategies needed to prosper today and well into the future.

For a list of available titles, please visit our Web site at www.Wiley Finance.com.

day trade online

online

Second Edition

CHRISTOPHER A. FARRELL

WILEY

John Wiley & Sons, Inc.

This revision is dedicated in the memory of my father, who lost his battle with cancer in December 2001, but won in the game of life.

---

*"I have fought the good fight.
I have finished the race.
I have kept the faith."*

CONTENTS

Preface   xiii

Acknowledgments   xix

Introduction   1

SECTION I
THE WORLD OF THE DAY TRADER   5

Chapter 1.   Exploiting the Excesses of Capitalism   7

The House Edge   9
The Bid-Ask Spread   11

SECTION II
INTRODUCTION TO DAY TRADING   17

Chapter 2.   Trading 101: Buying on Bad News and Selling
on Good News   19

The Mind-set of an Online Day Trader   19
A Buyer When the Market Needs Buyers   20
Hit Singles, Not Home Runs   20
Brokerage Commissions Can Destroy Profits   21
Buy in on Fear, Sell in on Greed   22
The Slow Execution   23
Is the NYSE an Easier Market to Trade?   24

SECTION III
HOW TO BEAT WALL STREET AT ITS OWN GAME   25

Chapter 3.   Exploiting Wall Street's Conflict of Interest: Market
Orders versus Limit Orders   27

Understanding Wall Street's Conflict of Interest   27
Price Makers versus Price Takers   29
The Bargaining Process   30
Price Negotiation—Market versus Limit Orders   32
Wall Street's Prey   34
Prelude to the Bid-Ask Spread   35

Chapter 4.   The Day Trader's Crystal Ball: Understanding the
Bid-Ask Spread   37

A Snapshot of a Moving Picture   37
The Mechanics of Price Movement—Understanding
What Makes a Stock Move Higher   39
Example 1: The Quote—Snapshot of a Moving Picture   41
Example 2: The Market Order to Sell—Hitting the Bid   46
Example 3: The Market Order to Buy—Lifting
the Offer   48
Example 4: The Limit Order to Buy—Bidding
for Stock   50
Day Orders versus Good-until-Canceled (GTC)
Orders   52
Example 5: The Limit Order to Sell—Offering Stock   54
Haggling Over Nickels and Dimes   56
Example 6: Moving the Stock Higher   57

Chapter 5.   The Role of the Specialist on the New York
Stock Exchange   61

Using the Specialist System to Your Advantage   64
What If There Were No NYSE Specialist?   66
Buyer of Last Resort   67
Is the Profit the Specialist Makes Justified?   68
A License to Steal?   68
The Specialist's Limit Order Book   69
Being on Both Sides of the Market   71
Narrowing the Bid-Ask Spread   72
Wide Spreads Protect the Specialist from Volatility   73
Handling a Large Sell Order   74
The Real Intentions of the Specialists   77
Beware When the Specialist Takes the Other Side of
Your Trade   77
The Day Trader as a Shadow Specialist   78
The NYSE's Fair Order Handling Rules   80
Never Reveal Your Hand   85

How Can You Determine Where the Specialist Lurks
   in the Stock?   85
Jockeying for Position   87
How Do You Know Where You Stand in Line?   89
When in Doubt, Ask the NYSE Floor   89
Tipping the Odds in Your Favor   92
Beware of the Specialist   93

SECTION IV
INTRODUCTION TO SCALPING THE NYSE: TAKING FOOD OUT
OF THE SPECIALIST'S MOUTH   **95**

Chapter 6.   The Day Trader's Secret Weapon: Exploiting
             the Bid-Ask Spread   97

             How Can You Make Money Trading Stocks that
                Don't Move?   98
             The Role of the Scalper   99
             Hit Singles, Not Home Runs   100
             Operating under the Radar   100
             Avoiding the Glamour Stocks   102
             Exploiting the Bid-Ask Spread   103
             Finding the Trade's Sweet Spot   103
             Simplifying a Complex Process   104
             Other Moving Parts to This Trade   105
             A Bet with the House?   109
             Too Much Work for Only $100 in Gross Profits?   110
             A Few Words on Risk   110

SECTION V
TRADING THE MARKET'S MOMENTUM: HOW TO PROFIT FROM VOLATILITY   **113**

Chapter 7.   Exploiting Market Volatility and Momentum: Strategies
             for Trading Volatile Stocks   115

             The Specialist and the Upper Hand   116
             Playing the Gap Open—A Strategy for Betting
                with the House   117
             Buying on Bad News   118
             Betting on the Specialist   119
             Parameters of the Gap-Opening Trade   122
             How to Tell If the Opening Trade Will "Clear"
                the Specialist's Limit Order Book   124

Selling before the Second Wave   125
Trading Tick for Tick with the Market Indexes   127
Why Limit Orders Don't Work in a Rally   127
Using the S&P Futures to Gauge the Sustainability
    of a Rally   129
Lightning-Fast Market Upsurge: How Offers Vanish
    in the Vapor Trail   129
Stock for Sale Becoming Scarce   130
Nasdaq and the Role of the Market Makers   131
A Few Words on Short Selling   135
Two Methods for Day Trading Nasdaq Stocks   136
The Apple Computer Trade   139
Buying Strong Stocks on Pullbacks   140
Opening the Stock Abnormally High   141
The Dangers of Buying a Strong Stock on the
    Opening Trade   141
Inflicting Heavy Damage on the Market Makers by
    Attacking Their Vulnerability   142

Chapter 8.   The Day Trader's Ticket to the Poorhouse: How I
    Managed to Lose $12,000 in Less than 24 Hours   145

The Pain of Missing a Trade   147
How Could the Stock Go Any Lower?   147
The Terrifying Feeling of Getting Caught
    in a Downdraft   148
A Feeling of Irresistible Greed   148
The Need to Break Even   150
Buying the Stock for the Third Time   151
Feeling of Devastation Leads to Useful Insights   152
Learning from the Mistake and Moving On   156
Can the Quoted Market Always Be Trusted?   156
A Fool and His Money Are Soon Parted   159

Appendix A.   The Day Trader's Arsenal: Online Brokers, Trade
    Commissions, Real-Time Quote Systems, and the
    Home Office   161

Choosing an Online Broker   161
Negotiate the Best Possible Commission Rate   163
Make Sure that the Broker Can Route Directly
    to the NYSE   163
Per-Share versus Per-Trade Commission Rates   164
Setting up at Least Two Accounts   164
System Crashes and the Late Fill   165

Customer Service, Back-Office Problems, and Trade
   Discrepancies   167
The Remedy—Keep Good Trading Records   167
The Home Office and the Virtual Trading Floor   169

Appendix B.   Considerations for Trading for a Living: The
   Allocation of Trading Capital, the Pattern Day
   Trader Rule, Using Margin and Trading Part-Time
   vs. Full-Time   173

Allocation of Trading Capital   174
The Pattern Day Trader Rule   177
Trading on Margin   177
Margin Calls   178
Part-Time versus Full-Time Trading   179

Index   183

PREFACE

It's 8:00 Monday morning, and I awake to the sounds of my alarm clock. I couldn't be happier: It is the beginning of another trading week. I roll out of bed, "commute" into the next room, and turn on my computer. The workweek has begun.

But this is not your typical 9-to-5 job. There is no office to go to, no rush hour subway commute, and no "good mornings" to co-workers. There is no boss in the next room. I don't produce a product, nor do I sell one. When people ask me what I do for a living, I pause. In fact, I don't really "do" anything. There are no projects and no deadlines. There are no co-workers, no staff, and most of all, no friends. I am known by account number only. I am in total isolation. The entire trading day I may not see or speak to another soul. The work is extremely intense. The pace is fast. It is a job unlike any other in the world.

Sometimes I do feel guilty. For over a decade, I have answered to no one. My day is spent in the comfort of my own home. People may criticize what I do, but on a good day I can make more money in a single afternoon than most of them may make in three months, without ever leaving the house. And on a bad day, I could lose that much or more. Still, I am not providing a service to anyone. Is the world a better place because of what I do? Sometimes I don't think so. Very few people understand. They think it's gambling: I tell them it's not.

I am a day trader. My job is to buy and sell stocks for a living. I do not work on Wall Street. My seat is not on the floor of the New York Stock Exchange, it is in cyberspace. This is rarefied air. These are untested waters. I am among a new breed of entrepreneur and this is a new frontier. But do I have what it takes? Mentally, am I strong enough?

I've been doing this for 11 years. In the past I have made very good money. But the past is for cowards. And there are no guarantees. Today I must make money.

It is now 9:30. The bell has rung and the stock market is open. I take my seat at the table with the world's biggest banks, brokerage firms, and mutual funds. The chess match has begun.

It is hard to believe that nearly a decade has passed since I first wrote *Day Trade Online.* In 1998, when I put pen to paper as a first-time author at the age of 25, never in my wildest dreams did I envision the amazing journey that I was to embark upon. So here we are in 2008, preparing a revision to a book that became not only a national bestseller, but has been translated into languages around the world as well. To say that I am both honored and humbled by the response to this book over the past decade is an understatement.

It is my hope that this book is even more relevant today than it was when it was first written. There has never been a better time to trade the New York Stock Exchange than right now. Over the past few years, the NYSE has undergone more changes than perhaps at any other point in its long and storied history. These structural changes to the market have benefited the investing public in ways that were once only dreamed of and, in the process, have created tremendous opportunities for speculators to profit—but only if they know what to look for.

This is a golden age for online trading. Undoubtedly, you have heard stories of savvy short-term traders, day traders, who have been able to make a living buying and selling stocks, sometimes in a period of minutes or even seconds. The goal of this book is to provide a comprehensive overview of how to be consistently profitable by trading stocks over the Internet. We will examine all aspects of this exciting arena, from what it takes to get started to an in-depth analysis of which trading techniques work, which don't, and why. Most importantly, the book will show you how to beat Wall Street at its own game by exploiting the buying and selling of the investing public in the same manner that the Street's most powerful brokerage firms and trading houses do.

The information provided here will reveal closely held and profitable short-term trading secrets that can only be learned from having worked on one of Wall Street's trading floors, combined with the real-life experience of someone who makes a living trading over the Internet. Quite simply, this is information that most stockbrokers, financial planners, and everyday investors do not possess. With this in mind, the emphasis is on simplicity. The best and most successful traders are those who keep things simple. This is a book on trading, not investing. Therefore, it is written in a practical, nontheoretical manner for the reader who might have little or no investment experience, but only the desire to learn more about one of the most exciting businesses of the millennium.

After graduating from Colgate University in 1995, where I majored in philosophy and religion, I began my career working for two large brokerage firms. First for Olde Discount in Detroit, then for Gruntal & Company, a firm founded in 1880, located at 14 Wall Street, right across the street from the New York Stock Exchange. At the age of 22, I was trading literally millions of dollars of the firm's capital. It didn't take long to learn how Wall Street made its money. There was a system in place, and there were traders such as myself whose sole job it was to exploit that system for profit. That's when I came to the realization that the knowledge I had, if used the right way, could make me substantial amounts of money. I also decided I had wasted enough time making other people rich.

This was around the same time online trading was beginning to come into its own. The landscape of investing was changing and, thanks to the Internet, trades were becoming extremely cheap. It was slowly becoming clear that it was no longer necessary to work on Wall Street to participate in this game. The rules were changing, and the Internet was the key.

That was all I needed to know. For me, this was the opportunity of a lifetime, and I wasn't going to waste another minute. At the age of 23, I left Wall Street and began an exciting journey that led me to write this book. And now, some 12 years later, I am reflecting back upon what I have learned.

I wrote *Day Trade Online* for several reasons. First, it was to show the investing world that there is an alternative to the buy-hold-and-pray strategy that most retail investors unfortunately utilize. In fact, as I write this in the spring of 2008, had you invested in the S&P 500 index on December 31, 1999, and held until now, over seven years later, you would have actually *lost* money. Of course, there is a place in every stock portfolio for long-term investing; but don't believe them when they say it is the only game in town.

Second, I wrote this book to reveal the ways in which Wall Street is in the business of trading against the investing public, and to show how their profitability is made *at your expense.* Many of these trading strategies were shrouded in secrecy for decades, and were known only by the highly paid traders at the large Wall Street firms that employed them. The investing public, in most instances, didn't even realize the extent to which they were being exploited. However, with the advent of online trading, the secretive world of stock trading became open for all to see.

Some things never change. The house edge that Wall Street has had over the public for decades is in part still there. Even with the advancements in technology and the drastic changes to the rules that govern trading, the public is still at an inherent disadvantage to the market makers and floor traders that handle the public's buy and sell orders. However, there is a way to turn the tables, to put the odds in your favor, and to beat the Wall Street trading firms at their own game. After you read this book, you will know how.

Third, I wrote this book to answer some of the common myths, misinformation, and misperceptions that exist with regard to stock trading. Among them, to show the reader that you don't have to trade the most volatile Nasdaq stocks to make a living as a day trader. As I explain in detail, sometimes the NYSE and its specialist system can be an easier market to trade. Furthermore, you also do not need a bull market in stocks to make money as a trader. Bear markets and sideways markets can be just as profitable.

My hope is that this book stands in contrast to the many critics of short-term trading, who, for as long as I have been trading, have said that day trading doesn't work, can't work, and never will work. This is based upon a fundamental misunderstanding of how the NYSE's specialist system works, and how an aggressive trader can exploit that system for profit. The idea that the individual, with his or her own capital, can exploit the short-term movements of the market in the same way that the big Wall Street trading firms do, the same way that the specialists on the floor of the NYSE do, goes against the grain of what these critics learned in Finance and Investing 101. So be it.

The critics of day trading base their argument on the idea that high portfolio turnover is devastating to long-term returns. Undoubtedly, you have heard the drumbeat of financial planners, academics, and financial magazine writers alike who proclaim that aggressively trading in and out of your stock portfolio is the pathway to ruin. You won't hear traders on Wall Street echo that sentiment. This is because they are too busy making millions trading in and out of the market to heed that advice.

The critics of day trading, however, are partially right. If you excessively trade when the odds are not in your favor, the money will go out of your pocket and into the pocket of the person taking the other side of your trades. But, if you are careful and trade only when the odds are in your favor, you will likely come out a winner over time. Case in point: I estimate that I have turned my own portfolio over some 5,000 times in 11 years. 5,000 times! I have paid upwards of 1 million dollars in online brokerage commissions, at $8 bucks per trade. Adding up the buys and sells, I estimate that I have traded over 3 billion dollars worth of stock (billion with a "b") and have traded several hundred millions shares. All of this from my home office, by myself, with a relatively small capital base by Wall Street standards. I hope that this proves that there is an edge in the marketplace. If there weren't, with my own level of high turnover, I would have been buried long ago. The point here is that the independent trader, with a modest capital base, can compete and thrive in a marketplace dominated by large Wall Street trading houses.

Unfortunately, day trading will always have a stigma attached to it. I often joke that the day trader is the ugly stepchild of Wall Street. Part of this lies in the fact that it, unfortunately, has always attracted some of the worst of characters: quick-buck artists and charlatans alike. The get-rich-quick mentality is the worst kind of mind-set to have when approaching the markets. In fact, it goes against everything that I try to teach in this book. This is a long-term endeavor, one of grinding out high percentage profits and putting your capital at risk only when the odds are in your favor.

There are literally thousands of trading opportunities per day. Some only last for minutes, or seconds, but they are out there for the taking if you know what to look for. No one is saying that it is easy or without risk. Nothing worthwhile ever is. There are two sides to every trade: a winner and a loser. And the odds are constantly changing. Sometimes they are well in your favor, and sometimes they are not. This book will help you differentiate between the two.

Thus, my sincere wish is that when you, the reader, finish this book, you will never look at the stock market in the same way again. Once you see the market through the mind-set not as an investor, but as a market maker, an NYSE specialist, you will view buying and selling in a way that you have never done before: from the perspective of the person taking the other side of your trade. Your time is very valuable and I take this responsibility very seriously. You will not be disappointed. I promise.

For additional trading tips, updates and information on the author, please visit his web site at www.farrelltrading.com.

Warning

This book is not a get-rich-quick endeavor. It is meant as a primer on how the stock market works and provides insight into methods for exploiting inefficiencies in how stocks trade for profit. It is not meant to be taken as an end-all, be-all on how to trade stocks for a living. This is a risky business with a high failure rate, in part because of some of the market mechanics and the destructive forces of the "house edge" that we explain here. Said another way, day trading is not for everyone. Anyone who thinks that all they have to do is read this book and then they will get rich in the market should not be trading in the first place. In fact, it is contradictory to the central message that I convey in this book, one of protecting your hard-earned trading capital, and putting it at risk only when the odds are in your favor. Proceed with caution and at your own risk.

NOTE TO READERS

As of the writing of this revision in the fall of 2008, the stress and strain that our markets are under due to the credit crisis is quite possibly a once in a lifetime event. Anyone who has traded for long enough has seen stressful times before, whether the Asian currency crises of 1998, the dot.com bubble and its bursting in 2000, and of course the September 11 terrorist attacks and the wars that have followed. Each period of crises offers incredible opportunities for traders, and this one is no different. From a trading standpoint, this market has offered some of the best trading opportunities that I have seen in my entire career. As long as there are supply and demand imbalances in the market, there will be opportunities for traders to profit, whether in bull, bear, or sideways markets. It has been reported in the media that in the midst of this panic, the NYSE specialist firms have put a substantially higher amount of their own capital at risk than in more normal market conditions. The fact that they are willing to put their money where their mouth is by buying into the investing public's selling during this market turmoil is further proof of the opportunities for profit that are possible. However, this is not a market for the faint of heart and there is, without question, a higher degree of trading risk and market volatility in this market than in any market I have seen in my career. Trade accordingly. Proceed with caution and at your own risk.

ACKNOWLEDGMENTS

On a professional note, I want to thank my publisher John Wiley & Sons, especially editor Pamela van Giessen, for their continued commitment to the success of this book for well over a decade. In addition, I want to thank editorial assistant Kate Wood and the many other people at John Wiley who have worked hard to make this revision a reality.

INTRODUCTION

Betting with the House

Trading the stock market is a little bit like poker. You can bluff, you can posture. You can pretend to do something different. If I have 100,000 or 5,000 to sell, I can show you 500 shares. As the bell is closing in on me, as the day comes to a close, all of the bluffing and the posturing disappear, and you do what you have to do.

—Art Cashin, Director of NYSE Floor Operations,
UBS on CNBC, Nov. 13, 2007

The stock market is perhaps more volatile today than at any time in history. Markets move suddenly and without warning, creating and destroying wealth in ways the majority of market participants simply do not understand. In the rarefied air of stock speculating, fortunes can be made and lost in a matter of seconds. The naive and inexperienced will quickly learn that it is not a place for the faint of heart. Still, many people would love to trade for a living, if only they knew how.

It is often said that the market will humble those who do not respect its power. There are many day traders who enter the financial arena for the first time without having any respect for or real understanding of the system or of the risks that are involved. These people will only last so long before the market inevitably crushes them. In fact, statistics show that the majority of day traders lose money. Before you risk even a single penny of your trading capital, you must understand what you are getting yourself into. Good day traders can make thousands of dollars in a single day. Bad traders can lose that much or more. You have to proceed cautiously. With that in mind, it is my hope that this book will act as a good primer so that you may successfully compete in the world of stock trading.

What is the key to making a living as a day trader? To answer this question, you have to look to Wall Street for answers. Wall Street is better at the business of making money than any other industry in the world. Look at the large brokerage firms, banks, and trading firms. How do they make their money? What is it they do to generate billions of dollars per year in profits by trading stocks? Where is the money coming from? I will devote a good portion of the next few chapters to answering these questions. Why is this important? Because as a day trader, you are doing the exact same thing with your money as Wall Street does with its money. Understanding how the system works is the first step in seeing how to exploit it for profit. And exploiting the system is the only way it is possible to make a living as a day trader.

Once you get a little insight into how Wall Street works, we will then formulate a specific strategy on understanding how stocks actually trade. The emphasis in the beginning is on the inherent disadvantages that face the day trader who trades over the Internet. We will spend a good deal of time on the mechanics of the market maker system, the specialist, and the bid-ask spread. This will lay the groundwork for formulating the differences between trading New York Stock Exchange (NYSE) stocks and National Association of Securities Dealers Automated Quotation (Nasdaq) stocks.

Finally, we will get down to the task at hand: day trading. I will use a more conservative approach that focuses on exploiting short-term inefficiencies in the way that NYSE-listed stocks trade, starting with lower-volatility stocks, before venturing into the volatile, high-risk, high-reward domain of more volatile stocks. This way, you will become acquainted with the principles of supply and demand in areas that are slower moving, instead of jumping headfirst into the volatile sectors of the market. When you finish with the book, my hope is that you will see that day trading is far different than you first thought it was.

The trading strategies outlined in this book encompass a wide area of the universe of stock speculation. This book will touch on many subjects, each important in its own right. I write from experience, and I only write about things that I think will affect the bottom line—trading profits. Along the way, your understanding of how the game works will hopefully deepen tremendously. You must be patient and give yourself time to understand these concepts. To the beginner, they are not easy. But they will come with time. The better you understand them, the better your chances success will be.

Here is a summary of the 16 major themes of the book:

1. Wall Street is in the business of trading against its customers, and earns its profits at the expense of the investing public.

2. The day trader earns his or her profits at the expense of Wall Street, by beating it at its own game.

3. Day trading has very little to do with long-term investing. The time horizon on the day trader is so short that, in general, the principles of buy-and-hold investing do not apply.

4. Day trading is the art of anticipating and exploiting temporary supply and demand imbalances in the trading of stocks. Some imbalances may last for several hours, minutes, or only seconds.

5. Opportunities for day trading exist because, in the short term, the stock market is inefficient, irrational, and imperfect. The system is flawed and can be exploited for quick profits.

6. The system is flawed because in stock trading, as in a casino, the odds are always with the *house*. Over the long term, the house always wins.

7. The house, in this case, is the Wall Street firms who control the trading in stocks, namely, the specialists on the floor of the New York Stock Exchange and the market makers on Nasdaq. The house always wins because of a mechanism called the *bid-ask spread. When the house wins, the investing public loses.*

8. The majority of day traders lose money. This is because the system is geared toward their failure. In other words, because of the bid-ask spread, it is very difficult for day traders to be consistently profitable by betting against the house—trading against the Wall Street firms. If you bet against the house long enough, eventually Wall Street will have all of your money.

9. Day traders should trade only when they have an edge, when the odds are in their favor. Even though the odds are usually against them, there are numerous times throughout the trading day when the odds swing drastically into the day trader's favor, and that is when they must place their bets.

10. The only time the odds are truly in their favor is when they trade with the house, by being on the same side of the trade as the traders on the floor of the New York Stock Exchange (the specialists). When the specialists are risking their own capital to buy, so, too, should the day trader.

11. Unlike the casino, the New York Stock Exchange has rules in place that allow individual traders to bet with the house. This gives traders the same edge and access to profits that Wall Street has always had. This is *buying on the bid* and *selling on the ask.* The investing public is generally not aware that these favorable rules exist, and that is key to the day traders' profits.

12. Buying on the bid and selling on the ask is called *exploiting the bid-ask spread,* and it is the way day traders take food out of Wall Streeters' mouths. The practice of exploiting the bid-ask spread is called *scalping.*

13. By exploiting the bid-ask spread, day traders can make consistent, lower-risk profits even in stocks that don't move. The stock does not have to go up or down for day traders to make money.

14. The fact that day traders can make money in stocks that don't move means they don't have to trade volatile stocks to make a living.

15. The recent changes to the structure of the New York Stock Exchange, including the move toward a hybrid-electronic trading model and the increased transparency of the NYSE specialists' order books, have benefited the investing public immensely. As a result, it has created trading conditions that are much more favorable to short-term speculators than they had been in the past.

16. Although the playing field is still not truly 100 percent level, these changes to the NYSE have decreased the trading edge that NYSE specialists have over the trading public, and in the process, have greatly increased the day traders' opportunities to "bet with the house."

So how do you bet with the house? A major portion of this book will be devoted to answering that question.

SECTION I

The World of the Day Trader

Day trading is the practice of anticipating and exploiting temporary supply and demand imbalances in the trading of stocks. What does this mean? It means that long-term trends and market conditions are not the primary focus. Neither is reading the Wall Street Journal *cover to cover, nor combing through piles and piles of analyst research. These will not put food on your table. Why? Although these may be helpful to the long-term investor, they will not increase the odds of a profitable trade when your time horizon is only hours, minutes, or even seconds.*

This is the short term, and the only thing day traders should be concerned about is the immediate supply and demand picture in the stock. Every trade must be a precise, well-calculated move, where trading capital is put at risk only when the odds of a successful trade are substantially in your favor. Otherwise, you are throwing your money away, as it is far easier to lose money in this game than it is to make it. Welcome to the world of the day trader.

CHAPTER 1

Exploiting the Excesses of Capitalism

Did you ever wonder how the top trading firms on Wall Street are able to make so much money year after year? Whether or not the great financial institutions would like to admit it, and whether or not the general public is aware it is happening, the Wall Street brokerage firms do to the individual investor exactly what the Las Vegas casinos do to their gambling patrons. In the gaming world, the house edge is probability, a slight statistical edge that the casino has over the gambling public. The more you gamble, the less likely you are to win.

While the casinos deal in craps, roulette, and blackjack, Wall Street deals in stocks, bonds, and commodities. In the financial markets, the effects of the house edge are more mysterious and dangerous, because unlike the casino, where most gamblers understand that the odds are stacked against them, on Wall Street it can go unseen, unfelt, and undetected by the ordinary investor. This hidden force is known as the bid-ask spread. The spread is the mechanism that transfers wealth from the investing public into the hands of the Wall Street brokerage firms. The odds dictate that the more you trade, the less likely you are to win. And when Wall Street wins, the investing public usually loses. The key to profitable day trading is to recognize this fact, and, like the card counter in blackjack, to place your bets only when the odds swing overwhelmingly in your favor.

Taken at face value, conditions seem ideal for the day trader. Low commissions, a fair regulatory environment, and technology that allows someone in Alaska to have the same split-second financial information as a trader on the floor of the New York Stock Exchange are but a few of the reasons. Information travels so quickly and efficiently that the day trader can witness and react to tiny, second-to-second price fluctuations in stocks that in the old days would go unnoticed. It is possible to exploit market moves in less time than it takes to pick up the phone, allowing those with the quickest hands to capitalize on opportunities created by markets that can change drastically in just a few seconds.

We have come a long way. For decades, the world of stock trading was dominated by a select few on Wall Street. The best and most profitable traders all held seats on the New York Stock Exchange. In the past, this was a necessity. These insiders had a virtual monopoly on financial information. Markets moved too fast for those who did not have the same access to quick trades and timely information that the floor traders had. If you were not on the floor of the exchange, you were on the outside, plain and simple. To make matters worse, only a privileged few could afford the high price of owning a seat. Day trading required a tremendous amount of money and resources just to compete. And the playing field was not level. The individual investor did not stand a chance in this environment. That is why, back then, the idea of the individual day trader competing on the same field with the Wall Street giants was unheard of.

In those days, the high commissions alone prevented most individuals from aggressively trading their stock portfolio. There was no such thing as discount brokers: Full-service brokerage firms were the only means for the individual to invest. If you bought 1,000 shares of a stock, you might pay a few hundred dollars or more for the order. Imagine buying 1,000 shares of IBM and paying a $500 commission! The stock would have to move a half point just to break even. And that doesn't count the commission you'd pay on the way out. There was simply no way to trade actively under the burden of such high commissions. If you were in the market, you were in it for the long term. You had no other choice.

But times have changed. Thanks to online trading, the individual who is trading from home now has access to the same profits the Wall Street brokerage firms have been making for decades. Online orders can be executed in as fast as one second, and can cost as little as a few dollars. By monitoring a real-time quote screen, the active day trader, if successful, can literally make a living on the same small, high-percentage profits that have made the large trading firms millions upon millions of dollars per year.

But that does not tell the whole story. Although the online traders have access to the markets today in a way that they have never had before, they are still at a slight competitive disadvantage compared to the "insiders in the marketplace—namely, the market makers and the specialists on the floor of the New York Stock Exchange. The independent trader is on the outside looking in. The fact that the majority of day traders lose money further supports this fact. Successful day trading requires an acceptance of this reality. This will become clear as you get further into the book.

THE HOUSE EDGE

The basic premise of day trading is that you are attempting to make a living by profiting off tiny inefficiencies in the stock market. In layman's terms, this means buying stocks and reselling them to someone else at a higher price. The best trades are the ones where you resell the stock for a profit seconds after you buy it. So how is this possible? The markets do not give away money. Especially not to you and me. It's because the markets are inefficient and the system can be exploited for profit.

Day trading, like many other lucrative professions, is an extremely competitive business. The profits certainly don't come easy. Day trading is a zero-sum game. The profits you make come directly at the expense of someone else. Sometimes it's at the expense of the Wall Street trading firms, sometimes at the expense of the investing public. Nonetheless, if you know what to look for, the profits are there for the taking—and if you don't take them, someone else will.

Let's draw an analogy to the casinos. Tens of millions of people visit the casinos in Las Vegas, leaving behind billions of their hard-earned money. How does this happen? The casinos did not steal the money. It's because of something called the *house edge*, a slight and virtually invisible statistical advantage that the casino has over its gambling guests. Every single transaction the casino engages in is the end result of exhaustive mathematical research to determine if the risk the house is taking is justified. Not a single penny of the casino's capital will be risked unless the odds are in the house's favor.

The key to success is that the casino doesn't get greedy. Its owners are perfectly content with paying out a majority of their profits and only keeping a small percentage for themselves. They do not do this because they like to give their money away. They just know that if you stay at the blackjack table long enough, chances are, you will leave with less money than you came with. Over time, this house edge will destroy even the best recreational gambler.

But as strong as the house edge is, some people have devised ways to overcome it. Undoubtedly, you have seen the stories of card counters and other hustlers beating the casinos at their own game. They do this by raising their bets as the odds tip in their favor. In the past, by counting cards, a player was able to gain a slight statistical advantage over the dealer in predicting which cards would be dealt next. This edge became more exaggerated and more profitable the longer the gambler stayed at the table. There were numerous people who made a living by doing this. These were the true professional gamblers.

The only problem with this line of work is that the casinos prohibit card counting. The casino management is not stupid. They are not about to give their hard-earned money away to people they consider card cheats. In fact, Las Vegas spends millions of dollars per year to protect itself from these "parasites." Consistently profitable blackjack players will last only so long at the tables before the casinos pull the plug. Well-known professional card counters can't even set foot in the large casinos without being asked to leave. Many have to resort to disguises just to go unrecognized long enough the make their profits, but it only lasts for so long. The casinos are devoted to protecting their house edge.

Yet these are the same casinos that welcome you and me with open arms. Every single service the Las Vegas casinos provide is aimed at keeping you at the tables. From the free drinks to the 24-hour room service to the fresh air that is pumped into the gaming rooms, you are made to feel as comfortable as possible. The casino is open 24 hours a day, but you can't find a clock anywhere. That way you are unaware of the time you have spent on the tables. This all revolves around the premise that, over time, you cannot beat the house. Unless you have an edge, or are doing something illegal, the longer you gamble, the less likely you are to win. The Las Vegas skyline was built with the hard-earned money that people like you and me have left behind at its tables.

There is another industry where the edge is more subtle and less understood, but produces the same results—Wall Street. In many ways, the successful day trader carries the same persona on Wall Street as the blackjack hustler does in Las Vegas. Day traders' profits are made by exploiting the system. The system they exploit is controlled by forces much more powerful than the individual trading over the Internet. The Wall Street establishment that sets the odds does not take kindly to the intrusion of the day trader. As the casinos will do anything and everything possible to destroy the card counters, so will the Wall Street market makers do all in their power to prevent the day trader from being profitable, because the profits of the day trader come directly out of the market maker's pocket. Like the unpopular guest sitting at the poker table with a weak hand, you must recognize that, as a day trader, the odds are inherently against you, and the other players will do everything legally possible to prevent you from being profitable. However, this does not mean the system cannot be beat.

The great thing is that throughout the trading day, there are an infinite number of times when the odds are in your favor. In the short term, the markets are irrational and incredibly inefficient. The markets are moved by fear and greed. This creates a tremendous opportunity for quick profits, if you know what to look for. The secret to success is to take the clues the market gives you and use them to interpret the intentions of the other players. When the odds move in your favor, you can beat the players at their own game. To do this, you need to understand the components of Wall Street's version of the house edge, known as the bid-ask spread.

THE BID-ASK SPREAD

How do the large trading firms afford to pay the rent on those high-rise buildings in New York's financial district, which is some of the most expensive corporate real estate in the country? How do they afford to pay their top traders multimillion-dollar salaries? The money is earned at the expense of the investing public. As you know, the essence of the stock market is a difference of opinion. For every buyer, there is a seller. The large banks and brokerage firms make a sizable percentage of their profits by taking the other side of customer orders. When the customer buys, one of these financial institutions is usually on the other side of the trade. The key is that, like a used-car dealership buying and selling cars, the trading firms buy low and sell high, skimming a few cents per share on the trade. Contrary to popular belief, Wall Street does not make its money by hitting home runs on huge, one-time gains. Like the casinos, it makes its money on small, consistent profits. This is done through the market maker system and the mechanism known as the *bid-ask spread.*

The market maker system is the glue that holds the financial markets together. Basically, the market makers are the intermediaries in the buying and selling of stocks. On the New York Stock Exchange, market makers are known as *specialists.* Each individual stock has one specialist who is its sole market maker. On Nasdaq, the market makers are the numerous firms that trade in the stock. There are several market makers for each individual Nasdaq stock. The various exchanges have slightly different methods, rules, and systems for trading stocks, but the underlying principles are inherently the same. The role of the market makers is to maintain an orderly market.

When it is said that specialists on the New York Stock Exchange *make a market,* it simply means that at all times and under all circumstances they are both buyers and sellers of the stocks they trade. There is always a price at which specialists will buy stock from the public and sell stock to the public. They are always willing to risk their own money to take the other side of your trade. If you want to buy 1,000 shares, the specialist is willing to sell you 1,000 shares from his or her own account. If you want to sell, the specialist is willing to buy the stock from you, assuming there is no one else in the market. This is another way of saying that he or she is adding liquidity to the market by buying when there are no buyers and selling when there are no sellers. The specialist does this by keeping an inventory in the stock. This is essential to ensuring that stocks can trade freely and with fluidity throughout the trading day.

But there is a catch. Specialists do not provide this service for free. The price at which a specialist sells stock to you is always going to be higher than the price at which he or she is willing to buy it from you. Consider this a price markup for maintaining an inventory in the stock. This markup is what enables specialists to skim the nickels, dimes, and quarters from the order flow, from the normal course of buying and selling throughout the trading day. The more trading volume, the better the odds that they will make money. Much the same way that the more gamblers are at a casino, the better the odds that the casino will be profitable. So how is this legal? It is very simple. It is legal because the NYSE specialists are exposing themselves to a substantial amount of risk. The risk they take is what justifies the compensation they receive. Imagine being forced to buy stock during a time when large mutual funds are dumping the stock. This is like trying to catch a falling knife. Even worse, imagine having to sell stock to fill an influx of buy orders on a stock that is going through the roof. Either case could easily steamroll the market makers, leading to huge trading losses.

For this reason, acting as a market maker is a very risky and dangerous job. Yet, most of the time, the trading firms involved in this part of the business are able to make huge profits because the bid-ask spread is able to soften their risk. As we said, to maintain an orderly market, the market makers must always "make a market" in the stock they are assigned to, by setting a price at which they will both buy stock and sell stock simultaneously, *even if they don't want to do either*. Obviously, they want to buy at cheaper price levels than they sell, but it is not guaranteed. This is called *keeping a two-sided market*. The market makers are risking their trading capital to ensure that investors will always receive a fair execution, buy or sell. This guarantees that, so long as customers do not put limits on their prices, at some price their orders will be executed. The specialist system is the grease that keeps the stock market running smoothly. When the markets are quiet, this does not seem like such a big deal. It is when the markets are volatile that the market makers really earn their paychecks.

As we said, market makers do not provide this service for free. They must be compensated for the risk they take. For this reason, they are not expected to simultaneously buy stock from the public and resell stock to the public at the same price. It is simply too risky to expect this. Why would anyone risk his or her own capital not to make any money? Capitalism doesn't work that way. Thus, market makers are allowed to maintain a spread in the stock. This is no different than the used-car dealer who buys a vehicle for $5,000 on a trade-in and resells the same vehicle for $6,000. The $1,000 profit is the dealer's *cost of carry* for the risk of taking on inventory. There is no guarantee that the dealer will be able to resell the car, so the profit is justified. Instead of a car, the market maker will buy IBM at 105 and sell it at 105.10. The buying price is known as the *bid*. The selling price is the *ask*. And the difference between the two is the *spread*.

The spread is determined by how volatile the stock is. When it is said that the spread is wide, this means that the difference in price between where the market makers are buying and where they are selling stock to the public is large. *The more volatile the stock, the wider the bid-ask spread.* This is justified because the specialists are unsure of the future direction of the stock. The wide spread is the market makers' only way to protect themselves in the event the stock moves against them. Although bid-ask spreads are generally only a few pennies wide, the markup or spread between where the market makers buy and sell can be much wider in some volatile stocks, or in volatile market conditions.

Imagine an extremely volatile or illiquid stock with a bid-ask spread of a $1. This means that, even if the stock doesn't move, the market makers might be buying from the public at $99 and selling at $100. This means they're making $1,000 for every 1,000 shares bought and sold. But there is no telling in which direction the stock is going. It could be on its way to $110—or to $90. Even the specialists don't know. Remember, the market makers *must* provide liquidity in a stock at all times. This means that, even if they don't want to, they are forced to be the buyer of last resort if they can't match the public sell orders with buyers. In volatile markets, this usually means that market makers accumulate large positions when the stock is falling (the public is panic selling, and the market maker is forced to buy from them) and they lighten up (or get short) the stock when it is running (if the public is panic buying, the market maker is forced to sell into the rally). Even the best traders can sometimes lose large sums of money under this kind of extreme volatility and market stress.

There are times when the opposite is true. The most profitable time for market makers is generally when the stock is trading in an orderly manner. This allows them to make a few cents per share without much risk. For example, in a $25 stock, this would be done by buying from the public at 25 and selling to the public at, say, 25.10. The spread is 10 cents. If the stock doesn't move and the buying and selling is equally distributed, the market maker will have made 10 cents per share on each trade: $100 for every 1,000 shares that trade evenly. Imagine how much is made if the stock trades several hundred thousand shares without moving too much volatility. That could be tens of thousands of dollars of trading profits to the market maker. Over the course of a year, it is this house edge of a few cents per share that compensates them for the infrequent times they suffer huge losses. That is how a few cents per share, over and over again, can translate into millions of dollars in trading profits in the course of a year.

Another way to look at the bid-ask spread is as a form of *risk premium.* Imagine that the stock, instead of moving in one direction, is trading in a choppy manner. This is generally how volatile stocks trade. Under these conditions, the market makers must keep the bid-ask spread wide to protect themselves from the onslaught of day traders and speculators who will try to profit in the event the market makers are "off their market." Most of the time, the wide spread makes it very difficult to "pick off" the market maker. Because the profit the day trader makes usually comes at the expense of the market maker, market makers will not just give their profits away. Their only defense is to make it as difficult as possible for day traders to predict movement in the market makers' stocks.

If the bid-ask spread is the market makers' advantage over the investing public, where does this leave day traders? In the best of all possible positions. Even though the specialists and market makers have the advantage, and even though they set the odds, the playing field is more level today than at any time in history. This is because the regulatory agencies are protecting the interests of the individual investors. Luckily, in the eyes of these agencies, even the day trader is protected in the same way as the small investor.

Let's be honest. Wall Streeters would get away with everything they could if there were nothing to stop them. Capitalism would not have it any other way. But there is something to stop them. There are rules in place that force specialists to give priority to customer orders over their own. On the New York Stock Exchange, these rules essentially let day traders take the same side of the trade as specialists in filling customer buy and sell orders. This allows day traders to trade just like specialists and to gain some of the advantages of the house edge, by participating with the specialists in taking the other side of customer orders. This enables day traders, like specialists, to make those nickels and dimes from the investing public's order flow.

As you can see, day traders are in a very precarious situation. They rely on their own abilities, and their own capital, to beat Wall Street at its own game. Although day traders have the rules on their side, they are able to exist, survive, and prosper only as far as their trading ability takes them, because the odds are not *with* success, but against it. Day traders are going up against much bigger forces, possessing deeper pockets and more information. That should not faze you, however. The game is difficult, but it is not without rewards. Undoubtedly, you have seen the colossal amounts of money Wall Street firms are capable of making in a single year. A piece of that same pie is there for you as a day trader. It is just a matter of going out and staking a claim to it in a way that is prudent.

> ### *Farrell Says*
>
> *Look to the bid-ask spread for clues. One skill that this book will teach you is the ability to tell the difference between a good supply-and-demand scenario to trade and a bad one. It has nothing to do with the long-term prospects in the stock. A good long-term investment can have a horrendous temporary supply-and-demand picture, and vice versa. A stock that is a terrible long-term investment may actually have a supply-and-demand equation that sets up for a profitable short-term trade. It all depends upon the bid-ask spread, where the buyers and sellers stack up at that given point in the trading day.*

Notice in Table 1.1 that both stock A and stock B are trading at the exact same price (25). The bid and ask is also the exact same (24.95 to 25.00). In other words, both have buyers willing to buy at 24.95, and sellers willing to sell at 25.00. Although at first glance they appear identical, a closer look reveals that both offer vastly different profit potential for a short-term trade. Why? The answer has to do with the size of the shares willing to be sold at 25.00.

Stocks move in the path of least resistance. Notice the ask size. Stock B has only one seller of 100 shares at 25.00. Not a big deal. It doesn't indicate either way if this is a good or a bad trade. Stock A, however, has 999,000 shares for sale at 25.00! The conclusion: Stay away from stock A. Unless there is a buyer for all 999,000 shares of stock, or the seller at 25.00 decides to cancel, stock A is going *nowhere*. It is impossible for this stock to trade higher than 25.00 until those 999,000 shares are gone. More on this later.

Table 1.1   The Bid-Ask Spread Indicated a Large Seller

	Stock A	Stock B
Last trade	25	25
Bid price	24.95	24.95
Bid size	1,000 shares	1,000 shares
Ask price	25.00	25.00
Ask size	999,000 shares	100 shares
Conclusion	Unfavorable	Neutral

SECTION II

Introduction to Day Trading

The best trading opportunities often last for less than three seconds. Three seconds before the market clears the imbalance, prices move, and the opportunity vanishes. In this game of seconds, you must realize that there are much faster players in the marketplace than you. Don't be fooled into thinking that technology and a split-second trade execution will put you on a level playing field with your competition. It will not. The hedge funds and the highly paid traders at the large Wall Street brokerage firms, in general, have faster executions, better access to market-moving information, and, of course, deeper pockets. These factors all conspire to put you at a substantial disadvantage in fast-moving markets, where being a fraction of a second too slow can literally be the difference between a winning and a losing trade. As a result, you must utilize trading strategies that neutralize the inherent edge that the faster, larger players possess. This sometimes means avoiding fast-moving or volatile markets altogether. Or, if you do choose to trade volatile stocks, it means concentrating on the opening "print," where all market participants are on equal footing. If you are not able to put the odds in your favor, you don't stand a chance of making a living at this game.

CHAPTER 2

Trading 101

Buying on Bad News and Selling on Good News

Buying a strong stock on the open on good news is a surefire way for the day trader to lose money. As a general rule of thumb, day traders should never be on the same side of a trade as the investing public on the open if the news moving the stock has been fully disseminated. If the public is buying, day traders must be selling.

THE MIND-SET OF AN ONLINE DAY TRADER

So what exactly does the day trader see that the long-term investor does not? While the long-term investor focuses on fundamentals, the day trader is trained to see the market only through the lens of supply and demand. What is the quoted market saying? Are there more buyers than sellers at that given moment, and at what price are they willing to transact? Is there is a large price gap between the buyers and the sellers? Is there a large seller looming in the stock? Is the stock more likely to trade higher or lower, given these circumstances? These are some of the questions that you must ask yourself repeatedly throughout the trading day.

Before you make your first trade, you must understand the nature of the markets and the special role of the day trader. Day traders serve one and only one function: They are middlemen in the buying and selling of stocks. As middlemen, day traders are not worried about the same things as investors. Investors wonder, How is the market doing? What will it do over the next few days, weeks, and months? Is the stock market overvalued, undervalued, or fairly priced at these levels? Which stocks are good investments right now? Day traders are not concerned about any of these issues. Why? Because they are outside of the parameters of supply and demand.

Think of how successful middlemen operate. It doesn't matter what they are buying and selling—stocks, bonds, cars, boats, or homes. Only one thing matters: selling the goods at a higher price than they were bought for. So long as they can do this, middlemen will put food on the table. The same is true of day traders.

A BUYER WHEN THE MARKET NEEDS BUYERS

Second to second, minute to minute, the market is in a state of flux. When a stock moves in any one direction, it is to rectify an imbalance between buyers and sellers. For every buyer, there must be a seller. So when the buyers and the sellers agree on a price, the stock trades. When they don't, the market readjusts its prices until they do agree. It's that simple.

This process of the stock price adjusting and readjusting to the buying and selling of the public is a very inefficient and choppy one. When a stock has trouble readjusting, that creates an opportunity for a quick trade. And this is where the day trader steps in. They do this by being temporary buyers when the market needs buyers and temporary sellers when the market needs sellers. This may seem to go against common sense. But remember, day traders make a living as contrarians, by taking the other side of the buying and selling of the general public, much the same way that the rest of Wall Street does.

HIT SINGLES, NOT HOME RUNS

A few words must be said about the profits that day traders make. Forget the notion that successful day traders make a living by hitting home runs, by making huge one-time gains. They do not. Anytime you could make that much on a single trade, you could lose that much as well. When you are playing with your own hard-earned trading capital, which will be risked and re-risked over and over again, you must avoid trades that could expose you to large losses. If you don't, the law of averages says that eventually you will get cleaned out.

For this reason, the focus is on razor-thin profits. These profits don't seem like much, but they can add up to thousands upon thousands of dollars at the end of the month. Small profits keep day traders in business. What is the secret? The key is to trade large enough volume to make these small gains profitable without exposing yourself to too much market risk—500 or 1,000 or more shares at a time. A profit of 10 cents on 1,000 shares is a profit of $100 before commissions. If you do that four times in a day, and protect yourself against losses, that is a gross profit of $400 before commissions.

BROKERAGE COMMISSIONS CAN DESTROY PROFITS

In my own experience, I may do upwards of 30, 40, or 50 trades in a single day. This means that I may spend upward of several hundred dollars on brokerage commissions, regardless of whether I turn a profit. As I said in the preface, I estimate that I have spent upwards of $1 million in brokerage commissions over my trading career. That is the cost of doing business.

Online trades cost less than $10 at most firms, and this low cost is absolutely essential to the day trader's livelihood. But that does not tell the whole story. The necessity of trading only when you have an edge is amplified the more trades that you do. Think about it: If you did 50 trades in a day and are paying $500 in brokerage commissions, and you fail to do better than break even on your trades, you will have lost $500 on the day. Transaction costs will eat away your trading capital if they are not managed properly.

My point here is simple. The day trader has very little margin for error. To make a living at this game, day traders must be right many more times than they are wrong. If not, transaction costs alone will kill you. This is one reason why so many day traders fail. That is the harsh reality of trading for a living, and it is exactly why you must be so prudent when picking and choosing trades and deciding if the odds are favorable enough to warrant putting your capital at risk.

BUY IN ON FEAR, SELL IN ON GREED

One of the central themes of this book is that the day trader should put capital at risk only when the odds swing drastically in his or her favor. One way in which this can occur is by buying on bad news and selling on good news. Good news and bad news alike are mechanisms for creating large supply-and-demand disruptions in the market, and by consequence, can create nice trading opportunities for quick profits.

There is one stipulation: These trades must be done at the open of trading. This may seem contrary to common sense, but you will be far more successful buying a stock at the open that has a very negative article in the paper than you will if you buy one that has a positive spin. This is because the markets will price in all available information immediately. The general public will react by dumping shares with reckless abandon at hearing bad news. This amounts to an overwhelming amount of market sell orders at the open, which must be paired with buy orders. If the buy and sell orders can't be *paired,* or matched, the stock cannot open for trading. If the stock cannot open for trading, the NYSE specialist will keep adjusting the price higher or lower until enough buyers or sellers are enticed into the transaction. Extreme supply-and-demand imbalances are precisely where the middleman is needed.

The basic premise of this trade is that the opening "print" will usually be where the selling pressure is most intense. Once that opening trade is paired off, the selling pressure may subside. What the general public does not understand is that this phenomenon is exactly what creates a market bottom. In many cases, this will be the stock's low trade of the day. Alert day traders will be buying on the low of the day, and hopefully selling the stock minutes later into the bounce that follows. How are they able to make a profit? Again, by buying when the market needs buyers, and selling when the market needs sellers.

On the contrary, stocks will react to good news by opening significantly higher on a buying imbalance. *For day traders, buying stock at the open on good news is a surefire way to lose money.* This is the same as selling on bad news at the open. While that created a market bottom, the influx of buy orders on good news usually creates a market top. As middlemen, day traders must be on the other side of this trade. If the public is buying, day traders must be selling. As a rule of thumb, *day traders should never be on the same side of a trade as the general public if the news moving the stock has been fully disseminated.* By the time stocks open at 9:30 A.M. in New York, most stories have had several hours to reach the investing public.*

THE SLOW EXECUTION

One of the biggest disadvantages faced by online day traders is the relative speed of their execution. There will always be faster players in the market than you. The problem with trading volatile stocks in fast-moving markets is that the whole investing world is watching them simultaneously. You are seeing the same exact supply-and-demand picture as everyone else. When it appears to you that the stock is headed higher, it appears that way to everyone else as well. So you find yourself in a race with the rest of Wall Street to get your buy order in as fast as possible—and anytime you are in a race with Wall Street, you will lose. Unless you are first, the price will inevitably move away from you before you can get filled. As a result, you will get filled at the worst possible price, and you will feel like the last one in and the last one out, as though you have been robbed. Inevitably, you will lose money. This is the reality of trading the market's most volatile stocks.

You must put this "slow" execution in context. When I say *slow,* I do not mean it in the absolute sense. I mean it in the relative sense. Most online market orders will be executed in less than two seconds, and in quiet markets, it can be even faster. Two seconds may seem like lightning speed to the novice; however, in the world of Wall Street, two seconds can be a lifetime. When stock is in high demand, there is only a limited number of shares for sale at each price level. The window of opportunity may be less than three seconds. The order that arrives first buys the stock at the best price. If your order takes even an extra second, the remaining stock at your price might be gone to someone else and you will be forced to pay a higher price. This split second could mean the difference between a $1,000 profit and a $1,000 loss. And no matter what you do, or how fast you are on your keyboard, there are

---

*Note to readers: There are other factors involved when evaluating whether buying on bad news is a good trade. Blindly buying every stock that opens down on bad news is not a steady path to riches. You have to be selective. You will be learning more about what to look for later in the book.

traders on Wall Street who can buy and sell stock faster than you can type in the stock symbol on your order entry screen.

IS THE NYSE AN EASIER MARKET TO TRADE?

The Nasdaq and the NYSE are two very different markets. The mechanisms through which each exchange handles supply-and-demand imbalances are unique. It is my personal preference to trade NYSE-listed stocks rather than Nasdaq stocks. Over the course of my career, 99 percent of my trades have involved NYSE-listed stocks.

In my own personal experience, I have found that the NYSE can be an easier market to trade profitably than Nasdaq. The rules in place on the New York Stock Exchange can be friendlier to the small investor, and, by extension, the online day trader, than those on Nasdaq. To put it another way, if you are in the business of trying to beat Wall Street at its own game, you have to go where you think you have the best odds. That is why this book is geared toward trading the NYSE, not Nasdaq.

Please remember that this is my opinion only. It does not mean that there aren't opportunities on Nasdaq to trade. There are! When I first learned the ropes on the trading floor at Wall Street's Gruntal & Company, I learned via the NYSE's specialist system, so perhaps I am partial to it. However, our markets are so deep and liquid that there is plenty of room for both NYSE and Nasdaq day traders. Keep in mind that there are many Nasdaq traders who believe that their market is superior to the NYSE, and their opinions are just as valid as mine. Successful Nasdaq day traders make great livings doing so. However, for the purposes of this book, NYSE stocks will be the focus. Chapter 7 touches on Nasdaq for those who want an introduction to trading that market.

SECTION III

How to Beat Wall Street at Its Own Game

Wall Street is in the business of trading against its customers. As a general rule of thumb, the Wall Street trading firms that take the other side of the investing public's buy and sell orders are buyers on weakness and sellers on strength. They are aggressive buyers into panic selling, and aggressive sellers into panic buying. When the public is fearful, Wall Street is greedy. It exploits the opportunity to accumulate positions at favorable price levels. And when the public is feeling greed and euphoria, Wall Street is cautiously taking profits by liquidating those positions at marked-up prices. To be profitable, the day trader must replicate this, by being on the same side of the supply-and-demand equation as the Wall Street professionals. If not, it will be impossible to make a living as a day trader.

CHAPTER 3

Exploiting Wall Street's Conflict of Interest

Market Orders versus Limit Orders

Whether you are a large brokerage firm, a hedge fund, or a small investor, it is virtually impossible to exit a large trade profitably unless you are able to sell into strength.

UNDERSTANDING WALL STREET'S CONFLICT OF INTEREST

Anyone who has been around Wall Street long enough will come to the conclusion that the work the firms engage in is an inherent conflict of interest. These financial institutions are in the business of advising their clients on the buying and selling of securities, while simultaneously taking the other side of the trades for themselves. Think about this for a moment. When a Wall Street brokerage firm tells its largest clients to buy a stock because it is a great value, who exactly is selling the stock to the clients? The brokerage firm itself. You have to ask yourself: If the stock is such a great buy, why is the brokerage firm not following its own advice? Why would it rather sell it to its clients instead of keeping the stock on its books in the hopes of future price appreciation? Shouldn't the brokerage firm be putting its own money where its mouth is? You have to believe with their teams of highly paid analysts, investment bankers, and other rocket scientists, these firms are in possession of far more information and knowledge as to the real value of the stock than their customers are.

But the customers don't see it in such a cynical way. The promise of a high return has a funny way of clouding perception. Investors rely on the brokerage firms for guidance, and depend on the firms' analysis and insight to steer them toward good investments and away from bad ones. Yet the trading desks at banks and brokerage firms would still rather sell the best stock pick of the year to their customers than keep a long-term position in the stock themselves. Why? It comes down to short-term trading profits. When their customers want to buy the securities, the brokerage firms are making substantial amounts of money on the turnover, by taking the other side of the trade. As the investing public is buying, Wall Street is selling, making money by accumulating an inventory in the stock at lower prices, and "flipping" it to their clients at a marked-up price. This markup is known as the *spread.*

Think about it in another way. As we've said earlier in the book, there is a winner and loser on every trade execution. When Wall Street wins, the investing public usually loses. *Whether you are a large brokerage firm, a hedge fund, or a small investor, it is virtually impossible to exit a large trade profitably unless you are able to sell into strength.* The brokerage firms know this all too well, using analyst recommendations to create strong buying demand that enables them to liquidate large positions for a profit. If the demand is strong enough, if the buy recommendation is compelling enough, it creates a buying panic as investors trip over each other to grab the stock.

For the public, this is a dangerous way to invest. Remember, as we said in the previous chapter, in the very short run, buying a strong stock on good news is a surefire way to lose money. The panic buying inflates the stock price, creating a short-term top in the stock. When investors are done buying, there is nothing behind them to support the stock price further, which can cause the stock to drop precipitously. *When the investing public is greedily buying, Wall Street is cautiously liquidating and taking profits.* That is the essence of stock trading, and in part is how Wall Street makes billions of dollars per year.

This is done by the entire gauntlet of Wall Street financial institutions. Big investment banks, full-service brokerage firms, Nasdaq market makers, NYSE member firms, specialists, even the discount and online brokerage firms—they all do it. They all trade against their customers for their own self-serving interests, namely profit. The more trading they can induce their customers to do, the more money they make in the process. That is why, regardless of what the market is doing, these brokerage firms always have an opinion. If the market looks bad, they advise their clients to sell. If the market looks good, they advise their clients to buy. Either way, Wall Street wins, because the firms are skimming small, high-percentage profits off the order flow, regardless of whether their clients make money.

These firms know that as long as customers buy the stock, like a boomerang at some point it will come back out of their accounts as a sell order. And when customers sell, they will immediately be putting the money to work by buying something else, thus generating even more commission revenue and trading profits for the firm that handles the trade. The only way the firms would lose would be if their customers stopped buying and selling. That is why hell would freeze over before these brokerage firms would tell their clients to stop trading, to hold cash for extended periods of time until market conditions improve.

But what about the discount brokers, who, unlike the full-service brokerage firms, aren't in the business of advising their clients on investment decisions? Naturally, because they make a large percentage of their money on trade commissions and margin interest, they want their clients to trade as much as possible, regardless of whether their customers make or lose money. Their goal is to make their customers feel as comfortable as possible with the trading process, with help desks, trade tutorials, user-friendly trading platforms, and promotions that include free trades. The more comfortable clients are with trading, the more likely they are to trade actively, allowing the online broker to collect a toll on the way in and on the way out.

PRICE MAKERS VERSUS PRICE TAKERS

Now that we have gained some insight into the contrarian trading psychology of the large brokerage firms, let's switch gears briefly to discuss where the day trader fits into this puzzle. As we discussed, the stock market is nothing more than a collective difference of opinion. For every buyer there is a seller, and for stock to trade, one of two things must happen: Either you agree to the prices of others, or they agree to yours. The advantage, the profit, and the edge lie in getting others to agree to your prices.

I like to call these two types of groups in the market *price makers* and *price takers*. The price makers make or set the prices in the stock market, and the price takers take or accept the prices the market gives them. The price makers are the Wall Street trading firms, and the price takers are the investing public. The day trader's edge—the key to making consistent short-term profits—is to be first and foremost a price maker, allowing participation in Wall Street's age-old game of making money at the expense of the buying and selling public.

But how does Wall Street do this? If it is taking the other side of your trades, what's the catch? It's actually quite simple. Wall Street earns its money when it takes the other side of your trade by dictating or setting the price at which the stock trades. Wall Street forces the investing public into agreeing to the terms and prices it sets, ensuring that Wall Streeters never risk a dime of trading capital unless it is in their best interests to do so. In other words, they are only going to buy stock from you at a price where they are reasonably sure that they can flip it for a quick profit. *This is done through the strategic use of limit orders.* The use of limit orders is also the key to making consistent short-term profits as a day trader.

THE BARGAINING PROCESS

To understand how limit orders work, let's look at an analogy. Think of the process of buying a used car. Let's say you are in the market for a Porsche. You've been doing your homework, and you've come to the conclusion that the particular year and model that you want, with about 100,000 miles, has a fair-market value of about $37,500. Imagine you are driving along and you see the exact car you are looking for on a neighbor's lawn with a For Sale sign on the window. To your delight, you find out the car has approximately 100,000 miles on it. You speak to the owner, who says the asking price is $40,000.

What steps do you take to get the best possible deal? Do you just accept the first price that the seller asks? I hope not! Is there better way to buy? Of course there is: Negotiate a better price, bid down, haggle, and make the seller lower the offering price. No one is stupid enough to just take the seller's first offer, unless it is a phenomenal deal. Why would you pay more money than you have to? The key is that you have a good idea of what the car is worth based on what you have seen and read in the marketplace. You are not going to pay the asking price because you know it is too high.

So, you tell the seller you'll pay $35,000 for the car, and not a penny more. You are bidding for the car at slightly less that it is worth. The seller now has essentially three choices. First, he or she could agree to your price—hit your bid—and sell you the car at $35,000. Second, he or she could refuse you outright and keep the sale price at $40,000. Or third, he or she could try to meet you halfway by coming back with a lower offering price of, say, $37,500. But you have stated that you are not going to pay any more than $35,000. Your tough stance has put the seller in a real dilemma. If you walk, maybe there are no other buyers and the seller risks never selling the car. You say the offer is only good for 10 minutes, after which you will walk. This puts added pressure on the deal. The beauty of this strategy is that the power is in your hands. You know what the car is worth, and you know you can always shop elsewhere if you can't agree on a low price right now. The last thing you are going to do is just accept the seller's terms. *In trading terms, by setting the price you bid for the car at $35,000 and no higher, you have used a limit order.*

What you have done by bargaining is put yourself in a no-lose situation. Either you buy the car at the price you have set, or you will shop elsewhere. *In other words, you are not putting your capital at risk unless the terms are favorable.* Your refusal to accept the seller's terms (of buying the car at $40,000) and determination to buy only at the price you have dictated makes you *a price maker.* Obviously, the seller would much prefer that you were not savvy enough to negotiate a better price. That way he or she could make a nice profit at your expense.

Imagine what it would be like if you were an active trader of cars and were unaware that you could negotiate a better price than the seller's first offer. Think of how much money you would leave on the table if you never made any effort to negotiate a better price for yourself. You wouldn't last in the business, because you would eventually be broke. No sane person would ever do business this way.

Yet, ironically, this is precisely the way most people buy and sell stocks. What the public doesn't realize is that they are doing precisely the same thing when they buy and sell stocks at the market as when they buy a car by accepting the seller's first offering price. By buying and selling at the market, these investors are agreeing to the terms of counterparty to the trade without attempting to negotiate a better price. And guess who is on the other side of the trade? A Wall Street trading firm that makes millions or billions of dollars per year by trading against the investing public. Do you think for one second that the price the firms set—and the public agrees to—is in the investors' best interests? No chance!

The market order is the investing public's most popular and most used means of buying and selling stocks. It also can be the most dangerous. *The investing public's reliance on market orders, and not limit orders, when they trade stocks is one of the great strategic follies in the world of finance because they are leaving money on the table each time they trade.* When the average investor is unaware or unsure of how they can negotiate a better price for the stock they buy and sell through the use of limit orders, it puts Wall Street at a significant competitive advantage over them. Unless you worked on Wall Street, perhaps you wouldn't realize the extent of this.

The concept of being able to get a trade executed at a better price than the quoted market is indicating is probably foreign to most people's preconceived notions of trading. As such, the last thing a Wall Street market maker wants is for the general public to be educated in the ways of stock trading. As long as investors still subscribe to the myth that the only way to buy and sell stocks is at the market, and as long as they fail to see that they can negotiate a better price, the financial institutions will remain rich and happy. This ensures that the public remains the food and the prey of Wall Street.

Buying 1,000 shares of stock should be no different than buying a used car. An active investor will likely spend far more money in his or her lifetime on stock trades than on buying a car. Think about it. If an investor buys 1,000 shares of a $25 stock, that is a $25,000 trade. Yet the irony is that most investors put far less effort into that purchase than they would into buying a car. By buying at the market, the investing public is unknowingly getting fleeced by the firms that specialize in taking the other side of the trade. All because the trade is being done on the firms' terms, not the investors'.

PRICE NEGOTIATION—MARKET VERSUS LIMIT ORDERS

It is always important to remember that something is worth only what someone else is willing to pay for it. This always puts the negotiating advantage, or edge, in the hands of the buyer over the seller, if the buyer puts a limit on the buying price. By setting the price, the buyer is determining what the item is worth. It doesn't matter what the seller thinks, because without a buyer, what is an item really worth? The same is true in stocks. A stock is worth only what someone else is willing to pay for it.

Getting back to the analogy of the used car, it is important to note that that transaction really had only one side. We had a seller, and we had an interested buyer. Unlike the used-car example, the curious thing about Wall Street is that the brokerage firms are on both sides of the fence. They are both buyers and sellers in the stocks they trade at the same time, regardless of whether they are bullish or bearish on the stock. The key to their profitability is that they always set both the price at which they are willing to buy stock and the price at which they are willing to sell. The key word here is *willing.* These firms are not ever going to buy or sell stock to the public at a price that is not to their best advantage. If it is not at their price, they would rather not do the trade. It's that simple.

The *limit order,* unlike the *market order,* is not the preferred choice of the individual investor. But it is the method of choice for the professionals who make a living buying and selling stocks. A market order is placed without price conditions: Buy X number of shares at whatever price the market sets. A limit order is nothing more than an order to buy or sell stock with a price limit attached to it. *The strategic use of limit orders is the key to the day trader's profitability.* If it is a buy limit order, the buyer sets the price, and is not willing to pay even a penny more than that price limit. Limit orders enable buyers to purchase stock cheaper than where the quoted market is indicating.

The tricky part is that when the firms set the price at which they will buy stock, there is no guarantee they will find a seller to agree to their terms. There is never a guarantee. But the firms don't care. The key to the equation is that they buy only on their terms, or they don't buy at all. It is a no-lose situation.

The way these large trading firms make their profits is the exact same way you will make yours as a day trader: by buying only at price levels where you know you can immediately resell for a small profit. That is why you have to be a price maker, and not a price taker. By using limit orders, your mind-set is simple. You are setting the price and then waiting. The trap is set. You wait patiently in the hopes that you find someone who is foolish enough to sell you stock at your price. If someone does, you will then turn right around and resell the stock higher yourself. If you can't find someone who will buy on your terms, you simply move on to another stock. Eventually, if you set enough traps, the odds are that someone will walk right into one of them. But what do you see that the sellers don't? Obviously, if the sellers knew what you knew, they wouldn't be foolish enough to agree to your low price. They would try to get a higher price for themselves.

What you see is exactly the same thing the rest of Wall Street sees—just how lucrative it can be to take the side of the public's market orders. The reality is that investors are leaving money on the table every time they place a trade. Even worse, the typical long-term investor doesn't have anyone in their corner to negotiate on their behalf. Remember, even the brokerage firms that manage the investing public's money trade against the very customers they advise. Customers are really on their own, and most of the time they don't even know it. That is why they walk right into the trap Wall Street sets for them.

Thus, the day trader is forced to compete with all of Wall Street for the profits created when the investing public buys and sells at the market. Every single profit that Wall Street makes is a profit taken directly out of the investing public's pocket. And, ironically, every single profit the day trader makes is one less profit reserved for Wall Street. The food on the day trader's table is food taken directly out of the mouths of the Wall Street firms.

WALL STREET'S PREY

With this in mind, you always have to be aware of the agenda of the other players in the market, especially the Wall Street firms. Who is really taking the other side of your trade? If you are a successful trader, the irony is that it certainly won't be Wall Street. This is because, if you are on top of your prices, the Wall Street firms will be too smart to take the other side of your trades. You and they will be buying and selling together. The investing public is Wall Street's prey, and by consequence, they are your prey as well.

This can be a tremendously profitable way to make a living. Wall Street would like to keep this game, this secret, all to itself. But the cat is out of the bag. The brokerage firms certainly don't want or need any day traders to be invading their turf. As such, the day trader feels like an unwelcome trespasser. But what can they do? Legally, you have every right to be in there trading side by side with the large Wall Street brokerage firms.

PRELUDE TO THE BID-ASK SPREAD

As you can see, the key to making profits as a day trader is the use of well-placed limit orders. Because you are essentially taking food out someone else's mouth every time you make a profit, you have to be extremely careful how you use these limit orders. The world of trading is filled with them. Many people have gone broke by letting their guard down. You have to be constantly aware of this fact.

In this chapter we have touched briefly on the differences between market and limit orders. But we have only begun to scratch the surface. Knowing how to use limit orders, and where to place them, involves much more than just knowing the difference between trading at the market and trading with a price limit. If you are going to make a living trading, you really need to have a firm understanding of how stocks trade. That can only come from an examination of the bid-ask spread.

CHAPTER 4

The Day Trader's Crystal Ball
Understanding the Bid-Ask Spread

Successful day traders are able to make thousands of dollars per day by extracting tiny profits from stocks in a way that very few people understand. Many times, the stocks don't have to move for day traders to make a profit. So what do day traders see that other people don't? What is their secret? The answer lies in exploiting the bid-ask spread. That is why understanding the mechanics of the bid-ask spread is the day trader's single most important task.

Yet very few people understand how this works. The uninitiated will waste precious time combing through piles of charts, graphs, and research in the futile attempt to predict price movement. Although this may be helpful to long-term investors, for the short-term trader it is a wasted effort that will not lead to profits, as it is outside of the immediate parameters of supply and demand. What these people fail to grasp is that they need to look no further than the bid-ask spread for answers. Hidden under this veil lie the market's best clues to predicting the direction that a stock might move in the next few minutes or seconds. Interpreting the bid-ask spread is the day trader's crystal ball.

A SNAPSHOT OF A MOVING PICTURE

Think of the bid-ask spread as a snapshot of a moving picture. The bid-ask spread is the most basic, yet misunderstood, component in the trading of stocks. For a day trader, interpreting the bid-ask spread is the key to making profits. The whole premise of this book is that, in the short term, the stock market is inefficient and can be exploited for quick profits. The markets are inefficient because of the mechanics of the bid-ask spread.

If there is one certainty in the world of day trading, it is that trading patterns and cycles constantly repeat themselves. In the course of your trading, you are going to be confronted with the same situations over and over again. A solid understanding of the nature of the bid-ask spread will enable you to predict price movements based on your experience with similar situations in the past. You may have only a few seconds to react. How you react will determine whether you make or lose money trading.

The best way to look at the bid-ask spread is as the mechanism within which the buying and selling of stocks occur. For NYSE-listed stocks, the floor of the stock exchange is the place where the buyers and sellers meet to negotiate the prices displayed in the bid-ask spread. As we mentioned in the last chapter, whether the individual investor realizes it or not, every single share of stock that changes hands does so on the basis of an agreement between buyer and seller as to the price and the number of shares. The beauty of trading from home is that this negotiation process is nameless, faceless, and anonymous. With today's technology, you do not have to be face to face with the other buyers and sellers in your attempt to get a better or more fair price. All the tools you need to communicate and negotiate effectively are found inside the parameters of the bid-ask spread. This is one reason why the New York Stock Exchange is the most effective and fair marketplace in the entire world.

Farrell Says

One of the best-kept secrets in day trading is the ability to transact at better prices than the marketplace is indicating. Through the use of limit orders, you can buy stock lower, or sell stock higher, than the advertised price that would be executed on a market order.

As a day trader, you play a crucial role in this negotiating process. Through the application of certain trading techniques, you will be able to step into the marketplace when the other buyers and sellers cannot agree on price or number of shares. By using well-placed limit orders, you will attempt to bring out other buyers and sellers in the stock by offering to buy and sell at better prices than are currently available in the marketplace. That is what makes markets, and what allows you to make profits.

THE MECHANICS OF PRICE MOVEMENT— UNDERSTANDING WHAT MAKES A STOCK MOVE HIGHER

The trading techniques used in the negotiation process are difficult to comprehend without having a firm understanding of the mechanics the bid-ask spread. This entire chapter is devoted to understanding the bid-ask spread and answering the most basic of all trading questions: What makes a stock move up or down?

It seems like a simple question, yet 99 percent of the investing public does not have the correct answer. Most would answer that buyers move a market higher, and sellers move a market lower. Some would even go as far as saying that a stock moves down because there are more sellers than buyers, and it moves up when more buyers than sellers enter the market. This is partially correct, yet the real reason is a bit more complex. The true answer lies in the bid-ask spread.

The essence of trading is that every single share of stock that trades has both a buyer and a seller. That is why it is not 100 percent accurate to say that a stock moves higher because there are more buyers than sellers. For the stock to trade, there must be an equal number of shares being bought and sold. The real answer is that the stock moves higher because of simple supply and demand: all you need to do to make a stock go higher is to buy all the stock available for sale at a given price level, then buy more at the next highest level where it is for sale.

The reason for this is that for each and every stock there is only a limited number of shares for sale at each price level. Your buying and the buying of others will cause the stock to tick higher if you are willing to buy more stock than is for sale *at a given price.* You and the other buyers will inevitably buy all of the stock for sale at the first price level, and then the remainder of your buy order will be bought at the next highest level or levels where stock is for sale. In other words, if the stock is in demand because of good news, the buyers will simply clean out the stock at each consecutive higher price level, causing the stock to trade higher.

Let's look at an example. Suppose you want to buy 10,000 shares of IBM at the market. The supply in the stock looks like this:

5,000 shares are for sale at 101

2,000 shares are for sale at 101.05

3,000 shares are for sale at 101.25

What happens when you want to buy 10,000 shares at the market, which is currently 101?

There are only 5,000 shares for sale at that price. So, you will buy those 5,000 shares at 101 (the current asking price), and then buy the remaining 5,000 shares at the next highest price level or levels at which stock is for sale, 101.05 and then 101.25. You will keep causing the stock to tick higher until you have bought all the stock on your order—in this case, all 10,000 shares.

The entire 10,000 shares were filled because the sellers sold you:

5,000 shares at 101, then

2,000 shares at 101.05, and finally

3,000 shares at 101.25

Your buying alone made the stock move up 25 cents from 101 to 101.25 as you "lifted" all the available stock at each price level. Assuming the stock opened the day at 101, if you checked the quote after your order was complete, it would read:

IBM : Last Trade **101.25** + .25

As you can see, IBM did not trade up 25 cents because there were more buyers than sellers. There was an equal number of shares willing to be bought and sold (10,000). It went up because of a scarcity of stock for sale at the current price level.

Another way to look at this is that if you are willing to buy stock, you are always going to be able to find a seller at some price. It's just a matter of at what price the seller is willing to sell you stock. If all of the sellers in IBM were willing to sell for $101 a share yesterday, and today, because of good news on the company, they adjust their sale price higher to $102, the stock will inevitably go up. As you can see, it didn't go up because there were more buyers than sellers. It went up because, with stock no longer for sale at 101, the potential buyers were forced to pay a dollar higher to get sellers to sell them stock. With an absence of sellers, any stock will naturally drift higher until sellers are enticed into selling. The stock will stop moving only when a price is reached where the buyers and sellers agree to exchange stock. This whole negotiation process plays itself out all day long in the mechanics of the bid-ask spread. This may seem a bit confusing now, but it will become clearer as we examine the components of the bid-ask spread.

EXAMPLE 1: THE QUOTE—SNAPSHOT OF A MOVING PICTURE

This first case study demonstrates a typical market scenario on the New York Stock Exchange. We are not going to make any trading decisions yet; this is only to show what the quote reveals. This is the most basic step in understanding the mechanics of price movement.

Let's say you are interested in trading in Chicago Bridge and Iron, listed on the New York Stock Exchange under the symbol CBI. You pull the stock up on your real-time quote screen, and the basic quote looks like Figure 4.1A.

What does this say about CBI?

There is a wealth of information about CBI to be found in this simple quote. Basically, this is the blueprint of the intentions of buyers and sellers in this stock at this point in the trading day. The breakdown looks like Figure 4.1B.

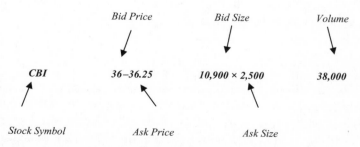

Figure 4.1A   The Jockeying of Buyers and Sellers

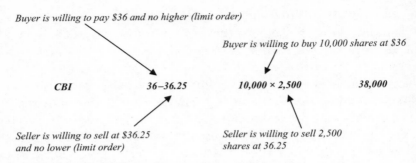

Figure 4.1B The Intentions of Buyers and Sellers

Farrell Says

The real-time stock quote is always going to reflect the very best prices in the market at that point in time: the highest price a buyer is willing to pay for stock (the bid) and the lowest price a seller is willing to sell stock for (the ask). This is what dictates the price at which stock trades.

The Bid

The bid is 36, or $36 per share. This is the highest price at which stock is currently willing to be bought. This is the absolute highest price buyers are willing to pay for stock at this time. Of all of the potential buyers of CBI in the entire world at this time, $36 is the best bid. However, this buyer or buyers, by putting a limit on the price, is stating that he or she is not willing to pay even a penny more than $36 for stock. This is a limit order, and as such, there is no guarantee the buyer will get the stock at $36. The buyer will first need a seller at the market to agree to the price before the stock can trade.

The Ask

The ask is $36.25 per share. This is the lowest price at which stock is currently willing to be sold. Of all of the people willing to sell CBI in the entire world at this time, 36.25 is the best offer. In other words, this seller is willing to sell stock with a price limit of 36.25, and is not willing to sell for even a penny less than $36.25. This is also a limit order, so here there is also no guarantee the seller will sell the stock at $36.25. The seller will need a buyer at market to agree to the price before the stock can trade.

Farrell Says

It is important to note that the only way you can transact at better prices than the market is indicating is through the use of limit orders, which allow you to bid for and offer stock inside the bid-ask spread.

As you can see, the bid and the ask are the two primary components of the market. If someone ever asks, "What is the market in a stock?" you now know that it is the highest bid and the lowest offer: in this case 36 to 36.25. In plain English, we have a buyer who thinks the stock is worth *no more* than $36, and a seller who believes that the stock worth *no less* than $36.25. In other words, the seller wants 25 cents per share more than the buyer is willing to pay. You are seeing the negotiating process in progress. The seller and the buyer simply cannot agree on a price, which is exactly why their buy and sell orders sit on the floor of the exchange and remain unexecuted. Both the buyer and the seller are holding out. The seller wants more money, the buyer wants to pay less. Each is refusing the other's proposition. If there were buyers willing to pay more than $36 per share, or sellers willing to sell for less than $36.25, the bid-ask parameters of the market would be updated to reflect that.

Although we know for a fact from the quote that there are not any buyers willing to pay more than $36, nor are there any sellers willing to accept less than $36.25 (if there were, the market would not be 36 to 36.25), it is important to note that in CBI, as in all other stocks, there could be hundreds of buy orders in the stock at prices below $36, and hundreds of sell orders at prices above $36.25. But we will never see those limit orders reflected in the immediate inside quote unless they are the highest bid and lowest ask, respectively, because they are considered away from the market. If you have access to a more sophisticated real-time quote platform, you will be able to see those buyers and sellers that are "away" from the market.

This is no different than the real estate market or the car market. If Porsche 911s are changing hands for $50,000 in the current environment, there are always going to be people who would love to buy those same Porsche 911s for $20,000 and people who would like to sell Porsche 91Is for $100,000, even though both are away from the market. The same is true with stocks. If CBI is trading around $36 per share, there are inevitably going to be numerous buyers below the market and numerous sellers above the market. There might even be a buyer of 10 million shares of CBI at $20, but that person will most likely never buy the stock that low because the stock is changing hands at $36. As such, because that buyer is so far away from the market, that buy order is insignificant to the price movement in the stock. A real buyer would not be waiting for the stock to get to $20 before purchasing it, unless he or she had an inkling that bad news was coming soon and the stock was going to drop precipitously.

Bid Size

The bid size is the number of shares the buyer is willing to buy. In our example, the bid size is 10,000. This means there are 10,000 shares of CBI willing to be bought at 36. It is important to note that this means a *total* of 10,000 shares willing to bought at 36 at this time. This could be only 1 buyer, or 20 different buyers willing to buy different amounts that total 10,000 shares. There is no way to tell the difference.

Ask Size

The ask size is the number of shares the seller is willing to sell. In our example, the ask size is 2,500. This means there are 2,500 shares willing to be sold at 36.25. As with the bid size, this could be one potential seller of 2,500 shares, or a combination of sellers totaling 2,500 shares.

Farrell Says

One of the basic principles of stock trading is that there are rarely equal numbers of shares willing to be bought and sold in a stock at the same time. The supply and demand in the stock is in a constant state of flux, as the market continually adjusts and readjusts it prices, trying to find price levels where buyers and sellers can agree. When they do agree, the market stops moving and achieves a temporary state of balance.

In this case, there are 10,000 shares willing to be bought (at 36), but only 2,500 shares willing to be sold (at 36.25). Most of the time, due to fluctuating market conditions, there will be large differences like this in the amount of stock willing to be bought and the amount of stock willing to be sold. This is known as a *lopsided market*. This is extremely important because it is one of the first indications of a short-term supply-and-demand imbalance, one that may precipitate a rally or a sell-off in the stock.

It is important to note that some real-time quote platforms refer to the bid size and the ask size in abbreviated format, leaving off the last two zeros. Therefore, 100 means 10,000 shares, 10 means 1,000 shares, and so on.

Volume

This is the last component of the quote. The volume is the number of shares traded that day since the opening bell. Volume is very important in gauging the activity in the stock. Not a single share can change hands without its being reflected in the volume. In this case, 38,000 shares have changed hands so far in the trading day.

Thus, the market is made. The highest bid (36) and lowest offer (36.25) set the parameters. In trading lingo, we would say that the market in CBI is 36 bid, offered at 36.25, 10,000 by 2,500. The market of 36 to 36.25 is known as the bid-ask spread.

As you can see, the bid-ask spread indicates the intentions of the buyers and sellers who are using limit orders. Limit orders are what dictate the parameters of the spread. This process ensures that the best prices will always be posted in the market—namely, the highest buyer and the lowest seller. By looking at the stock quote in real time, by seeing the market parameters change, we are witnessing the negotiating process firsthand. In the preceding example, the buyer and the seller could not agree to each other's terms. Both are considered price makers, because they are willing to trade only if it is on their terms and at their price. The buyer will only buy at 36, and the seller will only sell at 36.25. Both are stubborn, and would rather wait and take their chances than agree to the other's price. And, as we said in the last chapter, the key word is *willing*. Neither the buyer at 36 nor the seller at 36.25 is guaranteed to get the order executed. But both are willing to take that risk in the hopes of finding someone who will take the other side of the trade.

EXAMPLE 2: THE MARKET ORDER
TO SELL—HITTING THE BID

In Example 1, we learned the basics of how a stock is quoted. We will now look at the stock in further detail and see what happens when stock trades. We now know that the bid-ask spread ensures that buyers will always buy stock from the seller who is offering stock for sale at the lowest price at any given moment. Conversely, if there is a seller, his or her stock will always be sold to the buyer willing to pay the highest price for the stock. This ensures that both parties to the trade receive the fairest execution and the best possible price at all times.

Going back to the last example, the market in CBI was as shown in Figure 4.1C.

Now, assume an investor wishes to sell 100 shares. What happens next?

The investor essentially has two choices: either to negotiate a price or to take the price the market is giving right now. What occurs next depends on the intentions of the seller. For simplicity, we will assume the investor wishes to get an immediate execution. In this case, the investor has no choice but to sell at the price at which a buyer has stated intentions to buy stock. So, to get an instant fill, the investor decides to sell the stock at the market. Known as a *market order,* this order will be executed immediately. This stock will trade at the highest price a buyer is willing to pay the seller for the stock. No matter where a stock is trading, there is always a price at which a market order will be executed. A market order will usually take only a second or two to get filled.

The market order is the investing public's method of choice for buying and selling stock. The advantage of a market order is that, under all market conditions and circumstances, an immediate execution is guaranteed. The danger is that investors run the risk of the price

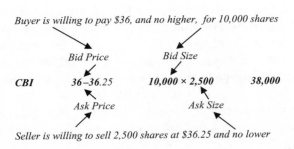

Buyer is willing to pay $36, and no higher, for 10,000 shares

	Bid Price	Bid Size	
CBI	36–36.25	10,000 × 2,500	38,000
	Ask Price	Ask Size	

Seller is willing to sell 2,500 shares at $36.25 and no lower

Figure 4.1C   A New Seller Enters the Market

changing before their order is executed. In both fast- and slow-moving markets, the market order can be very dangerous for this reason.

Farrell Says

Market orders can be dangerous because prices can sometimes move against you before your order is executed. This means that the price you actually receive can be much worse than the price you were expecting.

So, in our example, where will the order get executed if it is entered at the market? To answer that question, we have to ask: At what price is there a buyer willing to buy stock? We know from the bid-ask spread that there is a buyer willing to pay 36 for up to 10,000 shares. So, as long as the market parameters do not change before the order is entered, the stock will trade at 36, the bid.

The investor enters the order over the Internet:

Sell 100 CBI Market

The order is now sent down to the floor of the exchange for execution. When the specialist, or market maker, receives the order, he or she will immediately match the sell order with a buyer and the order will be filled. If you have real-time quotes, you can watch the stock trade. Figures 4.2A and 4.2B show you how it will look. Figure 4.2A changes to Figure 4.2B.

Remember, we had a buyer willing to buy 10,000 shares at 36 and no higher. The seller, by placing a market order, agrees to sell the stock to whoever is willing to pay the best price for it. There will be no negotiating in this trade, because it is at the market. In this case, the highest bidder was at 36. Therefore, 100 shares trade at 36. It is important to notice how the market in CBI has changed. Two components of the snap quote have changed: the volume and the bid size.

Buyer is willing to buy 10,000 shares at 36

36–36.25   10,000 × 2,500   38,000

Figure 4.2A   The Market Order

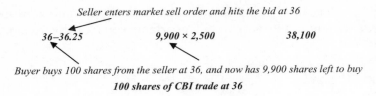

Figure 4.2B   Seller Hits the Bid

Volume

First, the volume has changed to reflect the 100-share trade. Before the trade was entered, 38,000 shares had changed hands. Now, with this 100-share trade, a total of 38,100 shares have traded since the opening bell.

Bid Size

Second, and more important, the bid size has changed. Before the seller entered the order, the bidder was willing to buy 10,000 shares at 36. As we mentioned before, there is no way to tell if it is just one bidder who wants 10,000 shares, or a combination of several bidders each wanting different amounts at 36 that together total 10,000 shares. Either way, 100 shares were just bought, and there are now 9,900 left on the order. That is why the bid size changed from 10,000 to 9,900. In market terms, the bid was hit on 100 shares.

EXAMPLE 3: THE MARKET ORDER TO BUY—LIFTING THE OFFER

The market in CBI when we last looked is shown in Figure 4.3.

Let's review what we have learned. So far, we know that the market parameters are determined by the highest price a buyer is willing to pay

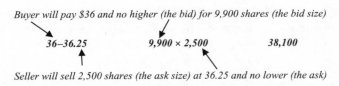

Figure 4.3   The Snap Quote in Real Time

for stock (the bid) and the lowest price at which the seller is willing to sell the stock (the ask). The highest bid and lowest offer are known as the bid-ask spread. From the snap quote, we know that there is a buyer for 9,900 shares at 36 (the bid) and a seller of 2,500 shares at 36.25 (the ask or offer), and that 38,100 shares have traded so far today.

At this point, let's assume there is a buyer looking for 1,000 shares of CBI. This buyer is a long-term investor who believes that the stock is cheap and is poised for an explosive move upward. Because of this, the buyer has no interest in haggling to save an extra 10 or 15 cents by trying to buy the stock cheaper than where it is for sale, which is 36.25 (the offer).

As with any investor or trader who is ever buying or selling stock, there is a certain element of greed involved. This buyer would like to have the stock in his or her account immediately, and is not willing to run the risk of missing the stock in the event it begins to run higher. Missing the stock could happen if the buyer tried to negotiate a better price through a limit order. Imagine trying to buy the stock at, say, 36.10, and then good news comes out and, in a flash, the stock runs to 40 before you are able to get filled. Therefore, the buyer is willing to take the price the market is willing to give in exchange for getting an immediate execution. Thus, the buyer enters a market order to buy:

Buy 1,000 CBI Market

When the order reaches the specialist on the floor of the exchange, 1,000 shares are immediately filled at 36.25. Remember, the lowest price at which a seller is willing to sell stock is the price at which the buyer will buy stock on a market order. Figures 4.4A and 4.4B show how the market in CBI changes.

Seller is willing to sell 2,500 shares at 36.25 and no lower

36–36.25   9,900 × 2,500   38,100

Figure 4.4A   Market Order to Buy

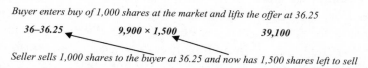

Buyer enters buy of 1,000 shares at the market and lifts the offer at 36.25

36–36.25   9,900 × 1,500   39,100

Seller sells 1,000 shares to the buyer at 36.25 and now has 1,500 shares left to sell

Figure 4.4B   Buyer Lifts the Offer

Notice which components have changed: the volume and the ask size.

Volume

The volume changes from 38,100 shares to 39,100 as 1,000 shares trade.

Ask Size

The ask size changes from 2,500 to 1,500. We had a potential seller willing to sell 2,500 shares at 36.25. Now that the seller has sold 1,000 shares to this investor, there are 1,500 shares remaining on the seller's order. That is why the ask size changed from 2,500 to 1,500. In trading lingo, the offer was *lifted* on 1,500 shares.

Farrell Says

There are some instances when market orders can be an effective way to trade. But, in general, for the day trader they offer the worst odds of a profitable trade in the marketplace. Said another way, the market order is a bet against the house, and short-term traders should use them sparingly.

EXAMPLE 4: THE LIMIT ORDER TO BUY—BIDDING FOR STOCK

When we last looked at CBI, the snap quote read:

$$36–36.25 \quad 9,900 \times 1,500 \quad 39,100$$

The last trade in the stock was 1,000 shares at 36.25. Now assume another potential buyer comes in looking to buy 2,000 shares. This time the buyer is a trader who was drawn to the stock after seeing the stock trade 1,000 shares on the offer at 36.25. Typically, unless convinced that the stock is running higher, most good short-term traders will attempt to purchase the stock at a cheaper price than where it is for sale. This is where the negotiation process begins.

How is this done? Quite simply, by entering a limit order. By doing so, the trader is putting a limit on the price he or she will pay for the stock. In plain English, the trader is saying the stock is worth a certain amount, and not a penny more. So, the trader is willing to buy the stock at the price he or she sets, but is not willing to pay a higher price. The problem and risk of using limit orders is that there is no guarantee of an execution. As we learned in the last example, using a market order ensures an immediate execution. What is not so sure is the price at which the order gets filled. The exact opposite is true of limit orders. The price is certain, but not whether we will buy the stock. Limit orders carry with them the risk that if we try to save 5 or 10 cents by using a limit order instead of a market order, the stock may run higher before our order gets filled. Then, if we really want the stock, we will then be forced to pay a much higher price than now. Thus, using a limit order means that the attempt to buy the stock cheaper than where the market has stock for sale comes with the risk of missing the market.

Let's see exactly how a limit order works. In this example, we have a trader who wants to buy 2,000 shares of CBI. The trader is aware that the stock is for sale at 36.25, and that 1,000 shares just traded at that price, but feels that there is a good chance to buy it cheaper if he or she is patient.

If this person is a true short-term trader, his or her intention might be to buy the stock and then try to immediately resell it to make a quick 10 cents. With that in mind, the trader decides that 36.10 is the absolute highest price he or she will pay for the stock at this time. Like any other trader or investor, this person would love to buy the stock even cheaper than 36.10, but knows that the chances of getting filled any cheaper than that are slim based on where the stock has been trading.

So here is the situation: The trader does not want to pay more than 36.10. Yet the stock is not for sale at 36.10, it is for sale at 36.25. And, to add to the difficulty, even up at 36.25 there is not enough stock for sale. There are only 1,500 shares for sale, and the trader wants to buy 2,000. Based on the supply and demand in the stock, if the trader is lucky enough to buy the stock at 36.10, he or she has bought a real bargain. Note to readers: Assuming you are able to buy stock at 36.10, there is nothing to say that the stock couldn't trade lower after your trade is executed. Whether the stock falls doesn't change the fact that it was still a good execution at the time you bought it. Why? Because you bought stock for 15 cents per share cheaper than where it was for sale. For the purposes of this discussion, we are only concerned right now about learning how to get the best possible execution under the current market parameters.

Over the Internet, the trader enters the order:

Buy 2000 CBI 36.10 LIMIT Day

DAY ORDERS VERSUS GOOD-UNTIL-CANCELED (GTC) ORDERS

It is important to note that there are two different types of limit orders: day and good until canceled (GTC). Day orders will be automatically canceled at the end of the day if not executed, and GTC orders will remain on the books until the trader or investor cancels them. To protect the investor, most brokerage firms will usually cancel GTC orders if they go unexecuted for 60 days. This ensures that an investor doesn't forget about an order and unknowingly buy the stock months or years later, when he or she is no longer following it.

This order states that the buyer is willing to buy 2,000 shares of CBI at $36.10 or less, good until the end of the day (unless the buyer cancels the order before the end of the day). How will the snap quote change?

Remember, the bid-ask spread is set by the highest price a buyer is willing to pay for stock (the bid), and the lowest price at which a seller is willing to sell stock (the ask). The current quote (see Example 4.5A) says we have a buyer willing to pay 36 (and no higher) for 9,900 shares only. Once this new order is entered, we now have a buyer willing to pay _more_ than $36 per share for stock. When the NYSE specialist receives the order, we have 2,000 shares willing to be bought at $36.10, or 10 cents per share higher than the previous highest bid of $36. Therefore, the market changes from 36 bid to 36.10 bid to reflect the intentions of this new, higher bid (see the change from Figure 4.5A to 4.5B).

It is absolutely essential to understand what has happened here. First of all, notice that the volume has not changed, but the bid and the bid size have. The volume hasn't changed because no stock has traded.

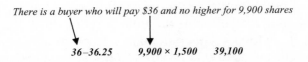

There is a buyer who will pay $36 and no higher for 9,900 shares

36–36.25   9,900 × 1,500   39,100

Figure 4.5A   Raising the Bid

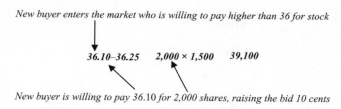

New buyer enters the market who is willing to pay higher than 36 for stock

36.10–36.25   2,000 × 1,500   39,100

New buyer is willing to pay 36.10 for 2,000 shares, raising the bid 10 cents

Figure 4.5B   A Bullish Change in the Bid-Ask Spread

The thing that has changed is the supply-and-demand equation in the stock.

Farrell Says

The first clues to reading the future direction of a stock come not from where a stock has traded, but from changes in the bid-ask spread itself. It is necessary that the day trader follow the reshuffling of buyers and sellers within the quote closely, as they can foreshadow a move in the stock higher or lower.

The Bid

Even though we now have a buyer willing to buy stock at 36.10, it is not for sale at that price. By posting the bid (36.10), the potential buyer hopes to bring out sellers who are willing to sell stock at that price. In a sense, by being the best bid, the trader is advertising to the entire financial world that he or she is willing to buy 2,000 shares of CBI at 36.10. This is important because, although no stock has traded, the bid-ask spread itself has changed *in a bullish way. In other words, the odds that the stock will trade higher have just increased slightly.*

Bid Size

Because we now have a new, higher bid (36.10), we also have a different amount of stock willing to be bought. We now have 2,000 shares willing to be bought at 36.10, which is why the bid size changed to 20. But why hasn't any stock traded?

As we mentioned earlier, the most important lesson to be learned from entering limit orders is that, by attempting to get a better price for your stock, you run the risk of not getting your trade executed. In our example, the stock was offered for sale at 36.25, not 36.10. It is still for sale at that price. Therefore, in the event the stock begins to run higher, the buyer may miss the stock entirely, as the stock may never trade below 36.25 ever again.

A No-Lose Situation for the Bidder

This is a great example of the negotiating process in action. This new buyer at 36.10 knows the stock is for sale at 36.25, but refuses to agree to those terms. The buyer is stating that he or she will pay 36.10 and not a penny more. If the buyer gets the stock at his or her price, that's great. But if not, it's no big deal. If the buyer can't get the price he or she wants, he or she would rather not buy the stock. This is a no-lose situation.

The great thing about this example is that, although no stock has traded, the bid-ask spread has just given us a clue, a glimpse into the future. If we were watching our real-time quote screen carefully, we saw something most people probably missed, a subtle change in the parameters of the bid-ask spread. This is a firm indication of possible future movement in the stock. As a day trader, some of your most profitable trades will come from limit orders.

As an alert day trader, you will immediately see that there is now a higher degree of buying demand in CBI even though no stock has traded. This is because there is now a buyer (at 36.10) who thinks the stock is worth more than 36 per share. The first signs of a potential move upward have been revealed.

In this case, although no stock has traded, the fact that the bid is now 10 cents higher than it was seconds earlier is a clear sign that there is now more buying interest in the market. Perhaps a serious buyer has entered the market. This may be the only clue the stock reveals before it moves higher. It is our job to form a conclusion and react to this information. And, as we know, we may get only a few seconds to react.

EXAMPLE 5: THE LIMIT ORDER TO SELL—OFFERING STOCK

The market in CBI when we last checked was:

36.10–36.25   2,000 × 1,500   39,100

As we saw in Example 4.5B, there is a buyer at 36.10 sitting on the bid waiting for someone to sell the stock at that price. Now we will see what happens when a seller of 1,300 shares enters the market. If the seller wants an immediate execution, he or she is guaranteed 36.10 per share for the stock unless the quote changes before the trade is executed. That is the best price at which there is currently a buyer in the stock. But this seller, like the trader who is bidding for stock at 36.10, believes that he or she can do better than what the current market is offering, and is therefore unwilling to use a market order to hit the bid at 36.10. Essentially, the seller would rather hold out for more money, fully aware that he or she is passing up a guaranteed fill at 36.10, to try to get a higher price. The seller is running the risk that the stock may trade lower before he or she is able to sell. As you know, using a limit order comes with a risk. Missing the market is the risk that comes with trying to negotiate a better price than the market is willing to give. If you are successful, the reward is getting more money on the sale of your stock than you would have by selling at the market.

We know from the quote that the lowest price at which stock is for sale is at 36.25. Since our seller refuses to sell at the market at 36.10, he or she essentially has three choices when placing a limit sell order:

1. Enter an order to sell above the current market—above 36.25; this could be 36.30, 36.40, 36.50, or even higher.
2. Join the offer at 36.25 with the other seller.
3. Underoffer the seller at 36.25 by offering the stock for sale at 36.24 or cheaper.

It should be noted that none of these options are guaranteed executions. There is nothing to say that the stock can't trade lower. Imagine how this seller would feel if, while he or she tries to squeeze an extra 5 or 10 cents above the 36.10 bid, the stock drops 2 points. Instead of saving $50 or $100, the seller might lose a few thousand dollars. That's the risk of entering a limit order instead of a market order.

One of the most important decisions the trader can make is the price at which to enter the limit order to sell. For simplicity, the trader decides that 36.20 is a good price at which to attempt to sell stock. Therefore, the order is entered:

Sell 1300 CBI 36.20 LIMIT Day

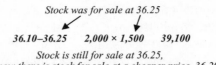

Stock was for sale at 36.25

36.10–36.25   2,000 × 1,500   39,100

Stock is still for sale at 36.25,
but now there is stock for sale at a cheaper price, 36.20

Figure 4.6A   Limit Order to Sell

36.10–36.20   2,000 × 1,300   39,100

New seller has under offered the other seller by 5 cents

Figure 4.6B   The Ask Is Lowered

When the order reaches the specialist, the market changes (see difference between Figures 4.6A and 4.6B).

Notice how the market has changed. The only thing that has changed is the ask and ask size.

This seller of 1,300 shares has underoffered the asking price by 5 cents. Before, we had a seller willing to sell 1,500 shares at 36.25 (the ask). That seller hasn't gone anywhere. We now have a seller willing to sell stock cheaper than 36.25, at 36.20. The volume has not changed, because no stock has traded. Only the parameters of the bid-ask spread have changed.

HAGGLING OVER NICKELS AND DIMES

As we know, the parameters of the market—the bid-ask spread—are entirely negotiated, set by limit orders. Pure supply and demand are at play. Here we have a situation where buyers and sellers are haggling over nickels and dimes. *Five cents a share does not seem like much to the average investor, but to the active trader it means everything.* When trading at high volume, over the course of the year, it may mean the difference between making a small fortune and losing money. Even in this case, if the stock trades at 36.20, the seller saves 10 cents on 1,300 shares, amounting to an extra $130 over selling at the market.

The New York Stock Exchange is essentially an auction market. An auction can be inefficient in the short term as traders and investors negotiate over prices. This is why the opportunities for quick profits are boundless. This fact enables talented traders to make substantial amounts of money in very short periods of time. The job of the day trader is to exploit these inefficiencies by taking part in the negotiating process. With this in mind, one of the most important skills a day trader can possess is knowing when to use limit orders and when to use market orders.

One of the most important facts about trading is that the individual is never forced to buy and sell at the market. Most of the investing public is under the false assumption that there is no room for negotiation, no room to get a better execution than the quoted market is indicating. They think they must accept the price the market gives them. When they sell, they get the bid; when they buy, they get the ask. They do not realize there is room for price improvement. The limit order does not exist as a viable alternative in the mind of the investing public. Ironically, the public's misled tendency to use market orders, and a lack of understanding of how to properly use limit orders, is what enables both Wall Street and the day trader to make profits at the public's expense.

EXAMPLE 6: MOVING THE STOCK HIGHER

Now that we have some idea of the mechanics of the bid-ask spread, we will demonstrate in detail the mechanism that makes a stock trade higher. Have you ever wondered what physically makes the stock trade higher? We talked earlier about how the answer lies in the bid-ask spread. There is only a limited amount of stock for sale at each given price level. All we need to do to move a stock higher is to buy all the available stock at a given price and then buy more at higher levels. Our buying alone will cause the stock to tick higher. Let's see how it looks on paper.

Let's go back to our old example. The market in CBI is now:

36.10–36.20   2,000 × 1,300   39,100

Now assume a buyer comes forward who wants to buy 2,800 shares of stock at the market. This is an investor who heard a bullish rumor that the company's business prospects were improving. This investor thinks the stock is going to fly, and is afraid to miss the market by trying to buy the stock cheaper than where it is for sale. This investor believes the stock could easily be at 45 by the end of the week. Therefore, the investor wants an immediate execution at the best available market price, and is not willing to bargain for a better price.

By entering a buy of 2,800 shares at the market, the investor is agreeing to buy the stock at whatever price the market has stock for sale. In exchange for a guaranteed execution that will take only a few seconds to fill, the investor forfeits the ability to negotiate a better price for the stock. Looking at the bid-ask spread, the investor knows that there are 1,300 shares for sale at 36.20. Because he has been watching the changes in the bid-ask spread closely, the investor also knows that there is a seller of 1,500 shares at 36.25. If the investor wasn't watching, but has access to a comprehensive real-time quote platform, he will also see the 1,500 shares for sale above it at 36.25.

So, the investor enters:

Buy 2,800 CBI Market

When the order reaches the floor of the stock exchange, the specialist immediately trades 1,300 shares at 36.20, the lowest price where stock is currently for sale (see the difference between Figures 4.7A and 4.7B).

What happened to the 36.20 stock? Simply put, the offer was cleaned out. Now the market reflects the next lowest offer, at 36.25. But so far, only 1,300 shares of the 2,800-share order have been filled.

The order is not done. We have 1,500 shares remaining. It is very important here to see how the market has changed. Remember from Example 5 that there were 1,500 shares for sale at 36.25. Then a trader came along who was willing to sell 1,300 shares at 36.20, underoffering the investor at 36.25. This seller at 36.25 did not cancel the order just

1,300 shares are for sale at 36.20

36.10–36.20   2,000 × 1,300   39,100

Figure 4.7A   Cleaning Out the Offer

Buyer lifts all of the stock at 36.20

36.10–36.25   2,000 × 1,500   40,400

Once the stock at 36.20 is taken, next best price at which stock is for sale is at 36.25

Figure 4.7B   The Stocks Tick Higher

because he or she got underoffered. The order still remains on the books.

So, now with 1,500 shares left to buy on the order, the bid-ask spread shows 1,500 shares for sale at 36.25. So, 1,500 shares immediately trade at 36.25 to fill the order.

There are 1,500 shares for sale at 36.25.

36.10–36.25   2,000 × 1,500   40,400

changes to:

Buyer completes trade by buying all available stock for sale at 36.25.

36.10–36.30   2,000 × 4,200   41,900

Seller at 36.25 is cleaned out.

Notice that the next cheapest price at which stock is available for sale is at 36.30.

Now imagine that a buyer of 100 shares enters a buy order after seeing this activity. With 4,200 shares for sale at 36.30, the specialist trades 100 shares at that price to fill this new buyer.

New Buyer completes the order by buying 100 shares at 36.30.

36.10–36.30   2,000 × 4,200   41,900

changes to:

Seller at 36.30 had 4,200 shares for sale—now has only 4,100 left.

36.10–36.30   2,000 × 4,100   42,000

This is a 10-cent stock rally.

Therefore, it took three different price levels to get a total of 2,900 shares executed. Three "prints" occurred: 1,300 shares at 36.20, 1,500 shares at 36.25, and 100 shares at 36.30. In the process, the stock ticked up 10 cents from 36.20 to 36.30 in a matter of only a few seconds. This is exactly what makes stocks move higher.

As this example demonstrates, the easiest way for a stock to move higher is if a buyer is willing to buy more stock than is for sale at a given price level. The buyer then lifts each consecutive higher offer until the order is complete.

As we said earlier, what we looked at here is merely a snapshot of a moving picture. This mechanism is constantly changing. These changes offer tremendous opportunities for price negotiation within the parameters of the bid-ask spread, as buyers and sellers reshuffle throughout the trading day. We never want to trade at the market unless we absolutely have to. Using limit orders, we are able to buy and sell stock at better prices than by trading at the market. This is the difference between making money and losing money. Remember, the day trader is nothing more than a middleman in the buying and selling of stocks. The beauty is that, compared to the investing public, the playing field is not level. The day trader who is skillful in using limit orders is in possession of trading techniques that give them a huge advantage over the buying and selling public. What we just saw in this chapter is information that a majority of the investing world does not understand. Their oversight is the day trader's opportunity to take the other side of the public's trades. This is the way Wall Street operates. It is the continual nickels and dimes that can add up to thousands of dollars per month, if we trade enough. But it is not an easy job. These small profits must be fought for and earned at the bargaining table. The limit order is our bargaining tool. Use it wisely.

Unfortunately, we are not the only price negotiators in the business of buying and selling stocks. On the New York Stock Exchange, there is someone much faster, better equipped, and more knowledgeable than the day trader—the specialist. The specialist is the one who controls the bid-ask spread, and is the best negotiator of all. And the specialist certainly doesn't like or need the day trader. The only way to make quick profits is to first deal with the specialist. That is why the next chapter is devoted to understanding how the specialist operates.

CHAPTER 5

The Role of the Specialist on the New York Stock Exchange

The New York Stock Exchange is the most fair and orderly market-place in the world. This is due to its unique system of trading known as the specialist system. Day traders must learn to use the specialist system to their advantage. When day traders trade NYSE stocks, some of their profits come directly out of the specialists' pockets. The bid-ask spread allows the specialists to earn their profits at the expense of the investing public; and, ironically, by exploiting the bid-ask spread, the day traders earn theirs at the expense of the specialists. A good day trader is one who takes food out of the specialist's mouth. However, the day traders are not trading against the specialists, but rather with the specialists, by reading and copying the specialists' every move and then stepping in front of them on their trades. The specialists are the best negotiators and traders in the market. Where specialists buy, so should the day traders. That is why it is absolutely essential that day traders understand how specialists trade and what the specialists' role is in maintaining an orderly market.

Knowing the mechanics of price movement and the bid-ask spread is essential to being able to read the markets. But that is only half the challenge. The New York Stock Exchange brings together traders and investors with varying degrees of ability and knowledge, as we have said, and the reality is that in this market there are bigger and better players than you. There are mutual funds, hedge funds, banks, brokerage firms, and day traders all competing against each other and conspiring to outsmart the market. The competition among these groups is fierce, which is exactly why most opportunities for quick profit last only a few seconds before someone capitalizes on them.

Farrell Says

Of all the players in the market, the biggest threat to the day trader is not posed by the hedge funds, banks, or brokerage firms. It is posed by the person who sets the odds in the stock, namely the specialist.

We have touched on the role of the specialist briefly in the earlier chapters. The role of the specialist is to maintain an orderly market. On the New York Stock Exchange, there is one specialist assigned to oversee all transactions in a particular stock. Each and every transaction that occurs on the floor of the exchange in that stock has to go through the specialist.

In the previous chapter, we used examples of various market and limit orders to show how the bid-ask spread moves to reflect changes in the intentions of buyers and sellers. As new buyers and sellers come into the market, and as stock trades at different prices, the bid, ask, bid size, ask size, and volume will change. It is the specialists' job to set and update the bid-ask spread and to ensure that the current market parameters are accurate. This can be a very difficult job in fast-moving and volatile markets, as the specialists' stocks get bombarded with limit and market orders at all different prices and sizes that must be reflected in the market.

In addition to ensuring that the general public's buy and sell orders are reflected in the market, specialists also take positions for their own accounts. Specialists are the best day traders of all. They will risk their own capital to take the other side of customer orders if the buy orders cannot be matched with sell orders. This ensures that stocks can trade freely and that liquidity doesn't dry up. The specialists' presence goes a long way in preserving stability and confidence in the market. Buyers and sellers know that under all circumstances there will always be someone who will take the other side of their trades at some price. In addition, they know their best interests are being protected in that they will always receive the best possible execution on their stock.

If a customer enters a buy or sell order at the market, the specialist in that stock is required to give an immediate execution regardless of market conditions. If the specialist cannot find buyers to match the sellers *at a reasonable price*, he or she will take the stock into position, risking his or her own capital to ensure that the customer gets a fair execution.

Note to readers: As of the writing of this revision in the summer of 2008, much has been said in the media about the diminished role of the specialist in the intraday trading of many listed stocks as the NYSE has moved to a more electronic trading model. This is a positive development for day traders. As a result, the day trader is on a more level playing field on the NYSE today than at any point in history, and there has never been a better time than now to trade the NYSE.

The NYSE's specialist system has a long and storied history. A firm grasp of how NYSE-listed stocks have traditionally traded, and an insight into the trading psychology of the specialist, are essential reading for any novice day trader, regardless of whether the specialists may play a diminished role in the future of trading on the NYSE. For the purposes of this discussion, we choose to focus on extreme supply-and-demand situations where the NYSE specialist's participation in the stock is required to keeping trading orderly in the stock. I believe that those examples offer the best glimpse into the mechanics of trading NYSE stocks. Not to mention, extreme supply-and-demand imbalances on the NYSE also offer some of the best odds for a profitable trade.

For this chapter, I would like to use a real-life example of a stock that, as of May 2008, is one of the most volatile stocks that trade on the New York Stock Exchange, Fairfax Holdings (FFH). The stock has one of the widest bid-ask spreads in the market, and is a good case study for our examples. *Warning: I am not saying to trade FFH. If you are an inexperienced trader, you will get your head handed to you on a platter in a stock like this.*

On that note, let's look at an example. If you pulled up Fairfax Holdings (FFH) on your real-time quote system, the market might look as it does in Figure 5.1.

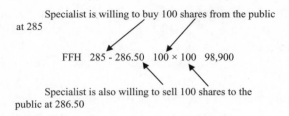

Specialist is willing to buy 100 shares from the public at 285

FFH   285 - 286.50   100 × 100   98,900

Specialist is also willing to sell 100 shares to the public at 286.50

Figure 5.1   The Specialist Is Setting the Odds

This quote tells you that there are 100 shares willing to be bought at 285 and 100 shares for sale at 286.50. Chances are, this is the specialist on both the bid and the offer. This means that as an investor, if you want to sell 100 shares at the market, the specialist is likely the one who takes the other side of the trade by buying your stock from you. By bidding 285, the specialist is indicating to the investing public that he or she is willing to buy stock at that price. Thus, if you sold your stock at the market, you would be immediately filled by the specialist at 285. You would be the seller, the specialist would be the buyer.

Why would the specialist want to buy your stock? Two reasons. First, because he or she has a mandate to maintain an orderly market at all times; but more importantly, *because he or she hopes to be able to turn around and resell the stock to someone else for a profit at a higher price*. The specialist is indicating the intention to do so by the offer to sell 100 shares at 286.50. The next person to enter a buy at the market will pay $286.50 per share. Who will sell the stock to this person? The specialist, because he or she just bought the stock at 285 seconds ago from you. The specialist can make $1.50, or $150, for every 100 shares traded this way all day long, even if the stock doesn't move. Not a bad gig to have.

USING THE SPECIALIST SYSTEM TO YOUR ADVANTAGE

The specialist has a specific job to do, and if he or she is a good trader, gets compensated very handsomely for the work. In the preceding example, the specialist ensured that buyers and sellers both received a fair execution for their stock. And the specialist got to skim a little off the top. But this job is not easy. The key to understanding the nature of the specialist is to be aware that he or she is forced to act in the best interests of the buying and selling public. Specialists will always ensure that you receive a fair execution, because that is their job. They have to answer to the regulatory bodies if a customer complains of receiving an unfair execution. Therefore, specialists will always give priority to your buy or sell order over their own. This creates a tremendous opportunity for day traders, because they can essentially use the specialist to their own advantage in their trading. This seems relatively simple, but in reality it is far from easy.

Farrell Says

The NYSE specialists are, first and foremost, day traders. They are out to make as much money as they can by trading. They risk their own capital in order to earn a living in this process of maintaining an orderly market.

So how is it possible for specialists to make money for themselves while also looking out for the best interests of the investing public? Specialists are able to make money for themselves through the bid-ask spread, by taking the other side of your trades. At all times and under all circumstances, they are willing to be both buyers and sellers in the stock they trade. Like any good day trader, the specialist attempts to grind out small profits all day long. *In other words, the specialist makes money by trading against the investing public.*

So what makes specialists willing to put themselves at risk to buy and sell stock at all times, no matter what the circumstances? They are motivated by profit. As the last chapter demonstrated, there is always a price difference, or spread, between where potential buyers and sellers are willing to transact trades. If the market in our example in Fairfax Holdings (FFH) is 285 to 286.50, there are buyers willing to pay $285 per share (the bid) and sellers willing to sell at $286.50 (the ask). And, as you now know, the specialist will often be on both sides of the spread. This means that, if the stock doesn't move, the specialist buys from customers at 285 and sells to customers at 286.50, making $1,500, for every 1,000 shares that trade evenly. Imagine if the stock trades 20,000 shares in a day this way. The specialist would net a trading profit of tens of thousands of dollars in a stock that didn't move lower than 285 or higher than 286.50! Not bad for one day's work.

WHAT IF THERE WERE NO NYSE SPECIALIST?

It is important to note that even though the specialist is profiting hand-somely on the trade, he or she is ensuring that the customer gets a fair execution. Imagine if the specialist were not in the stock. Stock would only trade at prices where buyers and sellers would agree. With no one willing to take the other side of any order, stocks would have wild intra-day swings. Inevitably, the stock would trade in a choppy and erratic fashion, thus undermining the orderly nature of the New York Stock Exchange.

Let's look again at the preceding example in Fairfax Holdings (FFH). Assume, for the sake of argument, that the specialist is bidding for 100 shares at 285 and offering 100 shares at 286.50. So long as the stock trades back and forth evenly, the specialist will be skimming $1.50 for each position he or she can buy and sell. But what would happen if there weren't a specialist monitoring the stock? The bid-ask spread might widen substantially, because absent the specialist, traders would have to find price levels where true natural buyers and sellers were willing to pay for stock. The bid at 285 might disappear, as would the offer at 286.50. What if the next highest buyer in the stock wasn't willing to pay more than 283 for stock? 283 would be the new bid. And what if there weren't any sellers willing to sell stock until up at 288? 288 would be the new offer. The market would look as it does in Figure 5.2.

A market that was 285 to 286.50 *now* becomes 283 to 288. The bid-ask spread has widened from 1.50 to 5 full points! Who loses when the

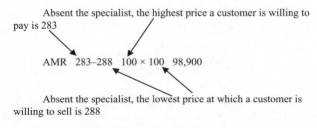

Figure 5.2 **What if There Were No Specialist?**

spread widens? *The investing public.* Without the specialist, someone who wanted to sell 100 shares at the market would get filled at 283 instead of 285, a full two dollars less than if the specialist was in the stock maintaining an orderly market. Conversely, a buyer of 100 shares at the market would have to pay 288 for stock instead of 286.50, because that is the only price at which stock is for sale. This is $1.50 per share higher than if the specialist were in the stock. This wide spread essentially cost both of these customers hundreds of dollars in lost profits. Whoever was bidding for stock at 283, and was able to buy it there, in this example made out like a bandit by putting the screws to the general public, because the specialist wasn't there risking his or her capital. If the specialist had been present, he or she would not have allowed this to happen.

BUYER OF LAST RESORT

As you can see, the profit that specialists make is their compensation for risking their capital to keep the market orderly. But their job isn't that easy. There are times when specialists are called on to be the buyer or seller of last resort. The most extreme example of this is when there is a huge sell-off in a stock. What happens if one day, there was some bad news in a stock with a very wide bid-ask spread? What if there were very few potential buyers for the stock, but there were 200,000 shares to be sold by the general public? Who is going to take the stock off these people's hands? If these sell orders are entered at the market, the specialist is obligated to give them an execution at some price. In a huge sell imbalance, the specialist will be unable to find buyers to match the sell orders. As a result, to ensure an orderly market in the stock, the specialist will be forced to buy a large piece of the 200,000 shares on the open. But there is a catch. *Specialists are able to set the price at which they buy the stock.* Remember, they are risking their own capital to maintain an orderly market, and they are not stupid. Like good day traders, they will buy only at a price where they believe they can make a profit. Though exposing themselves to a substantial amount of risk by taking on such large positions, specialists will most likely set a price that enables them to make a profit over the course of the day this way. They will buy the piece in one large 200,000-share block, or *print*, at a low price, then gradually feed the stock out to the investing public hopefully liquidating along the way at prices higher than where the stock was bought. This is why the opening trade is oftentimes the low "print" of the entire day in a stock.

IS THE PROFIT THE SPECIALIST MAKES JUSTIFIED?

The question may arise as to how fair it is that specialists are able to make such large sums of money at the expense of the public in an example like the preceding one. First of all, in this case, the specialist was taking on a huge risk by buying 200,000 shares from the public. In a sense, the specialist was looking out for panicked sellers' best interests by stepping up to the plate as the buyer of last resort. No one else was willing to buy the stock, and for good reason. What if, after the specialist opened the stock for trading, there were a second investor stampede out of the stock? The specialist could lose literally millions of dollars if the situation in the stock worsened, because he or she would still be forced to buy no matter how grim the circumstances became. Imagine what this situation would be like without the specialist. A more volatile, thinly traded stock like this could very easily lose a large percentage of its value if it were inundated with sell orders without any matching buy orders. So, as much as the specialist traded against the customers, he or she also acted in their best interests by guaranteeing them a fill on such a large sell order. That is why any profit the specialist makes in such a case is justified.

A LICENSE TO STEAL?

Part of the inherent advantage specialists have over the investing public lies in their ability to see the order flow. One of the prerequisites for being able to properly maintain an orderly market is having access to information the investing public is not privy to. In the past, it was often said that specialists had a license to steal, because they could act on privileged information for their own benefit and profit, so long as it is within the parameters of the market. This essentially meant that they were aware of buyers and sellers at price levels other than the current market. As these limit orders sat on the specialist's order book, the general public saw none of it. They could only see the highest bids and lowest offers posted, and didn't have access to lower bids or higher offers. These orders that only the specialist could see had a huge impact on the supply-and-demand picture, and thus the future price, of the stock.

Farrell Says

Much has changed since the days when the NYSE specialists kept the supply-and-demand information secret from the public. In the past few years, rule changes on the New York Stock Exchange have forced the specialists to make this privileged information, the limit order book, available to the investing public in real time. Currently, many real-time trading platforms have the capability to get this data feed for a fee. It is called NYSE Openbook. Ask your brokerage firm if it carries NYSE Openbook.

THE SPECIALIST'S LIMIT ORDER BOOK

Table 5.1 shows an example of a specialist's book in Fairfax Holdings (FFH) using the same market as before:

FFH   285–286.50   100 × 100   98,900

What the inside bid-ask spread doesn't reveal to the day trader is how many other buyers and sellers there are in FFH away from the market.

As you can see, having this secret information is vital to knowing the true supply and demand in the stock. Seeing the order book gives specialists a huge advantage in determining at what price levels they want to buy and sell stock for their own accounts. In this case, what does the specialist see here that the inside quote, 285–286.50, doesn't reveal? The inside quote does not tell you if there are big blocks of stock willing to be bought or sold at prices lower than the highest bid or higher than the lowest offer. In other words, is there stock in demand at prices lower than 285? Yes, there is. The bid-ask spread alone does not show the huge buyer that lurks in the shadows. Look at the buyer at 280. Goldman Sachs is willing to buy 50,000 shares at 280. If the stock never trades that low, the public won't see this buyer in the bid-ask spread until the stock gets to 280 bid, when you would see 50,000

Table 5.1   The Specialist's Book

Buyers

Shares	Price	Type	Firm
1,200	284	Day	Merrill Lynch
2,500	283.10	GTC	UBS
900	281	Day	Citigroup
50,000	280	GTC	Goldman Sachs
1,400	279.25	Day	Morgan Stanley

Sellers

Shares	Price	Type	Firm
400	288	Day	Schwab
100	288.40	GTC	TD Ameritrade
200	289.50	Day	E*TRADE

shares on the bid. However, those that have access to the specialist's limit order book will see it. Note to readers: Traders who have access to the specialist's limit order book via their real-time quote platform will not see the exact information that the NYSE specialist sees. They will see only price and shares, and not the identity of the specific firms that are bidding or offering stock. This ensures that all buyers and sellers, whether large or small, remain anonymous.

The significance is that, because of this large buy order, there is a very good chance the stock won't trade lower than 280 today. For the stock to trade lower, it will first have to trade through 50,000 shares at 280, provided Goldman Sachs doesn't cancel the order first. This fact alone will make specialists more confident in taking the other side of customer sell orders by buying as the stock nears that 280 price level. They can be aggressive buyers because they know there is decent buying support beneath them. In other words, the stock is not likely to go lower. In this case, the specialist is probably even thinking that Goldman Sachs might even raise their bid to a higher price if they get impatient. This buying alone could move the stock higher. Either way, at this point in the day, there is slight upward bias in the stock that the bid-ask spread by itself doesn't reveal. This fact magnifies the disadvantage that the investing public faces against the specialist if they are trading without all of the available price information. They are essentially fighting a battle with one hand tied behind their backs.

Using this same example, imagine if the roles were reversed and there were a huge seller sitting a dollar above where Fairfax was trading. If this is the case, the specialist will be less inclined to take stock into position, for fear that this seller has so much stock for sale that the stock will be unable to move higher. If this seller decides to unload, any buyer stepping into this stock, including the specialist, will feel like he or she has just unknowingly stepped in front of a freight train. Again, there is no way for you to tell without having the limit order book information. The stock would have a downward bias but the bid-ask spread gives no indication.

BEING ON BOTH SIDES OF THE MARKET

The key to the specialist's trading profits is being on both sides of the market at the same time.

The best way to understand how the specialist makes profits is to show specific trading examples. Let's say you pull up the quote for El Paso Pipeline Partners LP. The symbol is EPB, and the quote is as follows:

23.50–24.00 1,200 × 1,500 93,000

You know by now what the snap quote tells you. The bid is 23.50 and the ask is 24.00. The size of the market is 1,200 by 1,500 and the volume is 93,000. There is a buyer willing to buy 1,200 shares at 23.50 (and no higher) and a seller willing to sell 1,500 shares at 24.00 (and no lower). At this point in the day, 93,000 shares have changed hands.

The snap quote paints a surprising picture of the market in EPB. Look at the difference between the bid and the ask—50 cents. As already stated, the specialist is required to maintain an orderly market. In the case of EPB at this point in the day, assume the market is quiet. The active buyers and sellers in the stock, for whatever reason, have stepped away. In plain English, the buyers are not willing to step up, and the sellers are not willing to come down. The liquidity in the stock has temporarily dried up.

This is when specialists really earn their paychecks. With a bid-ask spread 50 cents wide, you would be at major disadvantage if you decided to buy or sell at the market. In fact, if you were to buy 1,000 shares at the market, and then immediately resell those 1,000 shares at the market, you would lose 50 cents, or $500 on the trade. You would buy the stock at 24 (where it is for sale) and then sell it at 23.50 (the nearest buyer).

NARROWING THE BID-ASK SPREAD

One could argue that this wide spread creates an extremely unfair market environment. Said another way, with bid-ask spreads so wide, the investing public would not be receiving fair market value for their stock. This is precisely when the specialist is needed most. The specialist will step into this market and narrow the spread. Chances are, the specialist would never allow the bid-ask spread to get this wide in the first place without first trying to close the gap.

The specialist would take a market that was:

$$23.50\text{--}24.00 \quad 1,200 \times 1,500 \quad 93,000$$

and narrow the spread, updating the market to:

Specialist is both a buyer at 23.70 and a seller at 23.80.

$$23.70\text{--}23.80 \quad 500 \times 500 \quad 93,000$$

How did the specialist do this? By being on both sides of the market at the same time. The specialist is now both the highest bid and the lowest offer. Remember, there were no buyers willing to pay more than 23.50 for stock, and there were no sellers willing to sell for less than 24.00. The specialist, by bidding 23.70, is now the highest bid, and is willing to pay 20 cents more for stock than the bidder at 23.50. In addition, by offering stock at 23.80, the specialist is now the lowest offer as well, and is willing to sell stock 20 cents cheaper than the seller at 24.00. The specialist has aggressively stepped up to the plate when no one else was willing to. As a result, the bid-ask spread has narrowed from 50 cents to 10 cents. Anyone who buys or sells at the market will now benefit greatly from the narrowed spread. This is a substantial benefit to the investing public. It is money saved. This benefit is due to the specialist.

WIDE SPREADS PROTECT THE SPECIALIST FROM VOLATILITY

What would prompt specialists to do this? In a sense, it is their job. They are required to maintain a fair and orderly market in the stock. Unless the stock is extremely volatile or illiquid, a 50-cent spread is not a truly orderly and liquid market. You might expect a spread that wide in an extremely volatile stock because the specialist is unsure of the future direction of the stock. Therefore, the specialist doesn't want to aggressively bid or offer stock for fear of getting picked off. But a less volatile stock like EPB, in most instances, doesn't require a wide spread to protect the specialist. A wide spread is unacceptable in a situation like this. If the stock is not volatile, the wide spread will hurt individual investors who trade at the market by forcing them to pay above-market prices for stock when they buy and to accept below-market prices when they sell. In this case, some investors might complain that they received an unfair execution. The New York Stock Exchange has a reputation to preserve and would frown on this. That is why the specialists will acknowledge their job and responsibility to step forward, risking their own capital to ensure that both buyers and sellers receive fair market value for their stock.

Farrell Says

Keeping bid-ask spreads abnormally wide is a weapon that the specialists use to defend themselves against intraday market volatility. By increasing their profit margins, they are less vulnerable to getting picked off by the public during a sudden market move.

But that is not the only motivation. Specialists are primarily motivated by profit. Remember, they are first and foremost day traders. By narrowing the spread, specialists put their trading capital at risk. And they will put themselves at risk only if they think they can profit in the process. A 10-cent-wide spread means that he or she will make $100 for every 1,000 shares that trade evenly. If there is enough trading volume in the stock, the specialist could make a nice paycheck in just a few hours this way.

As you can see, specialists can make a lot of money by trading actively in a stock when it doesn't move. They do this merely by taking the other side of the random buy and sell orders throughout the day. Day traders must attempt to mimic these moves, and skim small profits from the market orders of the investing public.

That is the real reason the specialist steps in. At all times, this specialist will make sure there is an active and liquid market in the stock. This means he or she must be the buyer and the seller if no one else is willing to do so. In this case, there were buyers and sellers already in the stock, but at unrealistic price levels. The buyer was only willing to buy stock too low, and the seller was only willing to sell too high. If someone agreed to these prices, it would only be because that person didn't know any better: 23.50 is far too cheap a price for someone to get stuck selling stock, and 24.00 is too expensive for someone to have to buy. Usually, it would be the unknowing, unsophisticated individual investor who would get the short end of the stick in this kind of market. Those are the people who trust that the market is fair, which is why they enter market orders in the first place. The specialist should not betray their trust and allow that to happen. In this example, preventing that from happening means the specialist must raise the parameters of the market by keeping a two-sided market, ensuring that buyers and sellers will receive fair market value on the executions.

HANDLING A LARGE SELL ORDER

The previous example demonstrated how a specialist could make quick trading profits by risking his or her own capital. By being on both sides of the market, specialists narrow the bid-ask spread in some stocks to the point where they are involved in every trade that goes through the stock, regardless of whether they are buying or selling. In other stocks, they will only step away if real buyers and sellers are keeping spreads tight. In such a case, they are not needed. At first glance, it seems like the specialists have an easy job, being able to make small, high-percentage profits all day long on the customer order flow even if the stock doesn't move. It is important to remember that anytime specialists keep a two-sided market, by being both the bid and the ask, they are at risk. There are no guarantees that the stock will trade in an orderly manner. Let's look back at our example.

Here is the market in EPB:

23.70–23.80   500 × 500   93,000

As the previous example showed, the specialist is both the bid and the ask. Let's now see what happens when a seller comes into the market and tries to pick off the specialist. Let's say this seller knows bad news is going to come out about the stock at the end of the trading day. He or she wants to unload 5,000 shares at the market. This seller wants out of the stock immediately and doesn't care at what price. He or she is trusting that the specialist, unaware of this bad news, will provide a fair execution. So the order is entered and reaches the specialist's booth on the floor of the New York Stock Exchange:

Sell 5,000 EPB market

This presents a real dilemma for the specialist. It is his or her job to maintain an orderly and liquid market in the stock. The specialist is obligated to give this seller an immediate execution, because this is a market order. With the sell order in hand, the specialist now has to find buyers in the stock who will take these 5,000 shares. But where are the buyers? The previous example indicates that there is a buyer of 500 shares at 23.70. This buyer is the specialist. But what about buyers other than the specialist? The preceding example also shows that there is a buyer of 1,200 shares below at 23.50. Aside from that, there isn't anyone else willing to buy the stock.

So this is a real problem. There is a seller who has decided to sell 5,000 shares at the market, agreeing to whatever price the market gives. The problem is that there seems to be no fair price at which there are enough buyers to match this sell order. The only real buyer outside of the specialist is this buyer of 1,200. But that only takes care of 1,700 shares (500 for the specialist and 1,200 for this public buyer) of the 5,000-share order. Regardless, the seller is guaranteed an execution at some price in the next few seconds.

This is where the specialist must step up to the plate. As the buyer and seller of last resort, the specialist is called on to take the other side of whatever remains of this 5,000-share sell order. Risking his or her own trading capital, the specialist will fill the entire 5,000 shares, buying 3,800 and pairing the remaining 1,200 against this buyer below the market. But at what price?

The price at which this stock will trade is entirely at the discretion of the specialist. Most likely, you will see 500 shares trade quickly at 23.70, followed immediately by 1,200 shares at 23.50. That leaves 3,300 shares that need to be filled because there aren't enough natural buyers to buy the stock from this seller. *The specialist can buy all 3,300 stock at whatever price he deems fair!* He or she is fully aware of the responsibility to give the seller a fair market price for the stock. Naturally, the specialist is only going to buy the stock at a low enough fair market price to increase the chance of a profit. The specialist is not going to run a risk unless he or she can make money on the trade.

Most likely, the rest of the stock would probably print at some price at or below 23.50, possibly 23.25. In that case, the seller will receive 23.25 for the last 3,300 of the 5,000-share order.

So the specialist honors the price quote for the first 500 shares, then matches the 1,200-share buyer with the seller, and then positions the rest of the stock for himself at 23.25. Is this a fair price? This is unquestionably a fair price. Other than the specialist, there were no buyers anywhere near where the stock was trading. Everyone wins in this kind of trade. The seller receives a fair execution, and the specialist buys at a level where he or she feels confident of making a small profit on the trade. The specialist hopes to be able to turn around and feed the stock out above 23.25. Many times, after a print below the market, the stock will immediately bounce. It is possible for the specialist to get out of all of his stock for a profit seconds later. This is his or her compensation for being the buyer of last resort. Remember, without the specialist, this seller might have driven the stock down a full point, because 23.00 or 22.50 might have been the only price level where enough buyers could be found for this 5,000-share sell order.

Farrell Says

Oftentimes, stock will bounce back to its prior price level immediately after the specialist absorbs a large block of stock from the public. This allows the specialist to liquidate the position for a quick profit.

Even though the specialist would love to be able to sell the stock quickly, the reality is that the specialist is now exposed to a substantial amount of market risk because he or she is long 3,800 shares of the stock. There really isn't anywhere to sell the stock right now if necessary. Therefore, the specialist is well aware that he or she may have to hold the stock in position for a while before being able to unload it. *And there is no guarantee that the specialist will be able to sell the stock for more than the purchase price.* This undoubtedly factors into the equation when determining the price. In addition, what would happen if this seller decided to sell another 5,000 shares at the market? Again, the specialist would inevitably have to buy the whole piece, as the buyer of last resort. The specialist could get buried by all the selling pressure, because the stock could easily drop to 22.50 or lower. And there is no way to tell how much more stock might come out for sale before the end of the day. This is the risk that specialists must take, and the uncertainty that they must deal with on a constant basis.

Farrell Says

The day trader must not be fooled into thinking that the specialists are only looking out for everyone else's best interests. Within the parameters of market, specialists will use every possible advantage to trade against the day trader for their own profit.

THE REAL INTENTIONS OF THE SPECIALISTS

Specialists are obligated by certain rules to watch out for the individual investor. And, in the grand scheme of things, the individual investor's welfare is far better off with the specialists than without, because of the individual's reliance on buying and selling at the market. Just be aware that there are two sides to every trade, a winner and a loser. By taking the other side of these customer market orders, the specialists give the individual a fair execution while still watching out for their own best interests.

BEWARE WHEN THE SPECIALIST TAKES THE OTHER SIDE OF YOUR TRADE

Thus, it can be said that the specialist ensures that market orders get executed fairly. But what happens if you are not trading at the market?

What if you want to enter a limit order? Does the specialist still look out for your best interests? In some instances, no. This is the fine line you must walk as a day trader. *When you enter a limit order, the specialist is usually not the one who takes the other side of your trade.* Therefore, the specialist looks at you as an adversary, as competition in the business of making money from the investing public. Specialists do not like day traders, and they will try to trade against you.

Farrell Says

The specialist always has a stronger hand and more knowledge than you do.

For this reason, you don't want the specialist to take the other side of your trade because it usually means the stock will move against you and you are off your market. Always beware, on a limit order, when the specialist is willing to fill your order from his or her own account.

Basically, when this occurs, the specialist is accepting your negotiating terms. This is very dangerous, because the specialist is the best negotiator of all and will only accept your terms when it is in his or her best interest and not yours. Whom do you want to take the other side of your trade? Someone who is smarter, better equipped, and more knowledgeable than you? Or someone with less information and less trading ability? Which of these two will lead to profits? You be the judge.

THE DAY TRADER AS A SHADOW SPECIALIST

Anyone interested in day trading would conclude that the specialist has a nice gig. Specialists have a huge advantage in the stock they trade, and as such, will usually make large sums of money over the course of the year by exploiting that advantage. Wouldn't it be great to be a specialist? The beauty of day trading NYSE stocks is that day traders, by using well-placed limit orders, can serve the same function as specialists. Day traders can buy and sell at the same exact prices, before specialists are able to buy even one share. Limit orders allow day traders to step in front of specialists to get their orders executed. And the specialists cannot do anything about it. They are forced by the rules to give priority to customer orders over their own. This allows day traders to make high-percentage profits, normally reserved for the specialists, off the market orders of the buying and selling public. In a sense, by trading this way, day traders are taking food out of the specialists' mouths.

If you, as a day trader, are taking food out of the specialists' mouths and the specialists really can't do anything about it, what is their defense? The only thing they can do is try to trade against you. Specialists have far more information about the stock they trade than you do. They are better equipped, more knowledgeable, and better able to react to market-moving information. When they can't profit off you, they will trade against you. Always beware when a specialist is trading against you, because you will inevitably lose money this way.

How exactly do specialists trade against you? Primarily in two ways. First of all, as mentioned earlier, specialists trade against you by taking the other side of your orders at the market. Anytime you enter a market order, you are fair game for specialists, because they are inevitably on the other side of your trade, only giving you a price that is in their best interests. Second, and more important for the day trader, specialists will attempt to trade against you when you use limit orders that are "off" the market.

Using well-placed limit orders is the day trader's key to making consistent profits. It is also the key to the specialist's profits. Remember, specialists use limit orders to earn their paycheck. It is the random market orders of the investing public that occur throughout the day that allow this to happen, providing the specialists with the order flow from which they trade. Without market orders, there is nothing for specialists to take the other side of. That is why they love an active market.

But what happens when the day trader also enters limit orders alongside the specialist? If the day trader is on top of the market and only bidding for stock at prices where he or she thinks a profit can be made, the specialist will be unwilling to take the other side of the trade. Why? Because it is not to the specialist's advantage to fill the order if it is at the same price where the specialist's limit order is. In other words, if the specialist is willing to buy at 23.70, and the day trader is also willing to buy at 23.70, the specialist is not going to take the other side of the day trader's order by selling. Why would the specialist sell stock to you at 23.70 if he or she is willing to buy stock at 23.70? The specialist will simply let the order go. He or she has no choice. When specialists can't profit off you, they will wait to see if market conditions move, and then do everything in their power to trade against you. Remember, they feel that you are now invading their turf. And, in reality, you are.

Farrell Says

By copying the exact moves of specialists, you serve the same function in the market as the specialists. How? By bidding for stock where the specialists are bidding, and offering stock where the specialists are offering.

Obviously, the specialists don't like the fact that you are there with them. They probably look at you as a parasite that they can't get rid of. But what can they do? Nothing, really. The New York Stock Exchange has rules in place that always give priority to customer orders over the intentions of the specialist. This essentially means that if a customer (or day trader) is willing to buy stock at the same price where the specialist is willing to buy stock, the customer gets priority.

THE NYSE'S FAIR ORDER HANDLING RULES

There is a reason the customer's order gets priority over that of the specialist. The New York Stock Exchange enacted these rules to keep the market fair for the individual investor. Think how unfair it would be if it were up to the specialist to choose whether the day trader or the specialist would get the stock first, assuming both were trying to buy at the same price at the same time. What would inevitably happen is that the specialist would allocate the stock to the customer's account when the stock was headed lower, and if the stock traded higher, the specialist would keep the stock and profit off it. That is why the New York Stock Exchange put these rules in place: to level the playing field so that individual investors were not unknowingly getting dumped on by specialists. All day traders do is exploit that rule to their advantage.

On the New York Stock Exchange, if a customer (or day trader) is willing to buy stock at the same price as the specialist, and stock trades at that price, the customer is entitled to the stock over the specialist. While the day trader may step in front of the specialist, under no circumstances can the specialist jump in front of, or front-run, the day trader. Exploiting this rule is the day trader's key to making consistent short-term profits.

This is an extremely important concept to grasp. Perhaps an analogy would shed some light on this. Think of the largest used-car dealership you know of. How does it make a profit? By buying cars from the general public at low prices and reselling to the general public at higher prices. The owner of the dealership profits from the spread between where the cars are bought and where they are sold. The general public, unfortunately, is at the mercy of this spread. The owner of the dealership is entitled to the profit because of the risk he or she takes. The dealer might not be able to resell a car after taking it into inventory. In addition, there is overhead and salaries to pay. The profit the dealer makes on the spread is his or her livelihood.

How do you think the owner of the dealership would feel if you went into the office and demanded to buy and sell the same cars at the same price as the dealer? Even worse, if you demanded first dibs on any car that came to the dealership to be sold? Suppose the dealer was prepared to bid $5,000 for a used car, and you were, too. And you said that, because you were a customer, you were entitled to the car over the dealer if you were both bidding the same price. This would never happen in a million years. The owner of the dealership would not appreciate your attempt to take food out of his or her mouth. Chances are, the owner would kindly ask you to leave before throwing you out on your head.

As crazy as it sounds, when the day trader bids at the same prices as the specialist, this is exactly what is happening. Look at the specialist as the owner of a used-stock dealership. The specialist earns a livelihood by buying and reselling stocks, just as the used-car dealer buys and resells cars. The rules that give priority to a customer over the specialist at the same price create a situation exactly like being able to step in front of the owner of a used-car dealership and have first crack at the car, at the exact same price the dealer is willing to pay. Think of the amazing possibilities for profit that this rule would allow.

If this could happen, and enough people knew about it, eventually the car dealership would go out of business. The customers would be taking food right out of the owner's mouth by intercepting his or her profits. The customers, not the dealership owner, would now be the middlemen in the buying and selling of cars. Although this rule doesn't exist in the world of car dealerships, it does exist in stock trading. So how is the specialist able to stay in business? Don't most people try to exploit this rule for their own profit? The answer is no. The specialist is able to stay in business because so few people understand how this rule works and that it even exists. That is why the day trader who knows how to exploit this rule can make significant profits.

But just like the car dealer, the specialists are not going to be happy when a customer or day trader attempts to take food out of their mouths. In fact, specialists will do everything possible within the rules to make it difficult for you to make money trading this way. Can you blame them?

As long as you are on top of your market, there is really no way the specialists can do you harm. It is only when you are off your market that they get the opportunity to pick you off and trade against you. So how can you be assured of being on top of your market? The only way is to buy at the exact levels where the specialists are buying, and to sell exactly where they are selling.

The specialists know the stock they trade better than anyone else, and as such, they know what are good price levels and what aren't. Day traders must realize that the specialists are only going to buy stock at levels where they feel they can make a profit, so copying them by picking the same price level to buy at is the easiest way to make profits day trading.

For an example of how this strategy works, let's use the original example of EPB but with a slightly wider spread. Imagine that, since we last looked, the market has widened out:

The specialist is a buyer at 23.65 and a seller at 23.85.

$$23.65–23.85 \quad 500 \times 500 \quad 98,000$$

As a good day trader, you will absolutely love a bid-ask spread like this. There is ample opportunity for profit in this example. The trading strategy is clear: You will bid alongside the specialist at 23.65. How do you know the specialist is bidding 23.65? That comes later in the chapter. No trade is without risk, but if the specialist is willing to buy 500 shares at 23.65, it is probably a safe level for you to buy as well. You are aware that the specialist knows the stock better than anyone else in the world. Specialists will not buy at a level where they think they will lose money.

Warning: As with the previous example in FFH, we are not advising here for you to trade EPB, or any stock for that matter. EPB is just being used as a hypothetical example to show how the process of trading works. Any stock you choose to trade is up to you entirely. Proceed with caution and at your own risk.

Bidding alongside the specialist is the day trader's short-term equivalent of an investor buying the same stock that Warren Buffett is buying. Billionaire Warren Buffett, of Omaha, Nebraska, is considered the greatest investor of all time. Many of the best investors in the world will throw caution to the wind and buy the same stock he is buying, even if they have not done any homework on the stock. They only need to know that Buffett is buying. They justify this by saying that if Buffett likes the stock, he must see something that other people don't see. Many investors have made a fortune investing with Warren Buffett this way over the last 30 years.

So, with this in mind, you will attempt to buy EPB at the same price where the specialist is attempting to buy, 23.65. Let's say you wish to buy 800 shares. Over the Internet, you enter the order:

Buy 800 EPB 23.65 DAY

Now, notice what happens when the order reaches the floor of the New York Stock Exchange. Because the specialist is bidding 23.65, he or she must let your buy order go in front. Therefore, the market will change.

Specialist is willing to buy 500 shares at 23.65:

23.65–23.85   500 × 500   98,000 (should be 23.65–23.85)

Day trader wants to pick off specialist and also buy stock at 23.65:

23.65–23.85   800 × 500   98,000

Specialist is obligated to give first priority to day trader's buy order at 23.65.

Specialist is forced to cancel own buy order at 23.65 as day trader steps in front.

As you can see, the specialist lets your 800-share order go in front of his own. If the 500-share bid were a customer order and not the specialist, the bid size would change to 1,300, not 800 (500 shares ahead of you plus your 800 shares) and you would be in line behind the 500 shares that were there first. However, because it was the specialist bidding for 500, your stock gets first priority at 23.65. This means that the next 800 shares that trade at 23.65 go to you before the specialist buys even a single share of stock.

If you are fortunate enough to buy the stock at 23.65, there is a good chance you will be able to make 10 cents or more on the trade. The strategy is to resell the stock at 23.75, 23.80, or 23.85, hopefully making $80, $120, or $160 on the trade. This is an example of a trade where the odds of success are in your favor as a day trader. And remember, the stock doesn't have to move outside of the parameters of the bid-ask spread for you to make a small profit this way.

Farrell Says

So, with the odds in your favor, how is it possible for the specialist to trade against you? Fortunately, there is only one way: smoke and mirrors. The specialist can try to scare you away from the trade by altering the appearance of supply and demand in the stock, by making it appear that the stock is heading lower when in fact it is not. The specialist will do this by manipulating the ask price or ask size, or both, in the attempt to give the appearance that the stock is weaker than it actually is. If it looks like the stock is going lower, you might be tempted into canceling your order. Remember, specialists will do all they can to trade against you within the parameters of the market. This kind of strategy is fair game for them because it does not violate any rules.

As a day trader, you will find that specialists generally will not bother you unless you repeatedly trade in and out of their stock. If you are an active trader in the same stocks, their specialists will probably get to know your trading strategy because they see every order you enter. For instance, after a while, the specialists will know that you are not an investor but a day trader who will resell the stock for a 10 cent profit as soon as you buy it. If you are trading in and out of the same stocks frequently, their specialists will probably get annoyed by your presence, because your trading is taking profits away from the specialists. Remember, the 10 cents you might make by exploiting the bid-ask spread is one less profit the specialist will make that day.

NEVER REVEAL YOUR HAND

This is why I sometimes prefer to move around and trade different stocks. If you are only in a stock once, and you are trying to buy at the same price where the specialist is buying, the specialist will be more inclined to leave you alone than if you trade in and out of the stock frequently. If the specialist is unfamiliar with you, the environment will be far more favorable for a quick profit than if he or she is familiar with your strategy. It's just like a poker match. You never want to reveal your hand to anyone, particularly not the specialist. The last thing you want is for the specialist to know when you are attempting to buy stock that the stock is going to be coming right back seconds later in the form of a sell.

HOW CAN YOU DETERMINE WHERE THE SPECIALIST LURKS IN THE STOCK?

The key to making money day trading NYSE stocks is to pick the same buy and sell levels as the specialist. It sounds easy enough, but before you can pick the same buy levels, you have to identify exactly where the specialist is in the stock. You certainly don't want to pick a buy level because you mistakenly think the specialist is bidding there, only to find out it is another day trader or customer like yourself. If that happens, you will be setting yourself up to get picked off. *Making this distinction is one of the most important skills you can develop as a trader.* Remember, when you look at the quote in the stock, you only see prices and size; you can't see who the players are, you won't know who is bidding for stock and who is offering stock. The only thing you know for sure is the number of shares willing to be bought or sold and the price. However, that does not tell the whole story. Is the specialist trying to accumulate stock, or is it one of the big brokerage firms? Does someone have an ax to grind in the stock? Being able to answer these questions is vital to predicting short-term movement in the stock.

The problem is that there is really no way to know with absolute certainty who is bidding or offering stock at any given time. Only the specialist and other traders on the floor of the exchange have access to that information. As a day trader trading from home, the only thing you can go on is the clues the market gives you. In trading, there are no certainties. At all times, you are basing your actions on your instinct, your best guess of what the situation is. That is all you can do.

So you will have to do some detective work. Study the stock. Examine the prints. Look where the trades have been. Are they little trades or big ones? Are they 100-share trades, or 5,000-share trades? Have they all been at the same price? Is stock trading on the bid or the offer? These clues will help you formulate your conclusion.

Farrell Says

The first and best clue to determine whether a buyer is the specialist and not a customer is revealed by the bid size and the ask size. The rule of thumb I use is that if the size of the bid (or ask) is a round number like 500 or 1,000 shares, there is a good chance it is the specialist and not a customer bid. If it is an odd number, like 2,700 or 5,500, you can be almost certain it is a customer bid and not the specialist.

Why do specialists normally bid in 500- or 1,000-share lots instead of larger amounts? Because they don't ever want to get blindsided by a large sell order they can't see coming. By bidding for only 500 shares, they are assured that a seller can only sell a maximum of 500 shares to them at the current price. If they want to buy more, they can. But if they don't, they aren't forced to. Because of the specialists' responsibility to be buyer and seller of last resort, they never want to accumulate large pieces of stock at one price level unless they are forced to. This helps keep their position light when the market is quiet. This way, if a large seller comes into the market, the specialists are able to drop the stock a few price levels to buy at their discretion. Specialists bidding for 5,000 shares instead of 500 might run into trouble because, if that is the market they are advertising, they will be forced to buy 5,000 shares at that price if a seller comes out. Under no circumstances are specialists allowed to back away from a trade, unless they cancel their bid before

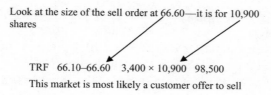

Look at the size of the sell order at 66.60—it is for 10,900 shares

TRF   66.10–66.60   3,400 × 10,900   98,500

This market is most likely a customer offer to sell

Figure 5.3   A Customer Offer to Sell

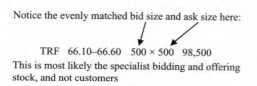

Notice the evenly matched bid size and ask size here:

TRF   66.10–66.60   500 × 500   98,500

This is most likely the specialist bidding and offering stock, and not customers

Figure 5.4   The Specialist Offer to Sell

the seller arrives. So, by bidding for only small amounts, the specialists' exposure to risk is somewhat protected.

Let's look at an example of how to tell the difference between a specialist bid and a customer bid in a new example (see Figures 5.3 and 5.4). Templeton Russia and Eastern European Fund (TRF) is a closed-end fund that trades on the New York Stock Exchange.

A specialist who really wanted to unload 10,900 shares would not reveal his or her hand to the investing public by advertising an intention to sell.

JOCKEYING FOR POSITION

You want to know where the specialist is in a stock so that you can mirror his or her moves. But it is extremely important to identify where the specialist lurks for another reason as well. When you are trading lower-volume stocks, position is everything. The New York Stock Exchange is a first-come, first-served market. This means that, when you are bidding, you always want to be first in line at the price level at which you are trying to buy stock. Otherwise, if your order does not arrive first, you will have to get in line behind any orders that arrived ahead of yours or be forced to raise your buying price. The only way you can be assured of being first in line when buying is when your bid replaces the specialist's bid, or if you raise the bid to a higher price. Where you are in line can determine whether you make money or lose money on the trade.

Remember, these are not market orders. They are limit orders, and as such they require a wholly different approach, because with a limit order there is never a guarantee that you will buy your stock. For example, let's say you have been watching TRF all morning. It has caught your eye because of two things: (1) the wide bid-ask spread in the stock, and (2) a large buyer sitting on the specialist's limit order book slightly below the quoted market. You are confident that, if you can buy it on the bid, the odds of being able to flip it for a profit are decent.

You immediately enter a buy of 600 shares on a 66.10 price limit. The market changes (see Figures 5.5A and 5.5B).

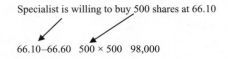

Specialist is willing to buy 500 shares at 66.10

66.10–66.60   500 × 500   98,000

Figure 5.5A   The Specialist's Bid

changes to

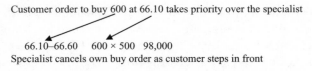

Customer order to buy 600 at 66.10 takes priority over the specialist

66.10–66.60   600 × 500   98,000

Specialist cancels own buy order as customer steps in front

Figure 5.5B   The Customer Steps in Front of the Specialist

Now imagine that a second investor attempts to join the bid at the same time as you and enters a buy order for 1,000 at 66.10. How will the market change?

Unlike the previous example where the specialist steps aside, in this case the new buyer will get in line behind you because the order arrived a fraction of a second later than yours to the specialist's post. Their 1,000 shares get added to your 600 shares, making the size of the bid now 1,600 shares.

$$66.10–66.60 \quad 1,600 \times 500 \quad 98,000$$

The second customer order reaches the floor for 1,000 shares at 66.10, but must get in line behind your bid for 600 shares, making the bid size 1,600 shares.

What has happened here?

In the span of two seconds, the bid at 66.10 went from 500 shares to 600 shares to 1,600 shares. You may have thought you were the only person watching the stock. Obviously, you weren't. Someone else is bidding alongside you at 66.10!

Farrell Says

This is a very important point about day trading: You are not the only one who is watching these stocks. Every opportunity that looks good to you usually looks good to other people as well. That is why it is imperative that you enter your orders as quickly as possible when you see the chance to make a quick profit. I cannot tell you how many times I have missed out on profits because I was a second too slow.

HOW DO YOU KNOW WHERE YOU STAND IN LINE?

The first question you must answer is where you stand in line. There are a total of 1,600 shares willing to be bought at 66.10. And only 600 shares of that are yours. If you were paying attention to the changes in the bid size, there is a very easy way to tell where your 600 shares are in line by examining how the market has changed. You must attempt to find out, because this could mean the difference between buying the stock and making a profit or not being able to buy the stock at all. Remember, there might be a few hundred shares that trade at the magic price of 66.10 all day, and you want to make sure you are first in line so that you are entitled to the stock if someone is willing to sell it to you there. If you find out you are last in line, you might think about canceling and moving the bid up a single penny so that you will have a better opportunity to buy at your price level.

WHEN IN DOUBT, ASK THE NYSE FLOOR

There are two ways you can find out where you stand. The way most Wall Street traders do it is by sending one of their firm's floor brokers out to talk to the specialist directly. The specialist will usually give this information out to friends and colleagues on the floor, who then relay the information upstairs to the trader. In this example, if the information came back that there were 1,000 shares ahead, it would mean you were not first in line. In other words, the other investor beat you to the floor. That is not the case here, however.

Unless this other order canceled, you would have to wait until at least 1,000 shares traded at 66.10 before you would be able to buy a single share. The reality is that, if this other trader had gotten in line before you, that person might have been able to have the stock bought and sold for a quick profit before you even got your order filled. All because that order reached the specialist's booth a few seconds before yours did. Those few seconds could be the difference between making a few hundred dollars on the trade and not making anything at all.

Unfortunately, when trading from home over the Internet, you don't have the luxury of being able to send someone down to the floor to talk to the specialist. That kind of service costs money. Sometimes the online brokers will call the NYSE floor as a courtesy for you. All you have to do is call up and ask. But that doesn't mean you can't find out on your own anyway. There is an easier way to determine the position of this order. All you have to do is look at changes in the bid size. In this case, if you were watching the quote carefully, the specialist updated the market this way:

$$66.10–66.50 \quad 500 \times 500 \quad 98,000$$

to:

$$66.10–66.50 \quad 600 \times 500 \quad 98,000$$

to:

$$66.10–66.50 \quad 1600 \times 500 \quad 98,000$$

Notice how the bid size has changed. It went from 500 to 600 to 1,600—in a matter of a few seconds. That alone gives you enough information to go on. *Your order was the first one to get down to the floor.* The other trader, who wanted 1,000 shares, got there after you. There is no question about this. The specialist was bidding for 500, then gave priority to your 600-share order when it arrived. Then, a second later, the other order for 1,000 reached the specialist, who put it behind your 600 shares on the bid.

Farrell Says

As you can see, you have to be alert and watch the quote as your order is entered. If your quote system has time and sales, you will be able to pull up the recorded changes in the market. Time and sales is usually available only on the more comprehensive quote systems: Therefore, if you don't have it, you have to be extra careful not to miss the changes in the market. If you do miss those changes in the bid size and ask size, you will be left guessing as to where your order stands.

The alert reader might be confused by why the bid size is 1,600 shares and not 2,100 shares. There were 500 shares bid for before your order arrived, then your 600 shares, plus another 1,000 shares from customer number 2. So that makes a total of 2,100 shares and not 1,600 shares, right? Wrong! The first 500 shares was the specialist. Therefore, the specialist simply cancels his or her bid for 500 shares and lets the customer orders for a total of 1,600 shares go instead. In essence, both traders have stepped in front of the specialist.

In these slower-moving markets, there will be only a limited number of shares that trade at a given price level where it may be easy to make a quick profit. The game of day trading requires that you be patient enough to wait to accumulate your stock at your price. It is very easy to buy stock at higher price levels where you won't be able to make quick profits because you will always be able to find someone to sell it to you there. *In other words, as the odds get worse, it gets easier for you to buy stock.* You alone could buy 100,000 shares of this stock if you had enough capital and were willing to take the price up a few dollars. But it certainly wouldn't be at a price where you could make a quick profit. *Remember, the market does not give money away.* You are going to have to fight for every precious share you buy at levels you deem cheap, and the last thing you want is for someone else to get to the stock before you. "Cheap" is always that level where the odds are good that you will be able to sell immediately for a quick profit, no matter what price that is. That is why it is absolutely imperative that you attempt to get your hands on as many cheap shares as possible when the opportunities arise. Position is everything. In some of the less active stocks that have daily volumes of less than 100,000 shares, you may only see 2,000 shares trade at your price level throughout the whole day. If there are two people both trying to bid for 2,000 shares at the same price, the difference between getting an execution and not getting an execution might be your place in line. And that place in line is determined by who gets there first.

TIPPING THE ODDS IN YOUR FAVOR

In this chapter I have outlined the basic principles behind exploiting the bid-ask spread. As you can see, by trading with the specialist, you tip the odds of success in your favor. Respect the judgment of the specialists. They didn't get where they are by being bad traders or making foolish decisions. They are the best day traders in that particular stock in the investing world, and they are going to buy only at levels where their instincts tell them stock is cheap.

It seems as though 99 percent of the investing world is unaware of the rule that specialists must give priority to customer orders over their own. The idea that you can buy stock at the same price where the specialist is willing to buy it seems outside of the periphery of most investors. Well, this book shows otherwise. You have to look at things inversely from the way you previously understood them. This is not an easy thing to do. Taken a step further, the fact that you can make money trading in and out of a stock that doesn't move by day trading is very hard to fathom because it seems to go against common sense. You'd be surprised to know how many people, even those working on Wall Street, have no idea this can even be done.

The irony of this fact is that the general public's oversight is exactly what allows you to make profits. Remember, for a limit order to be executed, there has to be a market order to take the other side of the trade. But who are the people buying and selling at the market? Don't they know they can save money by trying to negotiate a better price? You now know the answers to these questions. The actions of the specialists are what make Wall Street go around. As such, the last thing any Wall Street trader wants is for the general public to be educated in the ways of stock trading. As long as investors still subscribe to the myth that the only way to buy and sell stocks is at the market, the specialists, market makers, and brokerage firms will be happy. This ensures that the public remains the food and the prey of Wall Street. And, in the process, the public helps put food on the day traders' tables.

BEWARE OF THE SPECIALIST

Now that you know a little bit about how the specialist maintains an orderly market, and how to exploit the specialist's two-sided market for your own profit, a word of caution is appropriate. As you know, the reality of exploiting the bid-ask spread is that the day trader is taking food out of the specialist's mouth. This is a very dangerous thing to do, but it is the only realistic way for you to make consistent money if you subscribe to the belief of trading only when the odds are in your favor. Remember, the specialists do not like day traders. They do not want or need customers like you. As such, specialists are fully aware of your presence. You are not going to be able to hide from them. The only way you can protect yourself is to be very selective as far as what prices you put your limit orders in. Specialists will exploit any weakness you have in the attempt to drive you away from their markets. This means they will trade against you every chance they get. But the only chance you give them to do this is when your bid or ask is off the market. When this happens, the specialists will take the other side of your order, usually resulting in your losing money.

That is why it is absolutely essential that you only use this strategy on stocks where the supply and demand picture looks favorable. If you try to get in the specialists' way when it isn't, you will get crushed. I guarantee you will lose money. Remember, especially in volatile stocks and volatile market conditions, the specialist's advantage over the public becomes bigger as the supply-and-demand picture becomes more unclear. In those instances, other strategies are needed. We will deal with these in later chapters.

SECTION IV

Introduction to Scalping the NYSE: Taking Food Out of the Specialist's Mouth

As a day trader, you must leave no stone unturned in your quest for profits. But the New York Stock Exchange has several thousand stocks. Where do you even begin? Where do you look for your first trade? Surprisingly, some of the best opportunities, with the best odds, are often found in areas overlooked by the rest of the investing community.

Does a stock have to be volatile for you to make money trading it? One of the best-kept secrets in stock trading is that the answer is no. What the investing world doesn't understand is that you can make just as much money, or in some cases even more money, day trading a stock that is less volatile than one that is more volatile.

But if the stock doesn't move, where do the trading profits come from? Right out of the specialist's pocket. How do you do it? By doing the same thing to the NYSE specialist that the specialist does to the investing public: exploiting the bid-ask spread.

CHAPTER 6

The Day Trader's Secret Weapon

Exploiting the Bid-Ask Spread

I have spent the first sections of the book trying to give you an idea of the dangerous environment you will enter when you make your first trade. But there comes a certain time when you have to take the leap of faith, stop leaning on the advice of others, and start relying on your own ability and skill. Right now that time has arrived. It is time to get down to the task at hand: trading. All the preparation in the world cannot prepare you for that unique feeling the first time that your money is on the line.

Farrell Says

Warning! The scalping strategies outlined in this section of the book are suitable only for less volatile stocks. The more volatile the stock, the less likely that this strategy will be profitable. Although this chapter will discuss some things to look for, there are no set rules to determine whether a specific stock has a volatility level that is suitable for this strategy at the time you are trading it. The market is in constant flux. A stock that is good to trade one day may not be the next. This book offers insights on how to spot favorable

> *supply-and-demand situations, but it is entirely up to you to pick the right stocks, at the right time, under the right conditions. How well you do this will determine your success or failure as a trader. Proceed with caution and at your own risk.*

Contrary to popular belief, stock trading does not have to be like playing the slot machines, craps, or roulette. If your strategy is to make every trade relying on instinct, on gut, and on chance, your fate is sealed. Over the long term, you will not win. In fact, you probably will not last more than a few weeks. Unfortunately, this is the way many people approach trading. They begin by trading the most volatile stocks in the market, unaware of just how stacked the odds are against them. And they usually find out the hard way that they can't compete. These stocks simply move too fast for a beginner to get a good handle on the changing supply-and-demand picture in the stock. It seems there is always someone faster beating the online day trader to the punch in these volatile stocks. But there is a better way. Day trading slower-moving stocks can be just as lucrative, as long as you stick to the right stocks. To understand this, we will start by addressing the most basic questions.

HOW CAN YOU MAKE MONEY TRADING STOCKS THAT DON'T MOVE?

Think of the last time you glanced in your local paper to see how your favorite stocks had done the day before. Remember all the stocks that were unchanged, or only up or down 25 cents on the day? On any given day, there are literally hundreds of stocks that fall into this category. The investing public's first impression is that because there was no action in these stocks, there was no way to make any money in them. But did anyone make any money in these stocks? Was it a lost cause? No, it was not. I guarantee that in each and every one of these stocks, there were profits to be made, and all the while no one even noticed. But how did this happen?

Let's look at an example. Say you have been keeping your eyes on Dean Foods, listed on the NYSE under the symbol DF. You have noticed that for the last two days it has been stuck in a tight trading range, hovering around $23. In fact, the real-time quote reads:

*DF Last **23.30** Unchanged High **23.50** Low **23.10***

Most investors would agree that no money was made or lost in the stock so far on this day. The stock didn't even fluctuate more than 40 cents between its high and its low. This belief that no money was made is based on the fact that for long-term investors, their account's value remained unchanged if the stock didn't move. In other words, the 1,000 shares they own are worth no more today than yesterday.

The important thing to remember is that these people are investors, not traders. They have a much longer time horizon, and they tend to look at things in a different way. But traders see things differently. The short-term trader should not look at Dean Foods as a lost cause simply because of the lack of volatility. Smart traders see a potential for profit in the stock.

THE ROLE OF THE SCALPER

The first thing the day trader would look at is the trading volume. Dean Foods, on this morning, has traded over 100,000 shares on the New York Stock Exchange. For the 100,000 shares that traded, someone took the other side of every single trade. What does this mean? It means there is a very good chance that short-term speculators were active in the stock. Who are these speculators? The primary speculator is undoubtedly the specialist, the one who oversees all trading in the stock. Is there anyone else? Yes, a type of day trader called a *scalper*. Scalpers are so named because they exist by scalping razor-thin profits.

What does the scalper see that other people don't? Volume. When the scalper sees volume, he or she sees the chance to make small, high-percentage profits on the order flow. Anytime a stock trades a few hundred thousand shares in a day, and is not volatile, there is ample opportunity for short-term profit. So what is the secret?

There are four keys to success as a scalper:

1. Pick good entry and exit points to limit the risk of loss on the trade.
2. Get in and out quickly to maximize the use of your trading capital.
3. Trade a large enough position, say 1,000 shares, to make a small profit of 10 cents worth your time and effort.
4. Win more times than you lose.

Remember, profits of nickels and dimes add up quickly if you are able to keep your losses to a minimum. It is next to impossible to make money on every trade. There will be losses. So you need to make sure that the losses aren't so frequent or large as to squander an entire day's worth of trading profits.

HIT SINGLES, NOT HOME RUNS

It is important to note a theme mentioned earlier in the book. Look at Wall Street. What do the brokerage firms do differently than the investing public when they trade? It is very simple. The trading desks are not in it for the long term, nor are they trying to make big gains on each trade. The focus on small profits and high turnover is the mind-set that the scalper must also possess.

I remember when I was a trader at Wall Street brokerage firm Gruntal & Company. The firm would frown on any position that was held in your trading book for more than a few days. In fact, any position held for more than three weeks would have to be liquidated. The reasons are very simple. The firm did not want to have its trading capital tied up for extended periods of time on longer-term investments. As a trader, that is not what you are getting paid to do. It is not where the money is. The day trader can learn much from this.

This is what I mean when I say that Wall Street is not trying to hit home runs. That is not why these firms pay their best traders multimillion-dollar salaries. Remember, every time a trade is made, someone's money is on the line. And Wall Street firms are extremely careful about how and where their trading capital is put at risk. Every trade they make is a well-calculated risk. In addition, they are very content with taking small profits and not getting greedy. This is all because they know that, year in and year out, these small profits are exactly what keep trading firms in business.

OPERATING UNDER THE RADAR

Why does going for singles work so well? Because it is done in an environment where the rest of the world is trying to hit home runs.

Think about it. Why do investors buy a stock in the first place? Most are not in the game for small profits. They are in it for the long haul—to buy and hold it a few years, and hopefully sell at a significant profit.

Think about the specialist for a moment. Think how much money the specialist could have made in a stock like Dean Foods. Remember, the stock traded over 100,000 shares on the NYSE on this morning. If there was an absence of customer orders on the specialist's limit order book, there is a good chance the specialist was at risk on the majority of those trades, buying when there were no buyers and selling when there were no sellers. If he or she was careful, there is a very good chance the specialist made a decent profit with much less risk than you might think. And guess what—no one even noticed, because the stock didn't move. It was all done under the radar.

Farrell Says

Please keep in mind that, for this strategy for trading NYSE stocks, your trades must be routed to the floor of the NYSE for execution. If they are not, you put in jeopardy the ability to get a good fill at a good price. Sometimes, if you don't put a preference on the order, your online broker might route the order to another destination, like a regional exchange, instead of the NYSE floor. They do this to save on costs, and to steer business away from the NYSE.

When in doubt, ask your online broker where the orders are routed. If the order is not routed to the NYSE, demand that they reroute to the floor. They may do it for free, or they may do it for an added fee. If it is the latter, it might be time to change online brokers. Most higher-end brokers have trading platforms that can route directly to the NYSE.

The question you must ask yourself is: When trading for small profits, how much risk to do you want to expose yourself to? If your plan is to make only, say, 10 cents on a trade, why would you ever risk losing more than that? In other words, if your upside on the trade is limited to 10 cents, you do not want your downside to be 25 or 50 cents or more. If it is, you will eventually give back all of your profits.

In the end, no matter how many nickels and dimes you make, you will be at a net loss at the end of the day if you are giving back your profits in large chunks. What can you do? The answer is simple. For starters, if you are scalping for small profits, you must avoid volatile stocks.

AVOIDING THE GLAMOUR STOCKS

The reality is that the glamour stocks, the high flyers, the stocks that make the news every day, are simply too volatile for this kind of trading strategy. These stocks could move several points in a very short amount of time. Remember, to the online day trader, volatility can be your friend in certain rare instances, but most of the time, it can work against you. The bigger players in the market love volatility, because they have the resources and the means to take advantage of it. The small players in the market like you and me generally do not.

I have learned the hard way throughout my trading career that trading volatile stocks for small profits oftentimes doesn't work. Inevitably, in the beginning, it will seem very easy to get in and get out for a small profits over and over again. In a stable market, the high flyers are so liquid that it may seem like making dimes and quarters in them is easier than taking candy from a baby. In fact, you might be able to do this all day long. Do not be fooled, however. These stocks rarely stay calm for long. Eventually, you will get clipped.

Remember, as we have said earlier, a stock is constantly adjusting and readjusting its prices to find buyers to match with sellers. When the stock cannot find buyers, it readjusts its prices lower until it brings them out. The more volatile the stock, the more quickly this readjustment process occurs. The last thing you want to do is get caught on the wrong side of it as it is happening. If so, the stock you are trading will drop a point or two in the blink of an eye, at the worst possible time, when you are long 1,000 shares. You will give back a week's worth of profits in a few minutes. And when that happens, you will never want to trade these stocks again.*

---

*Note to readers: There are ways to be profitable trading volatile stocks. We talk about these in later chapters.

EXPLOITING THE BID-ASK SPREAD

There may be one question in the back of your mind: Why limit yourself to only a 10-cent profit when you can try to make more? Why not go for quarter- or half-point profits, or even higher? The answer has to do with the structure of the stock and the way in which it trades. Remember, the trading strategy is to exploit the bid-ask spread. You carefully pick a price to bid for stock at a level where the odds of flipping it for a profit are good. You cannot make more than 10 cents on this strategy on most trades simply because the bid-ask spread is not wider than 10 cents. Also, it is quite possible that the NYSE specialist will contain the volatility, and refuse to let the stock trade higher or lower than a certain range. This alone can prevent you from making anything larger than a small profit on the trade.

FINDING THE TRADE'S SWEET SPOT

One of the central messages of this book is to only put your capital at risk when the odds swing to your favor. It is quite possible that, in a stock like Dean Foods, you could spend the entire morning watching the stock for a favorable supply-and-demand situation, and it may not arise. And then, a split second later, the forces align to set up for a profitable trade. This is what I like to call the sweet spot.

What would cause the forces to align in your favor? It could be any number of factors. Perhaps a large buyer appearing, a large seller canceling, or even a subtle reshuffling of the buyers and sellers in the specialist's limit order book. Every stock has its own sweet spot. How quickly you are able to spot it, and more importantly, get an order executed at a favorable price level in the sweet spot, determines your success or failure as a trader.

To help find the sweet spot, let's look back at our example.

Let's check the quote for Dean Foods (DF) in real time once again. Here's how it looks:

DF Last **23.30** *Unchanged High* **23.50** *Low* **23.10**

The snap quote does not give a good indication of where the sweet spot in the stock is at this point in the trading day. For starters, you have to look at how the bid-ask spread has changed throughout the morning. By using the time-and-sales function on your trading platform, you are able to retrieve the time sequence of the bid-ask spread. Times and sales would reveal much more detail than this, but for our discussion, let's say that some of the data that you pull up are as follows:

23.20–23.30	*20,000 × 100*	*48,000* at *9:31* A.M.
23.25–23.35	*20,000 × 500*	*71,000* at *9:55* A.M.
23.30–23.45	*20,000 × 800*	*109,000* at *10:30* A.M.

Farrell Says

The time-and-sales function on your trading platform is one of the most important tools that a day trader can possess. It is absolutely essential to profitable trading. Think of time and sales as instant replay. It shows the time and size of the trades as they occurred, and what the bid and ask was at the time of the trade. Remember, the tape does not lie. The time-and-sales function allows you to examine and review the tape, to see how the changing supply and demand picture in the stock affected the stock's price. It is a great tool. Use it wisely.

SIMPLIFYING A COMPLEX PROCESS

Time and sales reveals two major things: (1) For the majority of the morning, the specialist kept the bid-ask spread 10 cents or wider in the stock. So what do you, as a scalper, conclude? *First of all, the fact that the specialist is willing to keep the spread wide signifies an absence of competition in the stock.* This is a positive development in the stock, because it indicates that there is some wiggle room in the stock to exploit the bid-ask spread. At face value, the strategy should be to join the bid or outbid the other buyers by a single penny to become the highest bid in the market. If your bid gets hit, immediately offer the stock out for sale on the ask, or a penny below the asking price. As buyers come in on market orders, you will hopefully be selling your stock to them up 10 cents or more from where you bought it. In its purest form, that is how you exploit the bid-ask spread.

Second, and more importantly, notice the size of the buyer in the stock: 20,000 shares. This is another bullish development in the stock because the buyer has been trying to buy the stock all morning. The buyer was there at 9:31 A.M., 9:55 A.M., and now at 10:30 A.M. One could assume that the chance of the buyer's still being there for a meaningful amount of time is pretty good. This is only an assumption, but the tape is offering us some basis for that conclusion.

OTHER MOVING PARTS TO THIS TRADE

I am aware that this explanation has simplified a very complex process that plays itself out thousands of times per day in the many thousands of stocks that trade on the NYSE. Do not be lulled into thinking that there isn't more to examine in this trade to find the sweet spot before putting your capital at risk. There is, and you can never be too careful.

There are more moving parts to this puzzle that need to be assessed before we place the trade. Now that the NYSE specialist's limit order book is open, transparent, and available for public view, you must take it into account before you put your money on the line on this trade. In other words, you must examine where the others buyers and sellers are lurking in the order book before placing the buy order.

Trading Dos and Don'ts

With this is mind, there are four general rules to follow before we take a glance at the NYSE limit order book:

1. If there is a big buyer either on the bid or slightly below the bid, that is a favorable condition. Pick price levels a penny or two above where this large buyer lurks.

2. Avoid entering the stock if there is a large seller sitting on the ask, or slightly above the market. No matter how big the buyers might be, and no matter how wide the bid-ask spread is, the presence of a large seller is a game changer. It changes the risk level, and the odds swing from favorable to unfavorable for the day trader. A stock that might have been a great buying opportunity seconds earlier now becomes a stock to avoid.

3. Don't be afraid to cancel an order if the supply-and-demand picture changes before you are able to buy the stock. The last thing you want is for your order to be hanging out there, vulnerable to getting picked off, if the market changes. Said another way, if the reasons for buying the stock have changed, get out of the way of the stock, because it could be moving against you.

4. Along those lines, if the supply-and-demand picture changes adversely after you buy the stock, it might be time to think about getting out of the stock, even if it is at a loss. This is one of the hardest decisions that any trader can make. The irony is that some of the best trades are ones in which you take a small loss. Reacting quickly and realizing you are wrong can save you thousands of dollars of potential losses.

A Quick Glance at the Specialist's Order Book

So you have examined the changes in the bid-ask spread for several hours. The market at 10:30 is as follows:

23.30–23.45   20,000 × 800   109,000 at 10:30 A.M.

Let's now take our analysis to a deeper level by examining the specialist's limit order book to see what it looks like.

NYSE Specialist's Limit Order Book in Dean Foods	
Buyers	**Sellers**
20,000 shares at 23.30	800 shares at 23.45
10,000 shares at 23.29	100 shares at 23.55
500 shares at 23.20	200 shares at 23.60
400 shares at 23.15	100 shares at 23.69

We have already talked about the buyer of 20,000 shares at 23.30. The interesting thing is that the specialist's order book reveals something even more bullish. Notice the buyer of another 10,000 shares a penny cheaper at 23.29. This strengthens the notion that the stock is not going to trade lower than the bid price of 23.30, unless these buyers get filled or cancel.

Another bullish development is on the sell side. Take a look at the sellers and the price gap between them. Notice that the sellers are sparse. Outside of the 800 shares at 23.45, you don't have much stock to weigh the price down. These two facts are the final two pieces in our puzzle. *We have now found the sweet spot the stock!*

So where do we bid for the stock? The answer is 23.31. The buyer of 20,000 shares at 23.30 is too large to get in line behind him or her. It is much more prudent to simply outbid by a single penny so that our buy order is now first in line. So you enter a limit order to buy 1,000 shares at 23.31.

So the market that was:

$$23.30–23.45 \quad 20{,}000 \times 800 \quad 109{,}000$$

becomes:

$$23.31–23.45 \quad 1{,}000 \times 800 \quad 109{,}000$$

As you know, there is no guarantee that you will be able to buy the stock at 23.31. One thing to note is that you are bidding for the stock in the hopes of bringing out a seller. If you are lucky enough to buy the stock, the odds of being able to flip it for a small profit are good. You are waiting for a seller "at market" to "hit your bid." If you are patient, there is a good chance you will buy the stock.

So you watch your real-time quote screen for prints in DF at 23.31. You wait 10 minutes, and still nothing has traded. Then, before your very eyes, you see 1,000 shares trade at 23.31.

You look at your real-time quote screen, and DF reads as follows:

$$23.30–23.45 \quad 20{,}000 \times 800 \quad 110{,}000$$

So what happened to your 23.31 bid for 1,000 shares? It is no longer there. Someone hit your bid. You bought 1,000 shares. Notice that the volume changed from 109,000 to 110,000 as your 1,000 shares traded.

The next step is to check your brokerage account to make sure that the stock is positioned in your account. You check your position screen and see that you now have 1,000 shares of DF in your account. Therefore, your money is now at risk. Now the fun begins.

Because you bought the stock at 23.31, you have some wiggle room within the bid-ask spread to decide where to sell the stock. The great thing about the bid-ask spread in DF right now is that there isn't any stock for sale until 23.45. You could get greedy and try to make 13 cents on the trade by putting it up for sale at 23.44, *but* sometimes keeping the spread "tighter" increases the likelihood of the stock trading.

Farrell Says

Sometimes by not getting greedy and being content with taking smaller profits, your odds of getting the trade executed increase. It is not a science but an art, based on market feel and the level of your trading experience. If you trade a stock for long enough, you will develop an instinct for picking price levels where you can get stock executed. Remember, you can enter trades all day long, but if you can't get the trade filled, your time is wasted.

So let's assume for our example that the goal for this trade is to make $100 before commissions, or 10 cents on the trade. Therefore, you now enter an order to sell 1,000 shares of DF on a 23.41 limit. Upon receiving your order, the specialist updates the market to reflect your offer. The market now looks like this:

23.30–23.41   20,000 × 1,000   110,000

Now the waiting game begins. Your hope is that by dropping the price from 23.45 to 23.41, you will bring out buyers. In other words, you just put the stock "on sale" at a savings of $40 per 1,000 shares. As a trader, you should feel comfortable about your chances of making this trade a success because you have done your homework prior to putting your capital at risk. You can take some comfort in knowing that as long as the large buyer of 20,000 shares at 23.30, and the buyer of 10,000 beneath it at 23.29, remain on the order book, your risk of loss is minimal.

So, you wait about 20 minutes, and then you see the bid-ask spread change back to what it was before, as 1,000 shares print at 23.41 on the NYSE. The market looks like this:

23.30–23.45   20,000 × 800   111,000

What happened to your stock, which was for sale at 23.41? It traded! Someone took the offer. You were lifted: 1,000 shares traded at 23.41.

You double-check your account positions and see that you no longer have a position in DF in your account. It took only a few minutes, but your objective was accomplished. You bought 1,000 shares at 23.31 and sold 1,000 shares at 23.41.

A BET WITH THE HOUSE?

One of the most important things you can do, especially as a novice trader, is to reflect back on each trade to assess whether the risk was justified. The first questions we must ask are: Was this trade prudent from a risk-reward standpoint? Were the odds in your favor? In other words, was this a bet with the house? The answer is yes. There are several reasons why.

First, we were successful in buying on the bid and selling on the ask. Taken at face value, exploiting the bid-ask spread put the odds of a profitable trade in our favor. Second, we examined time and sales prior to the trade to determine that the specialist's tendency, on this day, is to keep the bid-ask spread at least a dime wide. This also helped put the odds of success in our favor by giving us some wiggle room, some margin for error, in the event that things did not go as planned. Third, time and sales revealed that a buyer of 20,000 shares had been on the bid all morning. This large buy order acted as a backstop preventing the stock from going lower. And fourth, by checking the specialist's limit order book, we saw that there is even more buying pressure (10,000 shares a penny below the market at 23.29). Taken together, these four things helped swing the odds in our favor, making the trade justified from a risk-reward standpoint.

Thus, by using well-placed limit orders, and by carefully examining where the buyers and sellers were stacked on the order book prior to placing the trade, we were able to identify a sweet spot in the stock. Hitting that sweet spot enabled us to make $100 in profit before commissions in the process. The beauty of the trade is that you made $100 in a stock that basically didn't move. Think about it: The market is the same now as it was before, 23.30 bid, 23.45 ask, and yet you were able to grind out a small profit.

> ### *Farrell Says*
>
> *Although this example showed a trade size of 1,000 shares, beginning traders should experiment with 100-share lots at first. This will limit your risk of loss as you learn how to get into and out of positions. Do not raise the share size to more than 100 until you are consistently profitable on a gross basis before commissions. Remember, there is a learning curve involved. Don't get greedy. Pigs get fat; hogs get slaughtered.*

TOO MUCH WORK FOR ONLY $100 IN GROSS PROFITS?

The question must be asked: Isn't this a lot of work for only $100 in profits before commissions? The answer is, yes and no. If you spent the whole day watching the stock, and only got one trade filled throughout the day, then yes. But, to a seasoned trader, the answer is no. A bet with the house is hard work. Under the right conditions, this trade could be completed in only a few minutes or seconds. This would allow you to potentially go back in and repeat the trade again, assuming the supply and demand remained the same. Not to mention, the veteran scalper should be watching and trading in more than one stock at a time. In my own experience over the past decade, at any given time I might have 100 stocks or more on my watch list looking for favorable supply-and-demand situations.

> ### *Farrell Says*
>
> *The essence of scalping is the ability to replicate the same type of trade over and again.*

A FEW WORDS ON RISK

In the grand scheme of things, the Dean Foods day trader grossed $100 with a relative low risk of loss because the trades were made within a very tight range. But do not be fooled by this. The markets do not give away money. Anytime you are able to profit, there is always risk. There is an old cliche that says hindsight is 20/20. In hindsight, by the end of the day, it was very easy to see the level of risk that this trader faced. The stock didn't trade outside of a 40-cent range.

But the trade appeared riskless only after the fact. We didn't know going in what the stock had in store. Remember, the markets are based on fear and greed. How were we able to buy the stock and resell it for a profit? Only because someone agreed to sell it there. And why would that person sell on the lower end of the day's trading range? Obviously, that person was fearful that the stock was going lower, not higher.

My point in all of this is that you never know what the stock is going to do after you buy it. Regardless of how the trade turns out, you are always at risk the instant you buy the stock. Anything can happen. That bid for 20,000 shares a penny beneath us could have canceled right after we bought stock a penny higher, and it could've brought new sellers into the stock, causing it to drop 50 cents or more in a heartbeat. That's the nature of trading. The only control you have over this is in picking good entry and exit points based on a favorable supply-and-demand picture in the stock.

SECTION V

Trading the Market's Momentum: How to Profit from Volatility

Some of the best trading opportunities in the market come when the market is at its most volatile and its most uncertain. High volatility on the NYSE can create an extremely difficult environment for the NYSE specialist to maintain an orderly market in the stock that he or she trades. When this happens and the NYSE specialist is on his or her heels, the specialist will typically widen bid-ask spreads as protection from the onslaught of customer orders. In this case, the odds of a profitable trade can quickly swing into the day traders' favor if they are positioned properly. But this comes with a significant amount of risk. Any time there are extreme supply-and-demand imbalances in the market, there will be high risk, but there will also be tremendous opportunities for day traders to take advantage of the dislocations in the market. Knowing how the NYSE specialist trades in volatile market conditions is the first step in being able to exploit the process for profit.

CHAPTER 7

Exploiting Market Volatility and Momentum

Strategies for Trading Volatile Stocks

In volatile market conditions, the NYSE specialist's trading advantage over the investing public becomes more exaggerated as the supply-and-demand picture in the stock becomes more unclear. The more "clouded" the supply and demand appears, the more money that the specialist can make at the expense of the investing public. By exploiting the NYSE's specialist system, the day trader can use this volatility to his or her advantage. Remember, the larger the house edge for the specialist, the more profitable it can potentially be for any trader who is able to bet with the house.

The reality is that it is extremely difficult for most novice traders to be consistently profitable by trading in and out of high-volatility stocks. The forces of the house edge that we have talked about earlier in the book, including wide bid-ask spreads, slow executions, and lightning-fast market movements, are much more acute in volatile stocks than they are in less volatile areas of the NYSE. In fact, these forces can be more destructive to wealth creation here in volatile stocks than anywhere else in the stock market. In the land of momentum, a central theme of the book rings true: The only defense day traders have in this dangerous environment is to pick and choose their opportunities carefully, and to bet only when the odds are significantly in their favor.

THE SPECIALIST AND THE UPPER HAND

In the domain of trading high-volatility NYSE-listed stocks, the house edge is extremely powerful. This is because supply and demand can change so rapidly in volatile stocks that it can be very difficult to get a handle on what is happening. As we have said earlier in the book, some of the best trading opportunities may literally only last for one or two seconds before they disappear. In some volatile stocks, the time frame is sometimes even less than that.

These difficult market conditions are, in part, the result of the presence of the specialist. As stated earlier, on the New York Stock Exchange the specialist is required to maintain an orderly market. Each individual stock has one specialist who is assigned to oversee all transactions in that particular stock. The specialist risks his or her own capital to ensure that customers receive fair and instantaneous executions when buyers cannot be matched with sellers, provided the orders are market orders. As you know, specialists will only risk their trading capital at a price level that is advantageous to them. In other words, when they risk their trading capital, they do so at a price where they think they can turn a profit on the trade. Remember, the specialist is the best day trader of all.

The minute you enter the arena of high-volatility stocks, the rules change. As a general rule of thumb, it is next to impossible to consistently make money by exploiting the bid-ask spread in volatile stocks in that same manner that the scalper does in less volatile stocks. In rapidly changing market conditions, the specialists have the upper hand, which can put the day trader at a severe competitive disadvantage. Said another way, you cannot get in their way. If you do, you will most likely lose money. Why? Because the specialists have more supply-and-demand information at their disposal than you do, and they can "pick your pocket" if you are off of your markets. In other words, the online day traders will always be one step behind. And, when seconds, or fractions of seconds, are the difference between making and losing money, being one step behind always means losing money.

Farrell Says

This section on momentum trading, like the previous chapter on scalping, is written within the framework of having your buy and sell orders routed directly to the New York Stock Exchange for execution.

> *In most volatile and liquid NYSE stocks, there can be buyers and sellers on smaller, regional exchanges "off the floor" that compete with the NYSE for business. Those smaller exchanges are insignificant to our discussion here. The primary pool of liquidity in most NYSE listed stocks is right on the floor of the exchange, and for the purposes of our discussion here, that is the only thing that we are concerned about.*

It is important to remember one of the major themes of this book: You never want to bet against the house. Over the long term, you will not make a living as a day trader if you and the specialist are taking the other side of each other's trades. So, if you can't trade with the house all the time, how can you possibly make any money by day trading volatile NYSE stocks? If you recklessly throw your money at every trade, the answer is that, most of the time, you cannot. Outside of a few instances that I will mention in the next few pages, the odds are generally going to be stacked against you. It doesn't mean that there aren't opportunities. There are. It is just that there is a whole world on Wall Street of day traders and hedge funds who trade volatile stocks for a living. Everyone is looking at the same supply-and-demand information as you are, and the competition is brutal. With this in mind, there are a handful of momentum trades that allow you to trade with the house—to be on the same side of the trade as the specialist without being at a real disadvantage. One such strategy is called playing a gap open.

PLAYING THE GAP OPEN—A STRATEGY FOR BETTING WITH THE HOUSE

One way to trade with the house in volatile NYSE stocks is to be on the same side of the trade as the specialist when the stock opens. Remember, the role of the day trader is that of middleman. The day trader is a buyer when the market needs buyers, and a seller when the market needs sellers. An extreme supply-and-demand imbalance on the open of trading offers a great chance for a profitable trade. Imagine a company that has just released bad news. The bad news will inundate the stock with sell orders. For the stock to open, the sell orders must be matched, or paired, with buy orders. If the stock opens down 15 points on the news, the specialist will be forced into being the buyer of last resort if natural buyers cannot be found. The important thing is that when this happens, *the specialist will set the price at which he or she buys the stock*. And, as you know by now, specialists will set a price to risk their capital only where they feel they can make money, consistent with their role of maintaining an orderly market.

BUYING ON BAD NEWS

How does the day trader trade with the house when this happens? By joining the specialist in buying the stock from the investing public on the opening print, with the intention of reselling the stock minutes later for a profit. The reasoning is that, if the specialist is risking his or her capital to buy the stock, it must be a good price level at which to buy.

Let's look at a real-life example from earlier in my trading career in Computer Associates (CA), who issued a press release warning that earnings for the year would be far below expectations. (Note to readers: Computer Associates, as of the writing of this revision in the summer of 2008, moved from trading on the NYSE to Nasdaq.) This news came as a major surprise to the analysts who cover the stock. The result was that the stock was downgraded from a strong buy to a hold at several major brokerage firms. When a stock is downgraded to a hold, investors usually do not wait around for conditions to improve. They rush for the exits and sell. This is a true panic situation.

What some in the investing public don't realize is that when bad news is released before the market opens, the stock will immediately reflect the news. In other words, it is too late to sell: The price level at which the stock opens for trading that morning will have the bad news priced in. In this case, by 9:30 A.M. and the open of trading, it was fair to say that this bad news had reached everyone it needed to reach. In addition to being on the front page of all of the major financial newspapers, including the *Wall Street Journal* and *Investor's Business Daily*, it was talked about continuously on CNBC's *Squawk Box* from about 7:00 A.M. to the open of trading. In other words, the information was fully disseminated before the stock had opened for trading.

Anytime there is panic selling, the sellers do not care about the price at which the stock trades. They just want to get out of the stock at any price. This is an extreme case of a supply-and-demand imbalance.

Remember one thing: For every buyer there is a seller. This means the stock must open for trading at the price at which the influx of sell orders can be matched with buyers. If they can't match the sellers with buyers, they can't open the stock for trading.

By the 9:30 A.M. opening bell, the stock had over 2 million shares of sell orders at the market on the books. This means that all 2 million of these orders had to be filled on the opening print of the stock. In other words, the specialist now had an order in hand to sell a total of 2 million shares at the market. But who in their right mind would want to buy a stock when it is this lopsided? Conventional wisdom would tell anyone to stay away from the stock. *But conventional wisdom never put any money in the day trader's pocket.*

This is where the role of the specialist becomes very important. The specialist assigned to Computer Associates is obligated to maintain an orderly market. This means that, as long as the 2 million shares to be sold were entered at the market, the specialist is required to give them an execution at some price. If the specialist cannot match the sell orders with buyers, he or she becomes the buyer of last resort. As you know, buyers of last resort hold one advantage over the investing world: They determine the price at which the stock will be sold.

Think of the significance of this situation for one moment. Imagine being at a bargaining table where you are the only buyer and the sellers are in a state of panic. They want out at all costs. They tell you, as the only buyer, to name your price. Think of the edge you have over the sellers. They will accept any price you give them. This is what the specialist is faced with on a gap opening.

BETTING ON THE SPECIALIST

> ### *Farrell Says*
>
> *One of the central themes of the book is to put capital at risk only when the odds swing in your favor. As a general rule of thumb, gap-openings on the NYSE offer some of the best trading odds of the entire day.*

When the specialist has over 2 million shares to be sold and cannot find buyers, he or she will be forced to step up to the plate. As the buyer of last resort, the specialist will be called on to buy a large percentage of that 2-million-share sell order at his or her price. In the extreme, it is possible that the specialist may be forced into buying a half-million or a million shares. Think about this. If you were forced to buy 1 million shares of stock, but you could name your price, what price would you arrive at? Would it be high or low? In whose best interests would that price be? Yours or the seller's? That is exactly my point. In this type of trade, the odds are overwhelmingly with the specialist.

Joining the NYSE Specialist as a Buyer of Last Resort

The beauty of this kind of situation is that you don't have to be a reckless gambler to bet on the specialist. By placing a buy order in the stock before it opens for trading, you have, in essence, placed a very calculated bet on the specialist. You are risking your trading capital on your trust in the trading abilities of the specialist, and the inherent trading advantage that the specialist has over the investing public. When you enter a buy order at the market, provided it is entered before the stock opens for trading, you will buy your stock on the opening print at the exact same price and the exact same time as the specialist. You will join the specialist as a buyer of last resort.

One of the great things about this trade is that you do not need a split-second execution for it to be profitable. This is because your decision to buy the stock is made before the stock opens. It is not a race among day traders as to who gets the stock first. Whether you have a slow execution or a fast one, if you get the buy order in before the stock opens, you will get in on the action.

An Extreme Case of Buying on the Bid

In the case of Computer Associates, there was such a strong sell imbalance that the stock was delayed until 9:54 A.M., a full 24 minutes after the stock market opened for trading. The opening print was at 39.12, down over 15 points from where the stock closed the day before. Over 2.5 million shares changed hands on the opening trade. I bought 1,000 shares for myself. The ironic thing about this kind of trade is that, although it is entered at the market, it is much more like a limit order than a market order. This is buying on the bid in its most extreme form. How are you buying on the bid? Because you are buying into a sell imbalance, and are getting filled at the same discounted price as the specialist. In other words, both of you are on the same side of the trade. In the case of Computer Associates, I bought 1,000 shares at 39.12 and it is quite possible that the specialist bought at least 500,000 shares or more at 39.12 as well. Why did the stock take an extra 24 minutes to open? Obviously, the specialist had trouble finding buyers to match against these panicked sellers for 2.5 million shares. That is exactly why the stock was delayed.

The trade went exactly according to plan. Within a few seconds of the stock's opening at 39.12, it was immediately bid for at 39.18; four minutes later, at 9:58 A.M., the stock was trading up at 39.75; and by 10:00 it had broken through 40. That is where I sold. I had made over $875 in six minutes, and I was out of the stock by 10:00 A.M.

Goosing the Market

It is very important to understand what happened here. There was a very good reason the stock immediately traded up from its opening print of 39.12. To comprehend what happened, you have to put yourself in the specialist's shoes. As we have said, there is a very good chance that the specialist was the buyer of a very large block of that 2.5-million-share piece—quite possibly, 500,000 shares or more as it printed on the open. That is a huge position. Obviously, the specialist is not stupid. He or she would not have arrived at an opening price of 39.12 if he or she thought the stock would trade any lower than that price. Like any other day trader who bought stock on the open, the specialist bought 500,000 shares at 39.12 because he or she thought the shares could eventually be sold at a higher price.

If you had enough trading capital, what is the first thing you would do after you bought a half-million shares of stock? You would try to goose the market. In other words, you would immediately bid the stock up from 39.12 to make it appear the stock was headed higher. That is why the stock went to 39.18 bid to 39.75 bid to 40 bid in only a few minutes. Who do you think bid the stock up? Most likely, the specialist. Why? To make the stock appear like it has bottomed, so that other speculators would jump on the momentum. This would create a buying frenzy at these discounted price levels (remember, the stock was trading 15 points higher the day before) that would move the stock higher. The specialist would then sell into the demand, slowly liquidating the half-million-share piece for a profit. Imagine making an average of even 25 cents on a half-million shares! That is a $125,000 profit, all for a just a few hours of work.

Riding on the Specialist's Back

How was I able to make an $875 profit in only six minutes? By riding on the specialist's back. I was fulfilling a need the market had. Like the specialist, I was a buyer when the market needed buyers, and I was a seller when the market needed sellers. When the selling pressure was most intense, I was a buyer. When buyers finally stepped into the market, I was a seller. That is how I made my money. But that does not tell the whole story. *The money was really made because of a trust in the efficiency of the NYSE's specialist system. In other words, a trust in the ability of the NYSE specialist to "clear" an extreme supply-and-demand imbalance*. The price itself is almost inconsequential. Whether the stock opened at 41, 40, or 39 is insignificant. Regardless of price, wherever the specialist was willing to risk trading capital by buying stock was a good price level for me to do the same.

PARAMETERS OF THE GAP-OPENING TRADE

When you attempt to do a gap-opening trade, you must be very selective in the stock you choose. Anytime you are buying on bad news, you must be extremely careful how you go about doing it. There are four questions you must ask before entering a buy order:

1. *Is it a large, market-leading New York Stock Exchange stock?* It is absolutely essential that the stock trade on the New York Stock Exchange. This strategy is based on exploiting inefficiencies in the NYSE's specialist system of trading. It does not mean that it couldn't work on Nasdaq stocks. But for the purposes of this book, it is better suited for NYSE-listed stocks. In addition, it must be a market leader. If it is not a household name, I would strongly advise that you stay away from it. Why? The reason is simple. If the stock is a large, recognizable name, it is most likely widely held by mutual funds, hedge funds, and pension funds. As a result, there will always be buying interest in it, no matter what the price and no matter how bad the news. The

buying interest brings trading volume to the stock. Ideally, this strategy works best if the stock trades several million shares of volume. If it is a smaller, less-well-known company, one or two large sellers could crush the stock at any time if they decide to unload, because of the lower trading volume. In other words, it is a much more unpredictable situation, as a smaller stock can't withstand the selling pressure as well as a large stock can. As a day trader, you do not want to be in an unpredictable situation because it increases your risk exposure and lowers your odds of success. You do not want to leave anything to chance.

2. *Has the information that is moving the stock lower been fully disseminated?* This is another very important qualification for this kind of trade. Bad news brings out sellers. Anytime you are buying on bad news, you must make sure you are buying the stock at the precise moment the selling pressure is highest. As long as the news is released in the morning before the opening bell, the opening trade will undoubtedly be when the selling pressure is most intense. Why? Because anyone who has decided to sell the stock based on the bad news will most likely do so on the open. In a panic situation, people are not likely to wait. This is because when the investing public rush for the exits at the same time, as a group, they are their own worst enemy. This is exactly what creates a short-term bottom. How can you tell if the news has been fully disseminated? My rule of thumb is that if it makes the front page of the *Wall Street Journal*, or if they are talking about it on CNBC prior to the open, then the bad news has been fully disseminated.

3. *Is it an extreme supply-and-demand imbalance?* It is essential that you make the distinction between an ordinary sell-off and a panic sell-off. You do not want to use this trading strategy when a stock opens down only a point or two on bad news. You need a true panic sell-off—down 5, 10, 15 points or more. Why? Because the prerequisite for the success of this trade is that all the sellers rush for the exits at the same time—at the open. You need a panic sell-off to scare enough reluctant sellers, who might be sitting on the sidelines, into selling. This reduces the odds of the stock's heading lower after the opening print, because anyone inclined to sell will most likely have done so on the open, out of fear. It is this fear that creates the market

bottom, enabling the day trader to make a quick profit on the inevitable rebound.

4. *The million-dollar question: Is the opening trade going to "clear out" the sellers on the specialist's limit order book?* Answering this question is perhaps the most important component of this trade. If the opening trade fails to "fill" all of the limit order sellers that are trying to get out of stock, the stock is less likely to bounce immediately after the opening print. Remember, the sellers who use market orders are not of concern anymore. Why? Because they will have already been filled on the open, so they cannot weigh the stock down anymore. Our concern is with the supply of large limit orders on the order book at price levels slightly above the opening trade. It is the presence, or absence, of these orders that will determine whether the stock will trade higher or lower in the seconds and minutes after the stock opens.

HOW TO TELL IF THE OPENING TRADE WILL "CLEAR" THE SPECIALIST'S LIMIT ORDER BOOK

This is a very important concept to grasp, so perhaps more explanation is needed. If *the opening trade fails to "clean out" the largest sellers on the order book, it will be difficult for the stock to bounce after the opening print* Let's look at a hypothetical example. To keep things simple and easier to understand, let's imagine that the stock closed at $50, and, due to bad news, is indicated to open around $40 on the NYSE. And let's assume that there are 500,000 shares for sale at 40.00 on the NYSE.

At 10 seconds before the opening print, the NYSE limit order book would look something like this:

Buyers	Sellers
500,000 @ 40.00	500,000 @ 40.00
10,000 @ 39.99	600 @ 40.25
6,700 @ 39.70	1,000 @ 40.75

Let's imagine two scenarios—one in which the stock opens at 40.01, and the other in which it opens at 39.99.

A difference of 2 cents . . . . No big deal, right? Wrong! The difference between the stock opening at 39.99 and 40.01 in this example is night and day, and it might be the difference between you making and losing money on the trade. Why? It has to do with the way the limit order sellers are stacked on the specialist's order book prior to the opening trade.

In the first scenario, if the stock opens on NYSE at above 40.00, at, say, 40.01, the seller of 500,000 at 40.00 will be filled. However, if the stock opens 2 cents cheaper, at 39.99, the seller of 500,000 at 40.00 will not be filled! Remember, a seller of stock on a 40.00 limit is willing to sell at 40.00, or better. Thus, if the stock opens at 40.01, the order is filled a penny better than the limit. If the stock opens at 39.99, this seller sits on the order book at 40.00 unexecuted. *In other words, an opening price of 40.01 cleared the order book, while 39.99 did not.* Unless the seller cancels, or a buyer comes in to grab all 500,000 shares at 40.00, the stock cannot bounce higher than 40.00 until this seller is out of the way.

Farrell Says

The ability to assess whether the opening print will clear the order book is perhaps the single most important skill that a momentum trader can possess. As this example shows, although the difference of a penny or two doesn't seem like much to the investing public, to the short-term trader, it means everything to the supply-and-demand picture in the stock. It can be the difference between making and losing several thousand dollars on the trade.

SELLING BEFORE THE SECOND WAVE

In my experience with this type of trade, it is best to sell the stock into the first upsurge. This means that your intention should be only to hold the stock for a few minutes. This is because these kinds of situations are prone to a second wave of selling. There is no reason to wait around for this second wave. Take your profits in the initial updraft if you are fortunate enough to have the stock move in your favor.

In addition, I have found that this type of trade occurs more frequently than one might think on the New York Stock Exchange. Be alert and do your homework. The best way you can be alert to these kinds of situations is to watch CNBC's *Squawk Box* each morning and also read the headlines in the *Wall Street Journal* and *Investor's Business Daily*. If the company is not well known enough to make the headlines, you should refrain from using this trading strategy.

Farrell Says

In the 13 years that I have been trading the NYSE, the gap open trade has offered some of the best trading odds in the market if it is done carefully. But please use caution: Not every stock that opens lower is suitable for this trade. Remember, the markets do not give away money. If it were that easy, everyone would be doing it. You have to pick and choose your opportunities carefully, based on your reading of the changing supply-and-demand situation in the stock. How well you do this will determine your success or failure in momentum trading.

When you attempt to trade high-volatility stocks, I cannot stress enough just how fast these stocks will move in a rally. In the blink of an eye, they could easily move points. Why do they move so fast? Because fear and greed rule the markets, and the specialists are not going to allow themselves to get steamrolled if a stock moves quickly against them. The forces of human nature are extremely powerful. Market psychology is in a constant transition between these two dangerous forces. Fear brings out sellers, and greed brings out buyers. Think about it. The only reason anyone ever buys a stock in the first place is the belief that it will make them money. Fear usually does not enter the equation until after the stock is bought, when the money is truly at risk. For every buyer, there is a seller. So what you have is a volatile mixture of buyers buying stock on the urges of greed and sellers selling stock on the impulses of fear.

These forces manifest themselves constantly in the movements of the overall market. That is why the financial markets are prone to irrational selling and buying at any time, for no apparent reason. In light of this, regardless of the stock you are trading, you must maintain an awareness of the condition of the overall market's momentum at all times. Typically, if the stock you are trading is a high-profile market leader, it will move loosely with the momentum of the overall market indexes.

Table 7.1 Tick for Tick—IBM and the Dow

Market in IBM		Dow Jones Industrial Average
116–116.06	500 × 3,500	−74.06

Stock is lifted at 116.06 as the market begins to rally from down 74 to down 73.

| 116–116.25 | 500 × 1,000 | −73.10 |

Stock is also lifted at 116.25, and the bid moves higher as the market moves from down 73 to down 69.

| 116.25–116.50 | 1,000 × 1,000 | −69 |

As the market rallies, the bid-ask spreads widen, and offers disappear.

TRADING TICK FOR TICK WITH THE MARKET INDEXES

There is a saying on Wall Street that a rising tide lifts all boats. When the overall market is heading higher, more often than not the large-cap stock you are trading will move with the market. Why? Because these large stocks *are* the market. That is why it is absolutely essential that you check the market indexes continually while you are trading. Let's look at a real-life example in IBM.

In late summer and early autumn, I was trading IBM, one of biggest and most influential stocks in the Dow Jones Industrial Average. Table 7.1 demonstrates how stocks like this one move in tandem with the overall market indexes.

This snapshot of the market in IBM occurred during a span of about 45 seconds. My point in all of this is to illustrate the fast and orderly way high-profile stocks move with the broader market averages. Look at the Dow Jones Industrial Average. As the Dow began to rally from down 74 points to down only 69 points, IBM traded higher with the Dow step by step.

WHY LIMIT ORDERS DON'T WORK IN A RALLY

As the market was rallying, traders were lifting offers in IBM as the specialist was moving the market higher. Notice the market when the Dow was down 74 points. There were 3,500 shares of IBM for sale at 116.06. The split second the Dow upticked, a trader lifted the stock. Now stock was for sale at 116.25. As the Dow began to move higher,

IBM was moving higher as well. The stock for sale at 116.25 was also lifted. *Buyers will lift offers in market rallies.* That is why it is so difficult to buy on the bid when a volatile stock is moving higher. If the stock is rallying, any attempts to buy on the bid might go unexecuted, forcing you to "pay up" by lifting offers. You run the risk of missing the market if you try to bid for the stock at a cheaper price using a limit order, because other traders will step in front of you and move the market higher themselves.

Think about this for a second. Imagine if you tried to get cute and bid for IBM at 116. How would you buy the stock? Chances are, if someone were to hit your bid and sell you stock at 116, the market might be reversing and heading lower.

The irony is that what sometimes happens with limit orders in volatile stocks is that you miss the stock when it runs and you get stuck buying it when it falls. If the stock looks like it is reversing its tracks and heading lower, and you have a buy limit order at a slightly lower price, chances are you will be unable to cancel your buy order before your bid is hit. The stock will trade through you like a knife cuts through butter and head lower.

If you are careful and pick price levels to buy where there is decent buying support beneath you, buying on the bid is a good way to enter a position. Remember, buyers below you on the order book will help cushion any drop in the stock, and this will help put the odds in your favor. But if you aren't paying attention to the other buyers and sellers and the changes in the supply-and-demand picture in the stock, you will have trouble making a profit this way.

I hope this illustration gives you a good indication of how fast these stocks will move at the slightest indication the market is rallying. A high-profile stock like IBM will typically move faster than you can get your buy order entered over the Internet. The result: Even if you know the stock is headed higher, you might not be able to react fast enough to buy it at a decent price. That is one reason why trading momentum stocks is so difficult.

So, when can you make money trading these stocks? By selling into the strength. Remember, if you are a short-term trader, your intention in this kind of trade is not to hold the stock for the entire afternoon. You may even be inclined to sell it several seconds after you have bought it. You need to get caught in the updraft. For this to happen, you may need help from the overall market. If you are trading a stock like IBM, the market indexes usually must continue to rally for your stock to head higher. If the market indexes, like the Dow Jones Industrial Average and the S&P 500 Futures, fail to continue the rally after you have bought stock, your stock may be in trouble and you should thinking about selling and reevaluating. If you have just bought IBM, but the Dow is beginning to sell off, it might be prudent to think about selling the stock. More often than not, IBM will trade down when the market sells off.

USING THE S&P FUTURES TO GAUGE THE SUSTAINABILITY OF A RALLY

If you use only the Dow Jones Industrial Average as your gauge of a market rally, you will have trouble predicting if a rally is for real or just temporary. You will need another barometer as a guide in the treacherous world of momentum trading. The other gauge most day traders use is the S&P 500 futures contract. The S&P 500 futures contract is essentially a contract whose value is linked to the future value of the S&P index. It is traded in the futures pits in Chicago and electronically all over the world. As such, it is used as a leading indicator of the future direction of the overall market. If the S&P 500 futures are rallying, it will usually ignite a rally in the Dow Jones Industrial Average. If the S&P 500 futures begin to sell off as the Dow continues to rally, it is usually a sign that the Dow's rally is unsustainable. That is why it is very important to watch this crucial indicator before you place a trade.

LIGHTNING-FAST MARKET UPSURGE: HOW OFFERS VANISH IN THE VAPOR TRAIL

One of the most difficult things about trading a high-profile momentum stock is that there are literally thousands of traders looking at the stock at the same time. The competition is fierce. And everyone is looking for the same thing: supply and demand. Remember, when a stock rallies, there is only a limited amount of stock for sale at each price level. The stock may be inundated with thousands of buy orders simultaneously. It becomes a race among traders to see who gets the stock first. The winner makes money on the trade, and the losers lose money on the

Table 7.2   The Vapor Trail

Market in 3M		Dow Jones Industrial Average
99–99.37	1,000 × 10,000	+221

As the stock begins to rally, the specialist cancels his or her offers to sell stock at lower prices and reoffers the stock at a higher level, in this case up 35 cents of a point at 99.37.

99–99.62	1000 × 100	+224

In addition, as the market continues to rally, the specialist offers less and less stock for sale at each price level, essentially making buyers pay a higher price if they want to buy more than 100 shares. Originally the specialist had 10,000 shares for sale at 99.37. Now, a split second later, after canceling that order, he or she has only 100 shares for sale at 99.62. Less stock for sale, and at a higher price. A double whammy for the day trader who wants to buy a large block of stock.

99.50–100	1,000 × 10,000	+230

In a matter of only a few seconds, stock for sale at lower prices seems to disappear into thin air. To buy stock, buyers are now forced to pay 100 per share, when only 10 seconds earlier it was for sale at 99.37.

trade. It's that simple. That is why these stocks move so fast at the slightest hint of a rally.

Table 7.2 illustrates another example of just how fast a Dow stock will react to the market upsurge during a buying rally. The stock in this case is 3M.

One of the most difficult things about trading volatile stocks in an upsurge is that the offers seem to disappear into thin air. I call this the *vapor trail*. Like the last example, this one took place during a very short time frame—only a few seconds.

STOCK FOR SALE BECOMING SCARCE

As you can see, as the market moved higher, stock for sale in 3M became scarcer and scarcer. *The specialist created this situation to avoid getting caught short the stock as it ran higher*. In other words, the specialist did not want to get picked off by the short-term speculators in the stock. This could lead to huge trading losses for the specialist if the stock continued to run higher and higher as buy orders poured in. Remember, if the orders are market orders, the specialist must fill them at some price.

The point of this illustration is that at any given time, the specialist is fully aware of the situation in the stock. If the day trader who is watching the stock from home knows it is heading higher, the specialist probably knew 10 seconds ago. Specialists are not stupid, and they are always one step ahead of the day trader. They will adjust their markets accordingly. This is typically why high-volatility stocks move so fast in an upsurge. Specialists will keep raising their prices and make it harder and harder for buyers to accumulate stock at cheap levels. If the specialists know the stock is headed higher, they are not going to be foolish enough to sell you their stock at lower prices. They will mark up the stock accordingly because they know the speculators, in their greed, will pay any price to buy the stock. That is exactly how a stock can move a full point in a matter of a few seconds.

As you can see, trading high-volatility NYSE stocks can be very difficult because of the speed with which the markets change. But trading high-profile NYSE stocks is only half of the world of momentum trading. There is another segment of the market that we have not talked about as yet: the Nasdaq market.

NASDAQ AND THE ROLE OF THE MARKET MAKERS

Until now, the majority of this book has been devoted to trading stocks that are listed on the New York Stock Exchange. The Nasdaq, or over-the-counter, market is a slightly different animal. Most of the high-profile momentum stocks in the news are Nasdaq stocks. Google, Microsoft, Yahoo!, and Apple all fall into this category. No day trading book would be complete without mentioning the dimensions of the Nasdaq market.

Unlike the New York Stock Exchange, the Nasdaq exchange does not rely on the specialist system. Instead of having one specialist assigned to maintain an orderly market in a particular stock, Nasdaq uses *market makers*, or member firms that buy and sell on their own behalf. These member firms are linked electronically, and as such there is no physical exchange where the stock changes hands. It is all done in cyberspace. But as with the specialist system, these market makers are obligated to maintain an orderly and liquid market in the stocks they trade. Therefore, instead of having one specialist actively trading the stock, a Nasdaq issue may have upward of 10 to 20 different market makers.

Farrell Says

In my experience trading Nasdaq stocks, I have found that the market maker system can create more volatility than the specialist system on the New York Stock Exchange. This is because there is no one individual who is totally accountable for the movements of the stock.

Remember, on an NYSE stock, any complaints of unfairness fall directly into the specialist's lap. The specialist assumes all the responsibility of maintaining a fair market. Not true on Nasdaq: Instead, the burden falls collectively on the group of market makers. That is why, especially in the 1990s, there were numerous complaints accusing Nasdaq market makers of unfair trading practices from price fixing to collusion. Since then, Nasdaq has come a long way toward becoming a more fair and transparent marketplace.

On a typical trading day, most of the largest movers usually trade on the Nasdaq market. A stock like Google, at the time of this revision, can literally have intraday price swings of 20 to 30 points. If you get on the wrong side of this momentum, it can destroy you. That is why I believe the Nasdaq market is an extremely dangerous learning ground for the novice day trader. But, as with everything else, there are some times when the odds are in your favor. You must understand the landscape before you proceed, however.

The Stock Market of the Next Hundred Years

The Nasdaq market was often called *the stock market of the next hundred years*. This is because most of the issues that trade on Nasdaq are entrepreneurial in nature. With some obvious exceptions, companies that IPO on Nasdaq are not seasoned companies like those listed on the New York Stock Exchange, but instead are companies in rapid-growth industries, especially technology. This is usually the main culprit for the volatility, as the market tries to gauge the future prosperity of many of these start-up companies. In the past, it was not uncommon for some companies, particularly in the Internet sector, to go public without ever having turned a profit. Why would anyone buy stock in these companies? On the belief that they are the next Microsoft, Apple, or Google. These are typically the kinds of companies whose share prices are ruled by extreme fear and greed. Some of these start-up companies have been known to double or triple in a matter of only a few days (or hours), only to cancel out all of those gains in a quick bout of panic selling.

"Real" Day Trading Firms

There is a whole class of day traders who specialize in trading Nasdaq stocks. At its peak in the Internet bubble of the late 1990s, day trading firms were popping up in every major city in the country. Although many went out of business, the best of the day traders are still making a living the same way they were a decade ago. Many have rooms of traders, all looking for one thing: momentum. They have high-powered, high-tech systems that can alert them to profitable opportunities. These day traders are drawn to Nasdaq stocks because they are so volatile. Remember, when you have a fast execution, volatility creates profits, because you can get in and out of stocks quickly and efficiently. When you have a slow execution, volatility destroys profits. In a volatile market, the amount of money the very best of these day traders can make in a single afternoon using these trading systems is staggering.

The SOES Bandits

When these day trading firms began in the early 1990s, they were nick-named *SOES bandits*. They got this name because they exploited a Nasdaq loophole called the *Small Order Execution System (SOES)* to get lightning-fast executions. SOES was designed after the crash of 1987 to give the individual investor an immediate fill on 1,000 shares or less of a Nasdaq stock at the best possible price. What these bandits did was to use SOES to pick off the market makers by disguising themselves as members of the investing public when in fact they were professional traders. By doing so, they forced the market markets to "honor" the quoted market, allowing the SOES bandits to pick off the market makers for 1,000 shares at a time in fast moving stocks. The SOES bandits were the single biggest threat to the market makers' profits. The reason was that SOES was not originally intended for professional day traders.

In the glory days of SOES trading, it was not unusual to hear stories of SOES bandits making $50,000 or $100,000 in trading profits in a single day. Over the years, rule changes were implemented to protect the market makers against being picked off by SOES bandits. These rules changes spelled the death of the SOES bandit in the mid-1990s.

Tracking the Nasdaq Comp

If you are going to day trade Nasdaq stocks, it is very important that you keep your eyes on the Nasdaq Composite Index (the *Nasdaq Comp*) at all times. Like the Dow Jones Industrial Average to NYSE stocks, this is the main barometer for the momentum of the Nasdaq market. The large, market-leading technology stocks, including Google, Apple, and Microsoft, all move loosely in tandem with the Nasdaq Comp. It is extremely volatile, and is prone to breathtaking rallies and gut-wrenching sell-offs even in times when the Dow and the S&P 500 are stable.

Taking Food out of the Market Makers' Mouths

If there is one thing I have learned in my forays into trading Nasdaq stocks, it is that on Nasdaq, the market makers and the day traders have always had an adversarial relationship. Said another way, there is no love lost between the two groups. I remember when I was a trader at Gruntal, the Nasdaq traders on the trading floor all shared a dislike of the SOES bandits that bordered on animosity. This is understandable, given what was going on in the market at the time, and the risk of the SOES bandits "picking off" the market makers if they let their guard down.

My point is that you must understand your competition. To be successful trading Nasdaq stocks, you must understand the psychology of the market makers that are taking the other side of your trades. The fact that the market makers control the trading on Nasdaq adds a certain degree of risk.

For years, I was always concerned about the house edge, and the quality of my executions, on Nasdaq. The house edge existed because the market makers were not bound by the same fair order handling rules as the specialists on the New York Stock Exchange. Since then, however, many things have changed, and, in general, the edge that the market makers had over the day trader has been significantly reduced.

Even though the house edge is still there, there are a few ways to beat the market makers at their own game. One way to take food out of the market makers' mouths is to catch them off guard. That is precisely what the high-tech day trading firms have been doing for years. In the game of momentum trading, the day trader hopes that the market makers will have difficulty maintaining an orderly market if the stock is extremely volatile. Typically, when the stock appears to be poised for a run, the day traders will bombard the stock with buy orders. As they are buying, the market makers are required to sell. What inevitably happens is that the market markers are forced to bid the stock up to protect themselves from getting short the stock as it runs higher, creating a self-fulfilling prophecy.

Note to readers: Like the specialists on the NYSE, the role of the traditional large brokerage firms that act as market makers on Nasdaq has been reduced over time. This is due to a combination of improved technology, better order handling rules that protect the investing public, and less of a willingness to take market making risk on the part of the brokerage firms. These are all positive developments for the day trader. As a result, the day trader is on a more level playing field today on Nasdaq than at any point in history. Any discussion on day trading would not be complete without some discussion of the trading psychology of the market makers, regardless of their level of participation on Nasdaq in the future.

A FEW WORDS ON SHORT SELLING

I have yet to mention a trading strategy that is very popular among day traders—the concept of *short selling*. When you short a stock, you are essentially selling the stock before you own it. It is the exact opposite of buying the stock. Instead of buying low and selling high, when you short a stock, you are attempting to sell high and buy low. In other words, you sell the stock first before you buy it. It is a bet that the stock price will decline. If you short a stock at 100 and buy it back at 99, your profit is the same as if you bought the stock first at 99 and sold it later at 100. Why do traders like to short stocks? Because stocks typically fall faster than they rise.

Even in light of this, in my experience, shorting is a tough way to make a living for the novice day trader. There are many traders who share this belief. Again, the reason comes down to execution. To get a short off requires precision trading that takes skill and speed.

A few years ago, there were rules in place that prevented you from shorting on a downtick, or on a price lower than the previous trade. This rule was enacted to prevent traders from jumping all over a stock that was in free fall and driving it into the ground by adding to the selling pressure. Recent changes have allowed for a much higher degree of short selling in our markets. As of this writing, there are no longer any restrictions on shorting on a downtick.

The dangerous thing about shorting stock is that your risk of loss is unlimited. Imagine you short a stock at 15 and, to your horror, the stock opens the next trading day at 100. Though unlikely, this is not out of the realm of possibility. Imagine you own 1,000 shares. On a $15,000 investment, you will lose $85,000 if you *cover* or buy the stock back at 100. It would be no different than buying 1,000 shares at 100 and selling them at 15. That is why shorting stock is a very risky practice.

TWO METHODS FOR DAY TRADING NASDAQ STOCKS

There are two primary methods I have relied upon to make money day trading Nasdaq stocks: buying strong stocks on pullbacks, and finding stocks that have upward momentum in the afternoon and holding them overnight. These strategies also work well on high-volatility NYSE stocks.

Buying Strong Stocks and Holding Them Overnight

When you are trading high-volatility stocks on Nasdaq, be careful about holding positions overnight. Many day traders prefer not to carry a position in a stock overnight because of the volatility. The reasoning is that many of these high-tech companies can easily gap up or down points on the next open. In other words, there is no way to tell what the stock will do the next day, and that is a bet outside the parameters of supply and demand. Remember, *any bet made outside of the immediate supply and demand in the stock is a bet against the house.*

But there are certain rare times when the odds of a profitable trade may swing into your favor when you hold a stock overnight. There are two conditions for such a trade:

1. *Never hold a weak stock overnight.* Remember, momentum works both ways. A stock that is weak has a natural tendency to open weaker the next day.

2. *Only hold stocks overnight that go out strong.* The only way this trading strategy can be consistently profitable is if you buy a stock that is very strong in the afternoon. The reasoning is that the buying strength will spill over into the next day, as the good news that is moving the stock higher gets fully disseminated.

The strategy here is very simple. You buy the stock, hold it overnight, and then sell it on the open of trading the next morning. Momentum has a funny way of perpetuating itself, and it is a very powerful force. If you can get on the right side of momentum, you can make substantial amounts of money. Just be aware of the fact that you can lose money on this trade.

Screening Stocks for the Overnight Trade

When you are looking for stocks that fall into this category, it is best to keep your eyes out for any stocks that are movers. One place is to check the day's most actives. CNBC will also keep you informed of this kind of movement. A real-time news service will give you the best up-to-the-minute information to alert you to stocks that are moving.

There are two main reasons the momentum that carries a stock higher has a good chance of spilling over into the next trading day:

1. *Market makers get caught short the stock during the rally.* Remember, for every buyer there is a seller. On Nasdaq, the market makers perform the same function as the specialists on the New York Stock Exchange. This means they are obligated to maintain an orderly market. If the stock is inundated with buy orders, someone must step up to the plate to sell stock to the general public. Many times, a buying spree will flood the market makers, causing them to get short the stock as it is moving higher. In other words, because of a scarcity of sellers, the market makers

are forced into selling stock they do not own. This means they will eventually have to buy the stock back in the open market to cover, even if it is at a higher price. This is a very dangerous situation for the market makers to be in if the stock continues to run higher, as it can lead to significant trading losses.

Usually, a buying panic at the end of the day will catch the market makers off guard. This will cause them to carry substantial short positions in the stock overnight. Market makers are not investors. Like you and me, they are traders. They do not like to carry a short position for an extended period of time, especially in a stock that has strong upward momentum. Getting short a stock that is running is no different than being stuck long a stock that is falling. The market makers will attempt to cover their short positions if they fear the stock is headed even higher the next day. In its own way, this is a panic buying situation, except this time it is the market makers, not the investing public, doing the panicking. This will add additional buying pressure to the stock.

In addition, the market makers do not want to run the risk of accumulating a larger short position if the stock continues to go higher the next day. That is why the stock will tend to gap up on the open. If the market makers are forced into the uncomfortable position of selling more stock short, they will do so at a price that is advantageous for them (i.e., a much higher price). That is why it is not unusual to see a volatile Nasdaq stock open up 10 or 20 points on good news.

2. *The information moving the stock has not been fully disseminated.* It is very important to pick and choose your overnight positions carefully. My rule of thumb is to hold a stock overnight only if I think the good news that is moving the stock higher has not been fully disseminated. Why? Because the good news is the fuel that will drive the stock price higher. A front page article in the *Wall Street Journal, Investor's Business Daily*, or any of the other financial publications will bring buyers into a stock.

How can you tell if the information has been fully disseminated? If the stock is running in the afternoon, and there isn't anything on the newswires, it has not been fully disseminated. The ideal situation is to buy a stock that is strong in the afternoon and sell into a gap opening the next morning after the stock makes the front page of the *Wall Street Journal*. That is the sweet spot, and it is difficult to do. But, every once in a while, it happens. Conversely, if the good news has already been in the newspaper that morning, you should not hold the stock overnight. Why? Because the news moving the stock is already out. That is the difference.

Please note that this is the exact opposite of the trading strategy of buying on bad news that we discussed earlier in the chapter. When buying on bad news, you want to make sure the bad news is fully disseminated before you buy. If it is not, more selling pressure will be placed on the stock. When buying on good news, you want to make sure the news is not fully disseminated to the investing public, so that buyers continue to flock to the stock, thus causing it to trade higher.

THE APPLE COMPUTER TRADE

Every so often, the forces of the market align in such a way that a profitable trade is inevitable. I know from experience that this kind of opportunity does not come around often, so when it does, you must jump all over it. Following is a real-life example that occurred in Apple Computer (AAPL) that is relevant to the principles of holding a stock overnight.

There are many variations of the overnight trade, but the underlying recipe for success is the same: You want to buy before the news fully reaches the investing public and sell the instant it disseminates. In other words, you want to buy on rumor and sell on fact. Let me show you precisely what I mean using Apple Computer.

Several years ago, on a summer night, CNN was airing a story on its weekly financial program about the incredible turnaround at Apple Computer, and its return to profitability among dominant computer companies. This was a very positive news story, and I was convinced that the millions of viewers across America and around the world would inevitably bring buying interest into the stock the next morning.

Most of the time, when a company is featured in the media, you do not have the luxury of knowing ahead of time. If you did, you could make a substantial amount of money, because good publicity always moves the stock higher. But this case was different. CNN was advertising the lead story on Apple Computer's newfound prosperity several days in advance of the show.

On the eve of the show's airing, trading in Apple Computer was heavy. The stock was up *$1.50* by the close, undoubtedly moved up by traders anticipating exactly what I was anticipating: that the favorable news coverage would move the stock higher. Chances were that the stock would gap higher the following morning, as the investing public who saw the show would enter their buy orders in AAPL at the market on the stock's opening trade the next morning.

As it turned out, I was right. The news story delivered exactly what it had promised. The stock opened for trading up 75 cents the next day, and I sold on the opening print. The buying momentum created by the favorable story was simply too strong. Although there are no guarantees in trading, this was one that could be anticipated for several days in advance. This was one of the market's rare gifts.

The situation in Apple Computer sheds some light on the nature of momentum trading. To be profitable, you need to be on the right side of the momentum, ride the stock higher, and sell into the buying climax. In a sense, this is what I mean when I say that day traders make money by being buyers when the market needs buyers and sellers when the market needs sellers. But that is only half of the equation. The other half is that you have to be alert enough to spot these opportunities and to know the difference between buying on rumor and buying on fact. In this case, I bought on the rumor that the story would be favorable, and sold immediately after the fact. How did I make a profit? Simply by being one step ahead of the investing public.

BUYING STRONG STOCKS ON PULLBACKS

The other trading strategy that I have found works very well on Nasdaq's volatile stocks is buying strong stocks on *pullbacks*. A pullback occurs when a stock opens high, but falls back slightly in the 10 to 15 minutes after the open. Why do strong stocks pull back? It has to do with how the market makers react to a flood of buy orders. Remember, the market makers, like the specialists, are forced to be sellers of last resort if they cannot find true sellers to match with buyers. If good news comes out on a stock and the stock is inundated with buy orders at the market, the market makers are in a peculiar and dangerous situation. They will be forced into having to fill the influx of buy orders themselves, even if it means having to short the stock. Imagine a buying frenzy in a little-known and thinly traded stock. What if the stock trades only 50,000 shares per day on average, but on this day it has buy orders totaling over 1 million shares at the market that have to be filled when the stock opens? What are the market makers to do? Remember, every buyer has a seller. Someone always has to be on the other side of the trade. The market makers will be forced into shorting the stock to the investing public. Like the specialists, the only way the market makers can protect themselves is to open the stock as high as possible. Keep in mind that the market makers are setting the price at which the opening trade occurs. In whose best interests is that price determined? Yours or the market makers'? You know the answer to that question by now.

OPENING THE STOCK ABNORMALLY HIGH

If you are shorting stock, the higher the trade occurs, the better your chances of covering the short for a profit. It is the exact opposite of going long the stock. You are selling the stock before you buy it, so naturally you will want to sell high and buy low. The market makers will protect themselves and open the stock abnormally high when there is a buying panic by the investing public. The result? The stock may never again trade higher than it does on the opening trade, when the buying pressure is strongest.

In over a decade of trading, I have seen no better example of this than a stock called EntreMed Inc. (ENMD). In May 1998, there was a small article in the Sunday edition of the *New York Times* that hinted that this company had discovered a possible cure for some forms of cancer. The next morning, the stock was inundated with buy orders. Everyone wanted a piece of the company. The greed was overwhelming. What did the market makers do? They opened the stock at a ridiculously high level. That was the only thing they could do to protect themselves. After closing on the previous Friday at 12.06, the stock opened on the morning of May 4 at 83, up 71 points!

THE DANGERS OF BUYING A STRONG STOCK ON THE OPENING TRADE

Why did the stock open so high? That was the only price at which the market makers felt comfortable in shorting stock to the investing public. What happened next is a textbook example of the dangers of buying a stock on good news on the open. In the next several hours of trading, the stock proceeded to drop like a rock, hitting an intraday low of 40.75, over 40 points lower than where it opened! And remember, there was not bad news on the stock, there was good news; yet the stock still sold off after the opening trade. Why did it sell off so violently after the gap opening? Because the market makers let the stock drift lower after they got their short positions off. The market makers made a substantial amount of money on this trade, at the expense of the investing public. They shorted the stock at 83 and covered their positions at lower prices, buying back the stock to cover as it dropped. How would you feel if you were an investor who bought the stock at the market on the open of trading? After being filled at 83, you would have seen your investment cut in half by noon.

Farrell Says

As we said earlier in the book, it will be impossible to make a living as a day trader by buying strong stocks on good news on the open of trading. That is a very dangerous situation, and one of the worst forms of betting against the house.

This is proof of the tendency that strong Nasdaq stocks typically drift lower after the high opening trade. The reason? Once the market makers have filled the influx of buy orders by taking the other side of the trade, they are short the stock. The lower the stock drifts, the more money they will make when they attempt to cover their shorts by buying the stock back. All of a sudden, after the opening trade, the market makers have a vested interest in moving the stock lower. Provided there is not a second stampede of panic buying after the open, the stock can be gently guided lower as the trading frenzy dies down after the open.

INFLICTING HEAVY DAMAGE ON THE MARKET MAKERS BY ATTACKING THEIR VULNERABILITY

Here is where the alert day trader can participate in a buying spree that can level substantial monetary damage on the market makers. Once a strong stock begins to drift lower for a bit after opening high, day traders will typically attempt to inundate the stock with a second wave of buying. Why? Because the day traders know exactly how the game is played, and they are attacking the market makers at their weakest point. The day traders are certainly not foolish enough to buy the stock at the market on the open. They are well aware of the trap the market makers have set, and they are not about to step right into it. They know what the market makers' intentions are: opening the stock high and letting it drop like a rock after the opening print.

The day traders will strike when the market makers are at their most vulnerable. This is a very important situation to comprehend: The alert day traders are aware that the market makers are short the stock. As you know, the market makers are short because they were obligated to take the other side of the influx of customer buy orders on the open. They were forced into being sellers of last resort. Their only defense was to open the stock high in the hopes of covering their shorts (i.e., buying) as the stock drifted lower. The market makers will now try to cover their short positions at a profit. That is why they try to let the stock drift lower. But the day traders will not let them; instead, they bombard the stock with a second wave of buying.

The result? The market makers, instead of covering their short positions, are now short even more stock at lower price levels. This is a very precarious situation. If all goes according to plan, the day traders will make a substantial profit on this kind of trade at the expense of the market makers. How? Because the market makers are forced to join in on the buying to cover their short positions. Thus, the stock runs higher as the market makers cover their shorts. In essence, by buying, the market makers become their own worst enemy. Alert day traders will capitalize on the situation by selling stock into the upsurge, hopefully making a nice profit in the process.

This situation did not work in our EntreMed example because the stock opened so ridiculously high. But it should be noted that this tendency is exactly the reason the stock did open at 83. The market makers were very fearful of the potential for a second wave of buying sparked by day traders. Imagine if, after the stock opened at 83, the day traders waited 5 or 10 minutes and then began to bombard the stock with buying before the market makers were able to cover their first set of short positions. Now, instead of covering their shorts, the market makers would be short even more stock. That is how the stock could easily go to 100 in the blink of an eye.

CHAPTER 8

The Day Trader's Ticket to the Poorhouse

How I Managed to Lose $12,000 in Less than 24 Hours

Losses are a part of trading. No one is immune to them. What separates good traders from bad traders? Good traders are able to handle losses, learn from them, and move on. Bad traders are not able to do this. Keep in mind that trading performance is affected by your emotional well-being and your state of mind. Always remember that the markets are filled with opportunity. But they are also filled with danger. If you trade long enough, you will learn this the hard way. Large losses are a rite of initiation, because until you have experienced one, you will not know what it truly means to call yourself a trader. For it is only in losing money that you come to appreciate the two most important things an experienced trader can possess: an understanding of the nature of risk and a respect for the power of the market.

Eventually every trader will face his or her own demons. I faced mine in an afternoon of terror in the fall of 1998. Looking back upon it now, a decade later, as painful as it seemed at the time, it turned out to be one of the most important experiences of my trading career. It taught me a valuable lesson about risk control that has kept me out of trouble in volatile markets many times since. For almost two years, I had compiled a profitable track that I was extremely pleased with. This was achieved by trading for small profits of sixteenths of a point (as the market was trading in fractions at that time), limiting my losses, and refraining from trading stocks caught in downdrafts. In the last week of August and the first few days of September, I had weathered a nasty correction in the overall markets that saw the Dow drop more than 500 points in a single day. I actually turned a profit that day. That week was easily one of the most volatile in the markets' history, due to the now infamous "Asian Contagion" that swept global markets. I was able to survive in the midst of this volatility by keeping a level head, maintaining my composure, and not getting greedy. Then came my day of reckoning.

As is obvious by now, I don't like to take big risks. I like to trade only when I feel the odds are in my favor. However, this was one opportunity I couldn't pass up. What I learned was a very valuable lesson on how *not* to trade. I broke every single cardinal rule I've ever set for myself. In the process, I proceeded to lose more than $12,000 in the blink of an eye. In hindsight, I completely lost my composure.

For the better part of two months, I had watched Citicorp (CCI) stock with amazement (the stock is now Citigroup—listed on NYSE under the C—after the merger with Travelers). I had made a few profitable trades in the stock over the previous year, but I usually found them to be difficult trades. At the time, this was probably the most volatile stock in the Dow. On many occasions, I had witnessed the stock swing 10 points within the course of a single day. But this situation was different. The stock had been in a continual free fall from about 180 to 100 over the course of a couple of weeks. It seemed to be due for a huge upsurge. Analysts and portfolio managers alike were claiming that this stock would be a 200 stock in a year. Yet, day after day, it kept going lower. There were worries about Asia, a currency devaluation in Latin America, and rumors that the high-profile megamerger with Travelers was about to go bust.

As the stock broke through 100 earlier in the week, I kept weighing the pros and cons of taking a stab at it. I thought for sure that the stock could easily move 5 to 10 points in a day or two. I knew that if I did commit trading capital, this would not be a short-term trade. I would have to hold the stock overnight and hope I was right. I wasn't comfortable with this strategy. It seemed to me that buying a stock on a severe dip with a plan of holding it for a day or two was a form of short-term investing, not trading. And I was a trader, not an investor. So I decided not to get involved.

Over the next day and a half, to my dismay, the stock went up 13 points, to 113, apparently on a recommendation from a Morgan Stanley Dean Witter analyst. I felt sick to my stomach that I missed what was undoubtedly the opportunity of the year. I kept thinking about the 2,000 shares I would have bought. That would have been a $26,000 profit in about 36 hours, if only I had had the guts to do it.

THE PAIN OF MISSING A TRADE

I had always said to myself that, if the situation ever arose again, I would be willing to stray from my trading strategy and take on added risk to hit a home run. I kept questioning my own motives and my lack of initiative. Why didn't I just trust my instincts? I *knew* the stock would eventually come back, yet I didn't do anything about it when I had the chance. Words cannot describe the feeling of misery I felt. In trading, there is nothing more painful than missing a trade. So I swore to myself that if the stock ever dropped back below 100, I was going to throw caution to the wind and jump all over it.

To my surprise, the stock did make its way back down. When I missed it the first time, I was convinced Citicorp would never again trade below 100. The day the stock broke back through 113, it sold off and closed around 108. The next day, after opening down 3 at 105, it continued to go lower and hovered around 101. I felt like the gods of trading were on my side. I had been given a second chance! This time, I was not going to let opportunity slip by. The impulse of greed was simply too strong. The moment of truth had arrived.

HOW COULD THE STOCK GO ANY LOWER?

So I took a leap of faith and bought 1,000 shares at 101.50. I had thought about buying 2,000, but I wanted to play it "safe" instead. Visions of huge profits began to dance in my head. This was going to be a $20,000 month, which for a 25-year-old is a nice chunk of change. I would hold the stock for a day or two, if need be, and sell it up 10 points. Indeed, this could be a $10,000 day. The upsurge was inevitable. Over and over again I kept reassuring myself that this was going to be a huge windfall. The stock had lost 12 points in 24 hours, so how could it go any lower?

Within about 10 seconds after my order was filled, the stock began to break below 101. To my horror, the stock continued to fall. 100.87 . . . 100.62 . . . 100.06 . . . in less than five minutes' time, I was already down $1,500. And $1,500 was about my loss threshold. I should've sold right then and there, taken my loss, and moved on. But I didn't. Breaking every rule I have ever set for myself, I was riding a loss into the ground.

THE TERRIFYING FEELING OF GETTING CAUGHT IN A DOWNDRAFT

The stock continued its free fall for about 25 minutes. 100.06 . . . 99.87 . . . 99.25 . . . 99. In the blink of an eye, I was now down over $3,000. This is a very dangerous time for any trader. When you start to lose large sums of money in a very short time, it becomes very difficult to maintain your composure. I was beginning to fall apart. Irrational thoughts were entering my head. It finally reached the point where the mental anguish was so great that I had to sell. It was simply too painful to continue. I entered a sell of 1,000 shares at the market. I got filled at 98.

In a little over 30 minutes, I had managed to lose $3,500. In the grand scheme of things, $3,500 is not that much money. I should have stopped right there. But greed is a very powerful force. I was not done yet. *I felt that the stock owed me something*. The stock had taken my hard-earned profits, and I wanted them back. After taking such a large hit, my worst fear was that I would watch the stock finally move higher while I was sitting on the sidelines. That would be a fate worse than death. I knew that in trading, Murphy's law is alive and well. The second I sold the stock, it was going to rebound! I was not about to let this happen. I had to be long the stock.

A FEELING OF IRRESISTIBLE GREED

The stock drifted lower, and I bought it back at 97. This was the second cardinal rule I had broken: Never go back into a stock after you have just lost a large amount of money in it. Then, the stock started to move higher! It closed at 98.5, and I was still long the stock. I refused to sell for a small profit. I wanted to make all of my money back. This time, however, I had only bought 500 shares instead of 1,000. I should have bought 1,000, but my confidence was shaken. So, to get back even, I had my work cut out for me. I was forced into holding the stock overnight.

Something really strange occurs when you hold a volatile stock overnight, especially one you have just been on the losing side of. You have a tendency to do all you can to convince yourself your actions are justified. For me, it meant watching CNBC and *Moneyline* that night in the hopes someone would say something good about the stock. It also meant checking the news wires every few hours in the hopes of a positive press release by the company.

Finally, it meant going on the Internet to the Yahoo! Finance message board on Citicorp in search of moral support. Message boards are where investors and traders can express their opinions about a given stock. Each actively traded stock has its own message board. Usually, it is where people who share the same opinions on a stock commiserate about why they haven't made any money in the stock recently. These message boards are filled with rumors and speculation. This can be very dangerous, as it tends to reinforce stubborn bullish beliefs about a stock that is tanking. You can always find someone else who thinks a stock is going higher, no matter how bad the situation is. There was one message on the board that claimed that the stock was headed to 120 by the end of the next week. So much for message boards.

I find that when I hold a volatile stock overnight, I have trouble sleeping. I toss and turn all night worrying about what the next day will bring. It is a matter of hoping for the best and fearing the worst. This is no way to trade, nor is it any way to make a living. When you depend on profits to make a living, you will be surprised how your body reacts to stress—which is exactly why I don't like to hold volatile stocks overnight in the first place. The mental toll it takes is too great.

After a lousy night's sleep, I got up early to check how the S&P Futures had done overnight. A large-cap stock like Citicorp will usually trade with the momentum of the overall market. If the S&P Futures were up overnight, there was a good chance Citicorp would open higher. The S&P Futures, to my relief, were up fractionally. I was hopeful that Citicorp, after closing at 98.50, would open up at 100 or more. The last piece of the puzzle was to watch *Squawk Box* on CNBC. In the final few minutes before the opening bell at 9:30 A.M., Maria Bartiromo would report live from the floor of the New York Stock Exchange. This was the nerve center for the day's trading action. Maria usually mentioned in which direction the financial stocks are indicated to open. On this day, she said Citicorp would open higher.

With this in mind, with two minutes to the opening bell, I was preparing my strategy. Should I sell on the open or hold out for more? One of the most profitable strategies in trading is to sell into a gap opening. This is because the specialists will usually overshoot the market intentionally. This means that if there is an influx of buy orders on the open, the specialists will open the stock high to protect themselves. They are obligated to fill the buy orders even if they have to short the stock. They are more likely to open the stock higher if forced into a large short position. On many days, this opening trade is the high print of the entire day.

THE NEED TO BREAK EVEN

The main problem I faced that day was the need to break even. I felt that unless I recovered the $3,500 I had lost the day before, this day would not be a success. In fact, I refused to take a small profit in the stock. I was greedy, and felt that Citicorp owed me the $3,500 it had taken from me. The only problem with this is that, because I only owned 500 shares now and not 1,000, I would need to make twice as many points on the upside as I had lost on the downside. I would need to sell the stock at 104, seven full points higher than where I bought it. This was a recipe for disaster. But the stock was due for a run. So I decided not to sell on the open.

The stock opened at 100.12 and ran up to 101. I felt like things were finally going my way. The stock was four points higher than where I bought it, and I just needed another three to make back $3,500 so I could break even! Then things took a turn for the worse. To my dismay, the stock started to sell off. 101 . . . 100.50 . . . 100 . . . 99.50 . . . 99. Like the day before, it was dropping like a rock. The last thing I wanted to do was take a loss on this stock two days in a row. If it got below 99, I was going to lock in my profit. I saw it trade below 99, and immediately entered a sell at the market, breaking my own rules about never using market orders. I got a terrible fill down at 98.37.

In hindsight, this was a very bad day to trade. The market was in the midst of a major correction, currencies around the world were collapsing, and Citicorp was right at the forefront of this chaos. To make matters worse, it was the Friday before the Labor Day holiday.

The markets would be closed on Monday. There is always the risk of selling pressure going into long weekends, as traders like to lighten up their positions. Did the market know something I didn't? How could the stock go any lower?

BUYING THE STOCK FOR THE THIRD TIME

This is when things began to unravel. I was angry. I should have sold on the open at 100.12. Instead, like the day before, I rode the stock lower. Even after I sold at 98.37, the stock continued to trend lower. 98.37 . . . 98 . . . 97.62 . . . 97. If it got below 97, I was going to jump all over it again. But this time, it was not going to be for 500 shares. I was convinced I could make back more money. The lower it got, the more tempted I was. Then, I made a huge mistake. In total greed, instead of buying 500 or 1,000 shares, I bought 2,000! This was the beginning of the end. Here's how the rest of the day went:

Tarred and feathered—an example of how not to trade:

Bought 2,000 at 96.25

Sold 2,000 at 95.12 for a loss of $2,250

Bought 2,000 at 95.12

Sold 1,900 at 94.50 for a loss of $1,187.50

Bought 2,000 at 94.93

Sold 2,000 at 93.75 for a loss of $2,375

Bought 2,000 at 92

Sold 2,000 at 90.37 for a loss of $3,250

In less than 24 hours, I had managed to lose over $12,000—weeks' worth of hard-earned profits down the drain in the blink of an eye. To add insult to injury, the stock did manage a small rally right after I sold out the final time. I remember sitting in my home office in a state of total shock. This was easily the worst 24 hours of trading I had ever had. Since I began trading, I had managed to turn a profit almost every single day I traded. Now, I was sitting on a $12,000 loss for less than 24 hours' work!

As if losing that amount of money weren't painful enough, watching how the stock performed the next trading day was torture. The stock opened after the holiday weekend at 104, up over 11 points! I was right, but I was too soon. I knew the stock was ripe for a pop, but I had been caught on the wrong side of it. I calculated that I would have made $27,000 if I had held the stock overnight on my final trade. The problem was that it would have entailed holding the stock over the long Labor Day weekend, something I did not want to do. Murphy's law is alive and well in the markets. My instincts were right, but I was right at the wrong time. Some situations are not meant to be.

FEELING OF DEVASTATION LEADS TO USEFUL INSIGHTS

I recall a feeling of total devastation that lasted for several days. What an absolute disaster! I had disregarded every rule I have ever lived by in trading. What was I thinking? In hindsight, there were several factors that contributed to this debacle. If anything, it sheds some light on the dangers of day trading volatile stocks in fast-moving markets. I would like to share these insights with you.

Avoid Abnormally Wide Bid-Ask Spreads

The first problem with trading a volatile stock in a downdraft is the size of the bid-ask spread. Typically, in a large sell-off, bid-ask spreads become abnormally wide. This is because the specialists are unsure of which direction the stock will trade next. They keep the spread wide to protect themselves. As liquidity dries up, they are forced to take the other side of every trade. This wide spread is devastating to you as a day trader because you won't be able to play the spread. If you try to buy on the bid or sell on the ask, I guarantee you will miss the market and leave money on the table.

Yet you will leave even more money on the table by placing market orders when the spreads are so wide. That's exactly the problem. This is a catch 22 situation, where neither limit orders nor market orders are all that effective. In volatile situations, when bid-ask spreads are wide, the only time the specialist will ever let you buy the stock cheaper than the ask price is when the stock is heading lower. Thus, you are forced into a situation where, if you think the stock is running, you must either enter a market order to buy the stock, or put a limit order above the current quote. This is the only way to get a fill in a rising market. *Either way, this is clearly a bet against the house.* I would have to say that, as in a poker match, when spreads are wide in a fast-moving market, the day trader holds the weakest hand. Weak hands should not bluff; they should fold. I'll show you what I mean.

Here's how Citicorp looked after I bought it for the sixth and final time. After trading as low as 91, the stock appeared to make a quick upsurge. The problem is that this upsurge was exaggerated by a wide bid-ask spread. It takes only a few buy orders to make a stock appear to be moving higher, when in fact it is not.

The market looked like this:

91–91.50   1000 × 1000

Stock traded at 91.50, then again at 91.75. I reacted by entering a buy of 2,000 at the market, thinking the rally was sustainable. At the time my order was entered, the market was:

91–92   1000 × 1000

Can you imagine buying at the market when the bid-ask spread is $1 wide! There is essentially no way to make money on this stock unless it really begins to run. It is a losing trade from the start. But there is no other way to buy the stock if it is running. If you enter a limit order to buy cheaper than where the stock is for sale, one of two things will happen:

1. You will miss the stock as it goes higher.
2. You will buy the stock only if it is on the way down and headed lower.

That's the problem. Volatile stocks move higher because offers are lifted. The NYSE specialist wants you to use a market order so that it plays right into his or her hands. To make matters with my Citicorp stock worse, if I were to turn right around and sell seconds after I bought, I would have lost $2,000 because the highest bid was $91. And there was no middle ground.

In my case, after I got filled on 2,000 shares at 92, the stock began to trail off. I had stepped right into a trap that the NYSE specialist had set. The sell orders began to inundate the stock. This was about the tenth wave of selling that day. A seller hit the bid at 91 and offered more there. The market changed from:

$$91–92 \quad 1000 \times 1000$$

to:

$$90.37–91 \quad 500 \times 5000$$

Just like that, I was down over $3,250 on paper. I couldn't afford to lose any more money. My only exit would be to hit the next lowest bid, which to my horror was at 90.37. The liquidity in the stock seemed to dry up. If I tried to get cute and offer the stock out between the spread at, say, 90.70, I was sure I would get filled only if the specialist was picking me off, and the stock was heading higher. It was a no-win situation: Hit the bid and get creamed on the spread, or offer the stock out and get a fill only if it was trading through my price. And, if I didn't act, the stock could easily be at 89 in no time. I was forced to sell. I got filled at 90.37, losing $3,250. This put my two-day loss total at over $12,000.

Don't Trade on Old Price Information

The second problem with trading Dow stocks during volatile periods is that in times of extreme price movement and high volume, the specialist might be unable to update the supply-and-demand information in real-time. As a result, you might be seeing "old" price quotes. This delay might be only a fraction of a second, but it means you are seeing the trades print before the bid-ask spreads are updated. For instance, the bid-ask spread might read 90.37–91, but you might see the stock trading at 90.06 or even 89.90. This is not because the specialist is trading the stock below the market. It is simply because the bid-ask spread you see is a fraction of a second old, and the market changed before the bid-ask could be updated. If the volume is extremely heavy, the specialist could be so inundated with sell orders that he or she is forced to print the stock before updating the market. This is a dangerous time for the day trader. I absolutely hate to trade when this happens.

The Dangers of Attempting to Short-Term Invest instead of Trade

In addition to getting hammered on the bid-ask spreads, and getting lousy executions, there were a few tactical errors I made that led to the $12,000 loss. In hindsight, what I was trying to accomplish was a form of short-term investing, not trading. *In other words, the bet was foolish because it was made outside of the parameters of supply and demand.* After losing $3,500 the first day, I was determined to make the money back the next day. I had unrealistic expectations, thinking I could hold the stock for seven points. I normally trade for nickels, dimes, and quarters, so to think I could make seven full points was preposterous. *Taking small profits is the key to making a sustainable living as a day trader.* It is far easier to make a full point by making 10 cents over and over again than to make it all on one trade. Never, ever stray from a short-term trading strategy that has made consistent money in order to try to hit a home run. The nature of trading is such that you earn your profits one dime at a time, and if you are not careful, you will lose them in whole points. There is no such thing as easy money.

Cut Your Losses

Another error in judgment occurred in my refusal to cut my losses. When the bid-ask spread is so wide, you absolutely must cut your losses the second the stock goes against you. If the spread is wide, and the stock begins to go against you, you are in a no-win situation. As you can see, if you don't, the losses can be devastating. The problem is that the wider the spread, the more difficult it is to sell, because in the back of your mind you know how much money you are leaving on the table. But you don't have a choice, because that is what you face when you trade a volatile stock.

Don't Go Back into the Stock after Losing Money in It

Perhaps the biggest lapse occurred when I decided to go back into the stock after I had lost money in it. In my case, I went back five separate times! An emotional attachment to a stock is devastating to your profit and loss. Never go right back into a stock after you have lost money in it. *The stock does not owe you anything.*

Don't Buy Twice as Many Shares

Along those same lines, if going back into the stock was bad, buying twice as many shares was even worse! One thousand shares were no longer enough. Instead of 1,000, I had to own 2,000. As the losses mounted, I was determined to make back the money. If you are stupid enough to go back into a stock after you have just lost money in it, never, ever buy more shares than you did the first time.

Avoid Trading a Volatile Stock on the Afternoon before a Holiday Weekend

Last but not least, going long a tanking stock on the Friday afternoon before the Labor Day weekend was a recipe for disaster. Traders typically lighten up on positions going into long weekends, and they usually do it in the afternoon. Refrain from buying volatile stocks on Friday afternoons before long weekends. The market is more likely to go down than up during this time.

LEARNING FROM THE MISTAKE AND MOVING ON

It is my hope that you remember this example if you ever find yourself in a similar situation. If you trade long enough, it is bound to happen at least once. But, as I did, you will learn from the mistake. It is not the end of the world: It is a bump in the road and nothing more. It took a few days, but I was able to recoup the profits I lost in that 24-hour span. The point is that, no matter how much experience you have, there are going to be certain times when your self-discipline is going to be put to the test. Composure is hard to maintain and easy to lose. The forces of fear and greed can destroy you if you are not careful. I was lucky I didn't lose more than $12,000 during this debacle. But I made sure it would never happen again.

CAN THE QUOTED MARKET ALWAYS BE TRUSTED?

As we discussed, one of the problems that I faced in the Citi trade was that the supply and demand in the stock was changing faster than the quoted market was indicating. In times of extreme volatility, the NYSE's quoted market is sometimes not indicative of where the true buyers and sellers are willing to trade. In other words, the quoted market can sometimes not be trusted. This is a danger that you will inevitably face when trading in fast-moving markets, and you must be aware of it.

To shed some more light on this, let's take a real-life example that happened to me several years ago. Like the previous example, this was a valuable lesson to me in how markets behave during buying panics. It was Tuesday at around 2:10 P.M. That day was a special one because the Federal Reserve was set to announce the results of its Federal Open Market Committee (FOMC) meeting. The FOMC is the group that meets to decide what to do with interest rates. I was watching CNBC very carefully. The market consensus was split 50–50 between keeping interest rates unchanged and raising them. Anytime the market consensus is split, there will always be a big move the second the announcement is made. If the FOMC left rates unchanged, the market would soar. If rates were raised, the market would sell off.

My plan was simple: If rates were unchanged, I would buy 1,000 shares of Travelers (the NYSE symbol was TRV, but since merged with Citigroup) the second I heard the announcement. I would have to do so at the market, because the market would be moving too fast for a limit order. I was well aware of the danger of placing a market order. If rates were raised, I would refrain from placing any trades. At approximately 2:16, the announcement was made: "Fed leaves rates unchanged." As fast as I could, I entered a buy of 1,000 TRV at the market over the Internet. At the precise time my order was entered, the quote in TRV read 55.37 to 55.50. And the market was soaring. I was horrified when I got my fill report back a few seconds later. I was filled at 56.50, up a full point from where my quote indicated stock was for sale.

What exactly was going on? How could I have possibly been filled up at 56.50 if the quote was indicating stock for sale at 55.50? I quickly called the customer service department of my online broker and demanded an explanation. The representative phoned the NYSE floor and it turned out it was a fair fill. The stock was trading up at 56.50, not 55.50. The influx of buy orders at 2:16 P.M. had caused the stock to trade up a full point in only a few seconds, before the specialist could update the quote. The market had moved so fast that the specialist was unable to change the bid-ask spread in real time as orders were being filled. The moral of the story is this: Panic buying destroys wealth. This was a bad trade from the start, with poor odds and a poor risk-reward ratio. You will be unable to beat other traders to the punch when everyone is reacting to the same information at the same time. This was a bet against the house. And it was the last time that I ever tried to outsmart the market in a spree of panic buying.

Farrell Says

Do not blindly trust that the NYSE specialist will give you a fair fill when placing a market order in a buying panic! In most cases, you will not get a fair execution. This is when the odds of a profitable trade swing so quickly out of your favor that you must refrain from trading.

I learned a valuable lesson from that experience. What was I thinking? In retrospect, I had made a mistake every online trader makes at least once: I thought I could outsmart Wall Street. I thought I could get a jump on all the other traders who were looking at the same exact thing as I was. *What I learned is that no one will ever make any money by entering buy orders simultaneously with the rest of the investing world.* Remember, the whole world knew the market would go higher if the Fed kept rates unchanged. But no one knew for certain that keeping rates unchanged would be the outcome. So all the traders on Wall Street waited until after the announcement was made to enter their buy orders. This was a classic case of panic buying. And when there is panic buying, guess who gets filled last? The novice who is trading from home. Perhaps if I had a faster execution system, I might have been filled at 55.75 or better. Instead, I was filled at 56.50. A difference of half a second probably cost me $750.

That is the reality of trading in a stock that can literally move a full point in only a few seconds.

Remember how, in the last chapter, we discussed that when you are on the same side of the trade as the specialist, you can "trust" in the specialist system to give you a fair price? In this example, the opposite is true. When you are on the other side of the specialist's trade, you cannot trust that the price you receive will be fair. This was an extremely dangerous trade. Remember, for every buyer there is a seller. And this was a market order. Who was taking the other side of this trade, and at what price? The specialist was on the other side, selling when the rest of the investing world was blindly buying. But the specialist was selling on his or her terms, and at his or her price. Do you really think the specialist would be so stupid as to sell to me at a good price at the precise time that the FOMC announcement was released, knowing the market was heading higher? Of course not. Specialists are not in the business of leaving money on the table. That is exactly why the stock gapped up a full point in a few seconds. I got filled at 56.50 simply because that was the price where the specialist was willing to take the other side of my trade.

I hope this example paints a good picture of the inherent danger involved when momentum turns into panic buying. In times of panic buying, the day trader will be the last in and the last out, and will lose money 9 out of 10 times. The only remedy is to refrain from trading high-volatility stocks in these kinds of situations, when the odds of a profitable trade are not in the day trader's favor.

Farrell Says

This example highlights one of the central themes of this book. To make money as a day trader, you must be a buyer when the market needs buyers and a seller when the market needs sellers. Doing the opposite will cost you money almost every time. In other words, to send a market buy order to the NYSE when the specialist is flooded with panicked buyers makes you part of the problem, not the solution. As a result, with an absence of stock for sale at reasonable price levels, the specialist will reward your stupidity with an execution so poor that it will almost always result in a loss.

A FOOL AND HIS MONEY ARE SOON PARTED

So, we have reached the end. I hope you have enjoyed this journey as much as I have. You are now on your own. I wish you all the best in the uncertain times that lie ahead. Be careful, stay alert, and remember the things you read here. Never forget the central themes of this book: among them, be fearful when other traders are greedy, be greedy when others are fearful, and never, ever, bet against the house. Good luck, and may the gods of trading be with you.

APPENDIX A

The Day Trader's Arsenal: Online Brokers, Trade Commissions, Real-Time Quote Systems, and the Home Office

As a day trader, you will learn very quickly that part of the online trading experience is dealing with headaches. The second something goes wrong, you will realize how much your livelihood is dependent on the reliability of your online broker. There is nothing more annoying and frustrating than those times when you cannot place a trade because the system is down. Late fills, system crashes, back-office problems, commission and margin overcharges, busted trades, and trade discrepancies are all an inevitable part of life for the online day trader. And they always seem to happen at the worst possible time, when your money is at risk. You must prepare yourself accordingly.

CHOOSING AN ONLINE BROKER

The day trader's single largest business cost is brokerage commissions. That is why negotiating the cheapest possible commission rate is absolutely essential to your profitability. The most important decision the day trader can make is to choose the right online broker. The problem is that the investing world is saturated with online brokerage firms. How do you know which one to choose, when they all claim to provide the same services? The answer is simple: cost first, service and order-routing second.

Not all low-cost, online brokers are the same. There is a huge difference between paying $10 for a trade and paying only $7. This may not seem like a big difference to the average online investor, but to the active online day trader who makes a living trading, the difference between a $10 trade commission and a $7 trade commission could be tens of thousands of dollars at the end of the year. For some traders, that could be the difference between making and losing money over the course of a year. Think about it: If you did 5,000 trades in a year, paying only $7 per trade instead of $10 is a $15,000 difference over 12 months. That is why price must be your primary concern.

Over the course of my trading career, I estimate that I have spent upwards of $1 million in brokerage commissions. If you do 10,000 trades in a year, each dollar that you save on trade costs would put an extra $10,000 in your pocket. If you could negotiate that cost down from $10 per trade to $7 per trade, your savings could be $30,000 over the course of the year!

In the last decade, I have used at least 10 different online brokers. Each time I switched, it was generally because I was offered a better rate from a competitor. I do so many trades in a year that I need to reduce my transaction costs as much as possible. If I am deciding between a brokerage firm that charges $10 for limit orders and one that charges $7, I will most certainly choose the one that charges less.

Farrell Says

It is important to note that, when choosing a brokerage firm, you must compare the firms based on the price of limit orders, not market orders. As you know, the day trader's key to profitability is using limit orders, not market orders. The reality is that at most online brokerage firms, limit orders cost a few dollars more than market orders.

NEGOTIATE THE BEST POSSIBLE COMMISSION RATE

One of the best-kept secrets in the world of online trading is that all commission rates are negotiable. *Do not accept the advertised commission rate.* The online brokerage world is a brutally competitive business. The profits margins are very slim, and brokers rely on trading volume to be profitable. This means that if you are an active trader, the online brokers want your business! This puts you in the unique position of being able to play them against each other for price. When you are considering different online brokers, it would be prudent to call them up and discuss pricing over the phone. Tell them that you are an active online trader and you are looking for the right broker at the right price and that you are shopping around. More often than not, if they think that you will be doing a large amount of trades, they will be aggressive on their pricing to try to win your business.

MAKE SURE THAT THE BROKER CAN ROUTE DIRECTLY TO THE NYSE

Order routing is another key ingredient to choosing an online broker. If the trading system you are using doesn't offer you the ability to route directly to the NYSE, it might be better to look for another broker. One thing about online trading that has bothered me most over the past 10 years are antics involved in order routing. If you don't specify the destination of your order, the online brokers will often steer your order away from the New York Stock Exchange to a smaller, less-liquid regional exchange or electronic trading network to cut costs, because the NYSE charges the online brokers a fee to get trades executed on the floor of the exchange. This practice is fine for market orders, but not for limit orders. In my own experience, I have found that a limit order routed away from the NYSE will be less likely to get executed at a favorable price level.

Farrell Says

Watch where your online broker is routing your orders in NYSE-listed stocks. If they aren't being sent directly to the NYSE, demand that the

> *broker reroute them. If they won't, or they add a significant cost to doing this, it might be time to switch online brokers to one that offers you the ability to route directly to the NYSE. Remember, you can't exploit the NYSE's specialist system if the order doesn't get to the floor of the NYSE in the first place.*

PER-SHARE VERSUS PER-TRADE COMMISSION RATES

Another nuance in online brokerage commissions is the per-share versus per-trade fee structure. Most of the major online brokerage firms charge by the trade, not the share. In other words, if the commission structure is, say, $10 per trade, you will pay $10 per trade whether you trade 100 shares or 5,000 shares. (Keep in mind, that usually, any order larger than 5,000 shares results in a higher fee.) If you are trading only 100-share lots (as I recommend for beginners until you are consistently profitable), it might make more sense to go with a broker that charges by the share, not the trade. This will result is a significantly cheaper commission than $10 for that 100-share trade. For example, a per-share commission structure might charge you only $1 or less for a 100-share trade. Now, if you do 5,000 shares, you might pay much more than the $10 per-trade ticket on a per-share commission schedule. This is the trade-off. For small-lot traders, the per-share pricing could result in a substantial savings.

SETTING UP AT LEAST TWO ACCOUNTS

Unfortunately, when you choose an online broker, there is really no way to tell how reliable the firm's service is going to be. It is always going to be a case of trial and error. No one knows exactly what the future will bring, as so many smaller online brokers have merged with larger brokerage firms. For this reason, I have always made a point of keeping accounts open at at least two different online brokerage firms as insurance. That way, if there are consistent problems, I can merely move my money from the old firm to the new one. This ensures that, if I do decide to switch accounts, I will not have to miss weeks of trading while the new account is being set up. Remember, missing a few days of trading could mean missing out on a few thousand dollars.

SYSTEM CRASHES AND THE LATE FILL

So what might prompt you to switch online brokers? Once your account is opened and you are trading actively, the focus switches from cost to service. The online brokerage world, in the late 1990s at the height of the Internet trading boom, was notorious for technology and system failures, and no one was immune to these problems. Over time, as technology has improved, so has reliability. The situation has gotten much better, but the system can still crash from time to time. The problem can be much worse at some firms than at others. Unfortunately, you may find this out the hard way.

One of the most annoying aspects of trading online is the *late fill.* This occurs when you buy a stock, and minutes or hours later it is still not in your account. Why the delay? Because your online broker is having technical problems getting the execution report back from the floor of the New York Stock Exchange. The real problem is that, even if you are certain you own the stock, you may be unable to sell it until it hits your account. The online brokers have systems in place that will cancel an order if the computer thinks you are trying to sell a stock that is not in your account (not to be confused with short selling). The consequence of this is that you may be prevented from making a profit if the stock is trading higher than where you bought it, simply because you will be unable to sell it.

Even worse than the late fill is the *system crash,* when the entire Web site or trading platform goes down. In this case, you will be prevented from accessing your account to get up-to-the-minute information until the system is running again. This is a very dangerous situation.

When you don't get an immediate fill report on a market order, whether because of a late fill or a system crash, you have no idea at what price you bought or sold your stock, or whether the order is lost—or worse. When you trade slow-moving stocks, you can usually tell by the parameters of the market whether your order was executed at your price. But if you use market orders, when the stocks are moving so fast, you will have no idea where you might have been filled if you don't have the report back seconds after you enter the order.

This situation has happened to me many times over the past decade. It has occurred most often during those rare times when I place a market order in times of heavy volatility, market stress, and high trading volume. These are the times that online brokers are most prone to system problems. It usually goes like this: As the stock runs higher, I keep checking my account to see at what price I was executed. As the minutes go by, the stock continues to head higher, but I still do not have a fill back. Then I begin to get worried, because I wonder if the order is delayed or lost. Has my trade already been executed at a lower price, and is the broker just late in getting the fill back? Or is the broker having system problems that mean the order has not even been executed yet? The second situation is definitely worse because, with the stock continuing to go higher, the later the order is executed, the higher the price I will pay for the stock. That is always a danger of using market orders. There is nothing more frustrating than knowing I was on the right side of a trade but lost money anyway because the online broker could not execute the order properly.

Trading systems can get bogged down on days when trading volume is heavy. The heaviest trading volumes of the year usually occur during market crashes, which means Internet trading will be much slower during these rare, dangerous times. These are the times when the market moves 400 or 500 points to the downside. *The irony is that your execution will be at its slowest precisely when you need it to be at its fastest, in volatile markets.* It always has to be in the back of your mind if you dare to trade during market sell-offs.

Many of the advertisements on television for online brokers mention that, if you prefer, you can talk to a live broker instead of placing a trade online. Many people are under the impression that when the system goes down, they can simply phone their orders in. Good luck trying to get through when the system crashes—every trader in the system attempts to call in at the same time, and most firms do not have enough representatives to handle the calls. The consequence: You will be on hold indefinitely. There have been times when I have been on hold for over 45 minutes waiting to get an answer on a trade.

These are the dangers you will face when you trade over the Internet. They affect everyone. This technology is still in its infancy, and is prone to failure every so often. And, as you know, failures are always going to happen at the worst possible times. To calm my own nerves, I have accepted the fact that 99 percent of the time the system works well. As for that other 1 percent, that is when I give some trading profits back to the system. It is an inevitable cost of doing business. That is the price online traders must pay for the luxury of being able to trade from home.

CUSTOMER SERVICE, BACK-OFFICE PROBLEMS, AND TRADE DISCREPANCIES

There are a couple of other dimensions to the online trading experience that are not fun to deal with. Occasionally, if you trade actively, situations will arise involving mistakes or trade discrepancies made by online brokers—for example, getting hit with a commission overcharge. Maybe the trade only cost $10, but the online broker hit your account with a $20 charge. It could even be something more serious, like an unfair execution. Or maybe you thought you were entitled to a fill on a sell order, and you never got one. Even worse, 5,000 shares of a stock you never even heard of might end up in your account by error. I have even had experiences where I was credited with buying or selling a stock two or three days after the trade occurred. These kinds of things happen every so often, and you have to deal with them appropriately.

These problems and discrepancies are a fact of life for traders. My experience has been that eventually, no matter how bad the problem, the brokerage firm resolves it fairly. But that does not mean there are not headaches and stress in the interim. Trading is stressful enough. Dealing with back-office problems is a nightmare. This is why the big Wall Street firms have entire departments whose sole function is to resolve these problems. But that does not change the fact that you have to be on top of everything all the time. You cannot let anything slip by you. Remember, you are on your own. If you do not pick up on these mistakes, no one else will. It is your money on the line, and you have to protect it at all times.

THE REMEDY—KEEP GOOD TRADING RECORDS

There are a couple of precautions I take to ensure that I am protected in the event a mistake arises. I strongly recommend you do the same. These precautions are as follows:

1. *For each individual trade, keep a separate 3 × 5 card or piece of paper detailing the precise time the trade was placed, the order or confirmation number, and the market in the stock at the time the order was placed.* This ensures that you have a record of when the trade was entered, when it was filled, and the number of shares. If there is a discrepancy at a later date, this will be your

Table A.1   3 × 5 Transaction Card

11/12	Sell 2500	XYZ	23.07
1:39 P.M.	Confirm #964552809		
22.95–23.07	3400 × 1200	321,000 Volume	
2,500 Shares Filled at 1:41 P.M.			

only record of when the trade occurred and where the stock was trading at the time the order was placed, outside of the online broker's records. In the past, I have had situations where even a week later, I was still fighting with them over an execution. Remember, it's always your word against the broker's. That is why you want to do everything you can to keep accurate records. I usually keep this information on file for a few months just to be on the safe side. It looks similar to the illustration in Table A.1.

2. *Keep an accurate daily trading log.* This includes an itemized list of the trades made, the number of shares, the commissions incurred, the profit and loss on each trade, and total net profit and loss for the day. See Table A.2 for a sample trading log.

Table A.2   Example of a Daily Trading Log—November 12

Bought 2,500 XYZ 23	
Sold 2,500 XYZ 23.07	+175
Bought 3,000 Z 9.25	
Sold 3,000 Z 9.35	+300
Bought 2,000 AAA 22,01	
Sold 2,000 AAA 22.01	EVEN
Bought 2,000 XYZ 23.00	
Sold 2,000 XYZ 23.07	+140
Bought 2,000 Z 9.30	
Sold 2,000 Z 9.35	+100
Bought 3,000 AAA 22.00	
Sold 3,000 AAA 21.95	−150
Gross Profit before Commissions	+565
Less Commissions on 12 trades ($7 per trade)	
(does not include SEC fees)	−84
Net Profit after Commissions	+481.00

This trading log may be your only means of independently compiling your daily, weekly, and monthly profit-and-loss performance, outside of the records kept by the brokerage firm. But what if the firm's records are not accurate? If you get into the habit of logging your trading results after each and every trading day, it will give you a good reference point to double-check the accuracy of the values the online broker assigns to your trading account. This is extremely important because without it you will be at the mercy of the brokerage firm's accounting department. If you do several hundred trades or more in a month like I do, it is very easy to lose track of how much money you have made or lost in a given month. The brokerage firm will send you a month-end statement that is a summary of all of the transactions in your account, but you should never rely solely on the firm's recordkeeping ability. I make sure my records always match. That is the only way I know for sure that the broker's records are accurate.

Imagine making a $4,000 profit in a day that is not reflected in your account at month end. Where did the money go? Luckily, this is a rarity, but theoretically it could happen. If you didn't keep your own records, you would never know, because you would have no way to detect that something was wrong. Maybe the brokerage firm was so screwed up that it didn't detect it, either. This could be a real problem. The consequence? You would be out $4,000. That is my point: If this is your livelihood, you must be on top of everything. No one else is. The chance of this kind of error going undetected is slim. But I sleep much better at night knowing I have left nothing to chance.

THE HOME OFFICE AND THE VIRTUAL TRADING FLOOR

One of the most important things I have learned is that the environment you work in has a big influence on your ability to make profits. Wall Street firms spend millions designing state-of-the-art trading floors so as to bring out the optimal level of performance in their traders. You may be surprised to see this mentioned in a book on day trading, but the environment issue faces day traders as well. In trading, you have to give yourself every possible advantage. The fact of the matter is that you will be unable to trade to your highest level if you are stuck in an environment you loathe. It's that simple. That is why one of the biggest issues involved in trading full-time is making sure you have a pleasant work environment, especially if you trade out of your own home.

The home office is by far the most economical way to trade. In the world of day trading, you have to keep your overhead as low as possible because your earnings are so volatile. This may mean giving up the spacious office by the window that you might have in your current job in exchange for a far less glamorous work environment—your home. The plush office with the receptionist is not necessary in this line of work. Especially in the beginning, you don't want to have to pay rent for office space, because it will eat into your profits and put too much pressure on your trading. If you are successful after a few months, then go ahead and get an office. But I would not advise it at first.

Thankfully, today's technology allows you to create a virtual trading floor from your home. All the financial information you will ever need is right at your fingertips. All you need is a computer, cable television for financial news, an Internet connection, and a real-time quote system, and you are set.

Trading Equipment

The day trader needs four things to get started:

1. Desktop computer with significant speed and memory. You can pick this up for less than $1,500.
2. Cable Internet connection. This will probably run you about $40 per month.
3. Extensive real-time quote system. This runs about $200 per month plus exchange fees (unless provided free by your on-line broker). This must include the capability to receive supply-and-demand data directly from the New York Stock Exchange, including the NYSE specialist's limit order book.
4. Cable television to watch CNBC, Bloomberg, and/or Fox Business News all day.

Psychological Effects of Working from Home

Working full-time out of your house is an entirely different experience than working in an office setting. From a psychological standpoint, the difference is like night and day; you won't realize this until you actually try it. There seems to be a prevailing belief among people unhappy in their current jobs that working from home is the answer to all of their problems. They may not get along with coworkers, they may be unhappy with the long commute they face every day, or they may simply dislike working in such close proximity to the boss. I've been working out of my house for over 10 years, and I really enjoy the convenience it provides. I must admit there is something really great about not having to leave the house on those mornings when the weather is miserable. I can wake up at 8:00 A.M. and be fully ready for the markets to open at 9:30 without ever having to deal with a commute. When I worked on Wall Street, I was out the door at 7 A.M. to catch the subway and spent the better part of 45 minutes each day getting to and from work.

Just as it takes certain personality traits to be a good trader, it definitely takes certain traits to enjoy working out of the house. Some people need the structure provided by a corporate work setting. Hopefully, if you are reading this book, you do not. Thankfully, the notion of working from home, whether it be at day trading or some other home-based business, is finally getting a certain degree of acceptance and respect from the general public. Of course, there are always going to be people who think that, just because you work out of the house, you are not legitimately making a living—or you are not working at all. Take my advice: Ignore these people. The world is full of them, and they are generally people who work for someone else for a living. They are not entrepreneurs, and they don't understand risk. Best of all, they have no idea of the kind of money successful day traders can make.

So what kind of person takes well to working out of the house? The same kind of person who takes to day trading. Day trading and working from home go hand in hand. It's the entrepreneur, the risk taker, the self-motivated person who doesn't need to be told what to do by others that excels in this environment. In corporate America, there is always a lot being said about the necessity of being a team player. Well, chances are, most of you reading this book either are not team players or are sick and tired of being team players. Thankfully, day trading does not reward the team player.

The Isolation Factor

Every worthwhile attempt at achieving financial independence and wealth involves some personal sacrifices, and day trading is no different. Along with the independence of working for yourself, and the excitement of making quick profits, come some drawbacks. From a psychological standpoint, one of the toughest things you will have to endure is something I call the *isolation factor*.

There will be many days when you might not see or speak to anyone outside of your immediate family or significant other if you are trading from home. You will become so engrossed in the markets that you probably won't even notice this. But it can begin to take its toll on you mentally if you are not careful. I've heard horror stories about people who put their life savings into starting a home-based business, only to find, six months later, that they can't endure the isolation. After taking all that risk, they end up quitting a profitable business for reasons other than why they went into business in the first place. They don't give up working at home because of the money, but because they can't handle the isolation. These people are usually independent-minded, risk-taking individuals. At first, to this kind of personality, the isolation seems like a luxury. It's not the work that they despise, it's the boss breathing down their neck all day. So the idea of going out on their own appeals to them. But they learn the hard way that for them there is more to happiness than just being their own boss.

The only advice I can give in this regard is from my own experience. I have really enjoyed working for myself out of my home over the last decade. There is a tremendous feeling of accomplishment, and peace of mind, that comes from knowing that your success is entirely in your own hands. If this means working out of the house, and spending the working day in isolation, then so be it. Life is short, and you may not have the chance to do everything you want to do. And you are never going to know what it is like to trade from home unless you try it. I look forward to each and every day I spend trading. If that is an indication, then I stand as evidence that you can work from home and enjoy it.

APPENDIX B

Considerations for Trading for a Living: The Allocation of Trading Capital, the Pattern Day Trader Rule, Using Margin and Trading Part-Time vs. Full-Time

Rule changes enacted by the Securities and Exchange Commission (SEC) do not allow day traders to trade unless they have at least $25,000 in risk capital.

The single most destructive thing that a day trader can do is to trade with money he or she can't afford to lose. This is a recipe for disaster. For many, day trading from home is a dream job. The temptation of quick profits is very strong, and is often hard to resist. After reading this far, you might feel ready to quit the 9-to-5 world and join the ranks of day traders. As with many other things in life, however, the reality is not as sweet as the fantasy. Day trading is a different kind of work, but it is work. As with any business venture, you must plan ahead, be prepared, and proceed cautiously. If you are considering this career path, there are several important issues you must address.

ALLOCATION OF TRADING CAPITAL

As a day trader, the single most important tool you have is your trading capital. This is the lifeblood of your business. Obviously, you cannot trade without it. The problem is that the allure of day trading for a living is so strong that many people who are currently day trading are simply financially unfit to bear the risks involved. This, in part, contributes to the high failure rate among day traders that we have discussed in this book. There are several considerations that must be taken into account before you can decide how much money to allocate toward day trading. The first step is to make realistic assumptions about your lifestyle and your personal finances.

Obviously, you must first determine exactly how much trading capital you can afford to set aside for trading. This has to be considered *risk capital.* When I say risk capital, I mean money you can afford to have tied up for extended periods of time without having to dip into it to meet living expenses. This is the same kind of money you might use to start a business, or currently may have tied up in the markets in long-term investments. The idea is that, over time, you want your trading capital to grow untouched. Think of day trading as a battle, and your trading capital as your ammunition. Without enough ammo, you are dead. You do not want to be in a situation where you have to keep pulling money out of your trading capital to meet living expenses. This will severely limit your profit potential. As you get more experience and your level of skill improves, hopefully your profits will start to build up so long as the trading capital remains in your account. This increase in trading capital gives you substantial leverage to add to your gains. As you become a better trader, your profits will increase as your trading capital builds. This is what enables you to increase your profits month after month. Even the most profitable traders, if they have to draw from their accounts continuously to meet expenses, will have difficulty doing this.

Thus, risk capital must be money you can afford to lose. Under no circumstances should you take rent money, credit card debt, or money you need to live on and allocate it toward day trading. There are two reasons for this. The first is obvious; the second is more subtle, but far more destructive. For the simple reason that losses are a part of day trading, you have to make sure you can live without the money you are trading with in the event that you lose it. The markets have a strange way of destroying wealth at the worst possible times, when it is needed most. Every day trader hopes to eventually make back any money lost during a bad streak. The problem is that if this is money normally set aside to meet everyday living expenses, you are going to put yourself and your trading under a tremendous amount of pressure to turn a profit.

One of the most important lessons I have learned is never to force a trade. This is the tendency when you enter a trade because you must make money to meet your bills, and it is the easiest way to lose money. Your judgment is impaired, and instead of waiting for a trade where the odds are in your favor, you throw money at a stock in desperate hope that it goes higher. The minute you find yourself in a situation of *hoping* the stock moves in your favor, you are sure to lose.

There is another side to this as well. Your trading capital is your vehicle of risk. As with any business or investment decision, there is a certain degree of danger involved. One vital component of your success as a trader is your attitude toward risk. It sounds strange, but you cannot look at your trading capital in the same way you look at spending money. This is not money you buy groceries with, or go to the movies with. You have to tell yourself that this is not "money" at all, it is trading capital, a means to an end. Psychologically, that makes all the difference in the world, and will save you much mental pain and anguish. The reality is that you might make and lose more money in a single afternoon trading than you have ever spent in a single afternoon in your entire life. How you deal with this will make or break you. The bottom line is that you cannot get emotionally attached to the money you trade with. If you do, you will be unable to handle risk, and you will most certainly self-destruct.

We all love money. Traders, perhaps more than anyone, hate to lose money. Yet the best traders are the ones who separate themselves from their work. Even though your trading capital is real, hard-earned money, you must deal with it almost as if it were play money, merely a tool used to achieve success. It is only then that you can have some degree of detachment from the inevitable profits and losses you will encounter. Imagine a heart surgeon who is madly in love with the person he or she is operating on. The surgeon's performance is bound to be affected by emotion. The same is true in trading. The further your decision making is separated from your emotions, the more likely that you will be profitable. You will be unable to separate your emotions from your trading if you are risking money you cannot afford to lose.

Emotional attachment is a very dangerous thing. If you are trading money you cannot afford to risk, you will find it very difficult to cut your losses. It becomes impossible to cut your losses if you are married to your positions. In other words, you will let something other than the immediate supply and demand in the stock dictate when you buy and sell. The easiest path to self-destruction is to ride a losing position into the ground. Riding your winners and cutting your losses is one of the most important skills you can develop as a trader. The reason people hesitate to sell a losing position when they should is that they can't stomach the loss. It becomes even worse if they are losing money that was needed to pay bills. The fact that the stock has gone against them and the loss is already reflected even though the stock hasn't been sold is of no significance to emotionally attached traders. The all-consuming loss will begin to take on a life of its own. I speak from experience when I say that this type of thing can easily snowball out of control. I have seen an entire week's profits erode in an hour when this happens.

The same destructive psychology can come into play during winning trades. Inexperienced day traders, in addition to letting their losses run, have a tendency to lock in profits the second they are on the right side of the trade. This is because they can't afford to leave a profit, no matter how small, on the table, especially if the money is needed to meet bills. At this point, these people too are trading out of desperation. They *must* turn a profit. They force themselves to close out the position precisely when they should not sell. This type of trading leaves large profits on the table. The common denominator for all successful traders is having the self-discipline to book the loss in a losing position, and to refrain from selling a winning position until supply and demand, not your emotions, dictate that you sell. This is possible only if you are detached from the money you are trading.

One final thought on why you shouldn't trade your rent money: Day trading requires a tremendous amount of stamina. Burnout is common among people who have a hard time dealing with the pressure. You will sleep much better at night, and enjoy your weekends more, if you can separate yourself from your trading capital and your losses. Inexperienced traders, after losing $1,000 for the first time, will inevitably take the loss personally. Irrational thoughts are bound to cross their minds. Maybe they feel that if they hadn't made that last trade, they'd be able to afford a new television or go on a nice weekend trip. I know from personal experience that these kinds of thoughts will ruin you. The best traders look at their trading capital as a means to an end. Losses are an unavoidable part of trading. No one is right all the time. If you were, you'd be the richest person in the world.

The reason I've taken the time to explain this is that it plays a big role in deciding how much money to allocate toward day trading. The bottom line is that the urgency of having to turn a profit is going to affect your trading ability adversely. The more urgent the profit, the less likely it is to happen. Murphy's law is unfortunately alive and well in day trading.

THE PATTERN DAY TRADER RULE

In this book, we have talked about the inherent dangers that face the day trader, and how the destructive forces of the house edge put odds of success against them. Historically, the high failure rate among day traders speaks to this. The Securities Exchange Commission (SEC) is also aware of these dangers. A few years ago, in an effort to protect the investing public from the dangers of excessive day trading, they implemented the *pattern day trader rule*. In summary, any trader who makes more than four day trades in five business days is considered a pattern day trader. Pattern day traders must maintain at least $25,000 in equity in their account at all times.

TRADING ON MARGIN

It is very important to remember that the $25,000 minimum for trading is enhanced by the fact that you can trade on *margin*. Trading on margin is essential to profitable day trading. Trading on margin simply means you are allowed to take intraday positions up to four times the amount of cash you have in your brokerage account, and two times your trading capital on overnight positions. In the past, prior to the implementation of the pattern day trader rule, margin requirements only allowed you to take positions up to two times your equity capital during the day. Thus, when the SEC raised the trading capital requirements for pattern day traders, they also raised the leverage for those able to meet the stricter requirements.

> ### *Farrell Says*
>
> *All things considered, the pattern day trader rule implemented by the SEC benefited experienced day traders by doubling the amount of intraday leverage that can be used.*

Keep in mind that the brokerage firm lends you the money and charges interest. The beauty is that if you don't hold the positions overnight, you don't have to pay any interest. For the day trader, this is like free money. For example, if you deposit $25,000 with an online brokerage firm, as a pattern day trader, you actually have $100,000 worth of buying power. If you buy a $100 stock, you could buy 1,000 shares. If you resell the stock in the same day, you don't pay any margin interest. If you hold a stock overnight that is larger than the cash in your account, you are charged an interest rate that is probably around 8 percent annually, depending on interest rates at the time, the brokerage firm you are using, and the size of the margin balance. This interest will be more competitive as the amount you borrow increases.

There is a dangerous side to trading on margin, however. You are on the hook for 100 percent of any losses you incur on the borrowed money. It is a loan, and nothing more. It's the same as if your local bank loaned you money to open a business. Imagine if the business went belly-up. Not only would you lose your investment, but you would also owe the bank the balance of the loan, regardless of the profitability of the business. The same is true in trading. But the dangerous thing is that, unlike for a bank loan, there is no lengthy approval process for margin borrowing. So long as you have money in your account, and you are approved for pattern day trading, the broker will let you borrow against it intraday up to 4 to 1, no questions asked. Margin interest is a good source of revenue for brokerage firms. So what's the catch?

MARGIN CALLS

The brokerage firms are not stupid. They are fully aware of the risk they are taking by loaning you money. That is why they have *margin calls*. If you hold positions overnight, the brokerage firm's margin department will monitor your account to make sure the money loaned to you is protected. Let's look at an example.

Imagine you open a margin account with $100,000 cash and you qualify as a pattern day trader. The brokerage firm will loan you an additional $100,000 against the money overnight in the account. So you are actually playing with $400,000 of trading capital intraday, and $200,000 of capital overnight. Assume you buy 1,000 shares of a $200 stock and you hold the position overnight. Now imagine that, to your horror, the stock loses 70 percent of its value in one day. All of a sudden, the value of your holdings is cut to less than one-third. You had invested $100,000 and borrowed $100,000 from the brokerage firm to buy a $200,000 stock position. Now that stock position is only worth $60,000. The risk managers at the brokerage firm will get a little concerned that you won't be able to pay back the $40,000 of their money that you borrowed. It is not of their concern that you just lost $100,000 of your own money, which was the entire amount of your initial deposit. They just want their money back.

The margin call is when the broker forces you to deposit more money in your account as collateral against the margin loan. If you can't come up with more money, the broker will simply sell out the remainder of your holdings (whether you like it or not) and take back the money loaned to you, if possible. This is the brokerage firm's version of a bank foreclosure. This ensures that, in most instances, the firm gets its money back one way or another. This occurs only when the value of your account drops drastically.

There is another dynamic that protects the brokerage firm against losses from margin loans. Stocks under $5 are generally not marginable. This means you can't borrow the brokerage firm's money to buy stocks below $5. You have to pay for them entirely with your own money. This is because so many stocks trading below $5 are cheap for a reason: They might be on their way to being worthless. And the brokerage firm is not going to take that risk with its money.

PART-TIME VERSUS FULL-TIME TRADING

With this in mind, how much money should the beginning trader allocate toward trading? The pattern day trader rule forces you to have at least $25,000 in risk capital before you can trade. I strongly suggest that you have at least double that amount if you plan on trading full-time. I think $50,000 is about the minimum needed to give you a realistic chance of survival as a trader. For someone trading part-time who has a primary source of income, $25,000 is certainly enough trading capital to work with.

There are pros and cons to trading part-time. As long as you have online access and a computer, you can trade right from your current office or home office. The most important thing is that trading part-time will allow you to get your feet wet in day trading without risking too much trading capital or giving up the income from your full-time job. Losses are a part of trading, but you learn from those losses. The reality is that you really won't learn a thing until your money is on the line. That is when everything will begin to make sense. In the beginning, I would strongly suggest not risking more than 100 shares on each trade until you are consistently profitable.

There are several other issues to consider if you are deciding to trade part-time while still working at your full-time job. You are in this for the money. It has to be worth your while to justify the time commitment you are going to make. Even trading part-time requires a tremendous amount of concentration and effort. And, unfortunately, most of you happen to have your full-time jobs during market hours. Therefore, you will probably be trading from the same office or desk where you do your full-time job. The reality is that trading will distract you from your full-time job.

Farrell Says

Do not even think about trading part-time unless you are 100 percent focused on the markets during the time that you set aside for trading. If you are distracted by another job, or you are out of the rhythm of the supply and demand in the stock you are trading, the odds are likely that you will lose money. It will go out of your pocket and into the pocket of the person taking the other side of your trade. Said another way, do not ever trade when the odds are not in your favor.

Making money in the markets requires a tremendous amount of concentration. The last place you want to be when the market is crashing is in a two-hour meeting with your boss. People cite Murphy's Law because it comes true so often. The day the market crashes will inevitably be the day you are away from your quote screen and tied up in something else. So, with that said, I would suggest trading part-time if and only if your full-time job allows you to devote a sufficient amount of time during the day to trading without being distracted.

INDEX

A

Apple Computer, 131, 134
  overnight trade example, 139–140
"Asian Contagion," 146
Ask size, 16, 41, 44–45, 46, 48, 50, 56, 62,
  84, 86, 87, 91

B

Back-office problems, 167
Bad news, buying on, 118–119
Bargaining process, 30–32
Bid, buying on, 120–121
Bid-ask spread, 4, 7, 11–16, 28, 45
  exploiting, 4, 95–111
    complex process, simplifying,
      104–105
    glamour stocks, avoiding, 102
    house, betting with the, 109
    making money on stocks that don't
      move, 98–99
    operating under the radar, 100–102
    other moving parts to the trade,
      105–109
    risk, 110–111
    scalper, role of, 99–100
    small profits, focusing on, 100,
      103
    sweet spot, finding the, 103–104
  narrowing, 72
  prelude to, 35
  understanding, 37–60
    day orders versus good-until-
      canceled (GTC) orders, 52–54

limit order to buy, 50–52
limit order to sell, 54–56
market order to buy, 48–50
market order to sell, 46–48
moving the stock higher, 57–60
nickels and dimes, haggling over,
  56–57
price movement, mechanics of,
  39–41
quote, 41–45
Bid size, 16, 41, 44–47, 48, 52, 53–54, 62,
  84, 86–91
Brokerage commissions, 21
Buyer of last resort, specialist as, 67–68,
  119–120

C

Capitalism, exploiting the excesses of,
  7–16
  bid-ask spread, 11–16
  house edge, 9–11
Card counting, 10
Chicago Bridge and Iron (CBI),
  41–45
Citicorp (CCI), 146–154
Citigroup, 130, 146, 157
Commission rate
  negotiating the best possible,
    163
  per share versus per trade, 164
Computer Associates (CA), 118–119, 120,
  121
Customer service, 167

D

Day orders versus good-until-canceled (GTC) orders, 52–54
  bid, 53
  bid size, 53–54
  no-lose situation for the bidder, 54
Day trader's arsenal, 161–172
  accounts, setting up at least two, 164
  commission rate
    negotiating the best possible, 163
    per-share versus per-trade, 164
  customer service, back-office problems, and trade discrepancies, 167
  home office and the virtual trading floor, 169–170
    isolation factor, 171–172
    trading equipment, 170
    working from home, psychological effects of, 170–171
  online broker, choosing an, 161–162
  routing directly to the NYSE, making sure that the broker can, 163–164
  system crashes and the late fill, 165–166
Day trading, introduction to, 17–24
  brokerage commissions, 21
  day trader as buyer and/or seller, 20
  fear and greed in buying and selling, 22–23
  mind-set of an online day trader, 19–20
  slow execution, 23–24
  small profits, 20–21
  trading on the New York Stock Exchange, 24
Dean Foods (DF), 98, 99, 101, 103, 106–109, 110
Dow Jones Industrial Average, 127, 129, 134, 146

E

El Paso Pipeline Partners LP (EPB), 71
EntreMed Inc. (ENMD), 141

F

Fairfax Holdings (FFH), 63, 65
Federal Open Market Committee (FOMC), 157

G

Gap open
  parameters of, 122–124
  playing the, 117–118
Good news, buying strong stocks on, 141–142
Good-until-canceled (GTC) orders, day orders versus, 52–54
  bid, 53
  bid size, 53–54
  no-lose situation for the bidder, 54
Google, 131, 134
Goosing the market, 121–122
Gruntal & Company, xv, 100

H

Home office, 169–172
House, betting with the, 1–4, 109
House edge, 9–11, 134–135

I

IBM, 127
Isolation factor, 171–172

L

Late fill, 165–166
Limit order book, 69–71, 106–109
  determining if the opening trade will "clear," 124–125
Limit orders, 42, 43, 45, 78, 109
  to buy, 50–52
  failure of in rallies, 127–129
  market orders versus, 27–35
    bargaining process, 30–32
    bid-ask spread, prelude to, 35
    price makers versus price takers, 29–30
    price negotiation, 32–34
    Wall Street's conflict of interest, understanding, 27–29
    Wall Street's prey, 34–35
  to sell, 54–56
Lopsided market, 45
Losses, 145–159
  break even, the need to, 150–151
  downdraft, getting caught in, 148
  greed, 148–150
  learning from your mistakes, 156
  missing a trade, 147

trusting the quoted market, dangers of, 156–159

useful insights on, 152–156

abnormally wide bid-ask spreads, avoiding, 152–154

buying a stock after losing money on it, 155

buying twice as many shares, 156

cutting your losses, 155

short-term investing instead of trading, dangers of, 155

trading on old price information, 154

trading a volatile stock on the afternoon before a holiday weekend, 156

M

Margin calls, 178–179

Margin, trading on, 177–178

Market indexes, trading tick for tick with, 127

Market makers, 12, 131–135

inflicting heavy damage on by attacking their vulnerability, 142–143

Nasdaq Composite Index, tracking the, 134

opening a stock abnormally high, 141

SOES bandits and, 133–134

taking profits from, 134–135

Market orders

to buy, 48–50

ask size, 50

volume, 50

versus limit orders, 27–35

bargaining process, 30–32

bid-ask spread, prelude to, 35

price makers versus price takers, 29–30

price negotiation, 32–34

Wall Street's conflict of interest, understanding, 27–29

Wall Street's prey, 34–35

to sell, 46–48

bid size, 48

volume, 48

Microsoft, 131, 134

Momentum trading. *See* Volatility, profiting from

N

Nasdaq, xvi, 2, 3

and day trading, 24

two methods for, 136–139

market makers on, 12, 131–135

SOES bandits and, 133–134

Nasdaq Composite Index, tracking the, 134

New York Stock Exchange (NYSE), xiv, 2, 3, 4, 8, 9, 38

as an auction market, 56

and day trading, 24, 38

fair order handling rules, 80–85

Openbook, 69

rules, 16

specialists, 12, 60. *See also* Specialists role of, 61–93

typical market scenario on, 41–45

O

Online broker, choosing an, 161–162

Openbook (NYSE), 69

Over-the-counter market. *See* Nasdaq

Overnight, holding stocks, 136–139

P

Pattern day trader rule, 177

Price makers versus price takers, 29–30

Price movement, mechanics of, 39–41

Pullbacks, buying strong stocks on, 140–141

Q

Quote, 41–45

ask, 42–44

ask size, 44–45

bid, 42

bid size, 44

volume, 45

R

Risk, 110–111

Risk capital, 174

Risk premium, 14

S

S&P 500 Futures, using to gauge the sustainability of a rally, 129

Scalping, 4

introduction to, 95–111

bid-ask spread, exploiting, 103

Scalping (*Continued*)
    complex process, simplifying,
        104–105
    glamour stocks, avoiding, 102
    house, betting with the, 109
    making money on stocks that don't
        move, 98–99
    operating under the radar,
        100–102
    other moving parts to the trade,
        105–109
    risk, 110–111
    scalper, role of, 99–100
    small profits, focusing on, 100
    sweet spot, finding the, 103–104
Securities and Exchange Commission
    (SEC), 177
Short selling, 135–136
Small Order Execution System (SOES),
    133–134
Specialists, 12, 47, 60
   betting on, 119–122
   joining as buyer of last resort, 120
   limit order book, 69–71, 106–109
   role of on the New York Stock
      Exchange, 61–93
   absence of, 66–67
   being cautious of, 93
   bid-ask spread, narrowing, 72
   buyer of last resort, 67–68
   as competition for day traders,
      77–78
   day traders as shadow specialists,
      78
   determining where specialist is in
      stock, 85–87
   fairness of profit of, 68
   jockeying for position, 87–89
   knowing where you stand in line, 89
   large sell order, handling a, 74–77
   limit order book, 69–71
   market, being on both sides of,
      71–72
   NYSE's fair order handling rules,
      80–85
   privileged information of, 68–69
   real intentions of, 77
   talking to the specialist directly,
      89–92
   tipping the odds in your favor, 92
   using the specialist system to your
      advantage, 64–66
   wide spreads as protection from
      volatility, 73
   upper hand and, 116–117
System crashes, 165–166

T
Templeton Russia and Eastern European
    Fund (TRF), 87
Trade discrepancies, 167
Trading dos and don'ts, 105–106
Trading for a living, considerations for,
    173–181
   margin calls, 178–179
   margin, trading on, 177–178
   part-time versus full-time, 179–181
   pattern day trader rule, 177
   trading capital, allocation of, 174–177
Trading equipment, 170
Travelers, 157
   merger with Citicorp, 146
Two-sided market, keeping a, 13

V
Vapor trail, 130
Virtual trading floor, 169–170
Volatility, profiting from, 113–143
   bad news, buying on, 118–119
   gap open
      parameters of, 122–124
      playing the, 117–118
   limit order book, determining if the
      opening trade will "clear,"
      124–125
   limit orders, failure of in rallies,
      127–129
   market indexes, trading tick for tick
      with, 127
   market makers, inflicting heavy
      damage on by attacking their
      vulnerability, 142–143
   market upsurge, 129–130
   Nasdaq
      and the role of market makers,
      131–135
      day trading Nasdaq stocks, two
      methods for, 136–139

opening a stock abnormally high, 141
pullbacks, buying strong stocks on, 140–141
S&P 500 Futures, using to gauge the sustainability of a rally, 129
second wave, selling before the, 125–126
short selling, 135–136
specialists
    betting on, 119–122
    and the upper hand, 116–117
stock for sale, scarceness of, 130–131
strong stock, dangers of buying on the opening trade, 141–142
Volume, 45, 48, 50

W
Working from home, psychological effects of, 170–171
    isolation factor, 171–172

Y
Yahoo!, 131

CATHERINE BERGOIN

DECORATING PORCELAIN

The american technique

ANGO

Original title: *Peinture sur porcelaine: Technique américaine*
Copyright © ANGO éditions inc. 1998
4519, rue Saint Denis
Montréal QC H2J 2L4 - Canada

General Editor: Gérard & Josiane Boulanger
Photos: Jacques Vigouroux
Layout: ANGO éditions
Filmsetting: ANGO éditions
English adaptation: John Tittensor

Printed by Colorcraft, China

ISBN 1 894 185 01 3

Contents

Author's preface   **5**

1   **Basic material**   **7**

2   **Mixing paints,choosing brushes**   **11**

3   **Starting work**   **17**
Loading your brush   *17*
Basic brushstrokes   *17*

4   **Creating a design**   **23**
Leaves   *23*
Branches   *26*
Backgrounds   *27*

5   **The "traditional" American technique: Flowers**   **29**
Wild roses   *30*
Violets   *36*
Convulvulus   *37*

Showcase: Flowers   **38**

6   **The "impressionist" American technique: Flowers and fruit**   **43**
Daisies   *46*
Hortensias   *50*
Geraniums   *55*
Pansies   *56*
Tulips   *61*
Roses   *63*
Grapes   *68*
Vine leaves   *69*

7   **Having fun: A Mountain Landscape**   **73**

8   **Firing and Retouching**   **77**

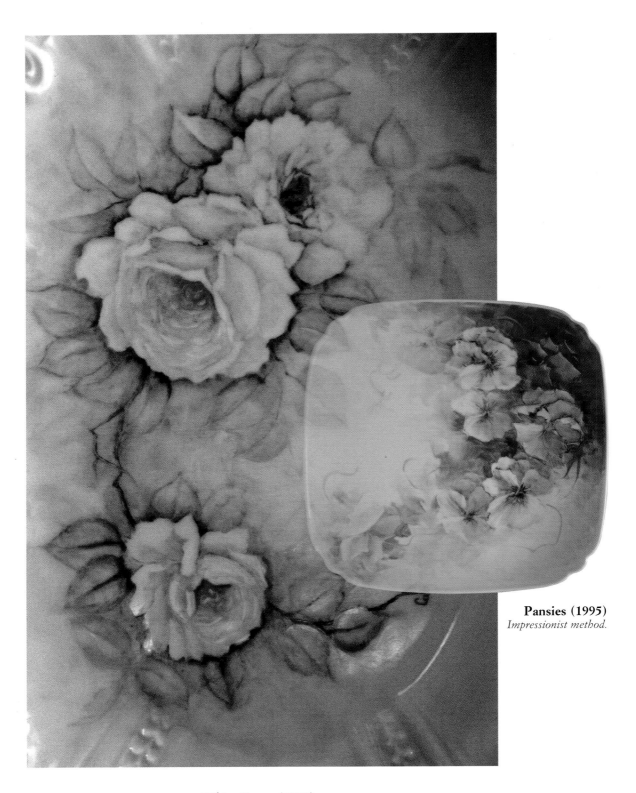

Pansies (1995)
Impressionist method.

White Roses (1990)
Traditional method.

Author's preface

Traditional or Impressionist?

T he "American technique" of porcelain decoration - also known as Soft Painting and the Diffusion Technique - is American in name only. When I was studying this method in Germany in 1989, my teacher told me that it was in fact of Russian origin: refugees fleeing the Revolution of 1917 had brought it to the USA, where it was combined with a South American technique.

If you like digging around in antique and junk shops you may come across 19th century porcelain pieces painted in this way. Whatever its origins, one thing is certain: this is the most difficult of the porcelain painting techniques and if you have already mastered other methods, you'll quite simply have to change your style. Fortunately it is also by far the most rewarding of all the techniques in terms of freedom of expression and pure pleasure. It really allows the artist to put his soul into his work; the infinite number of color mixes obtainable means that your designs will always be totally personal.

I'll explain the technique in detail later on, but you need to know from the outset that it is based on a special medium which *never* dries until fired; so in contrast with other methods, it allows for all the retouching you like - until you come up with your masterpiece! But take care: this advantage can also be a drawback for perfectionists, who are never entirely satisfied with what they have done.

Another interesting aspect of the American Technique is that you work by contrast: from light to shadow, or the reverse. For example, without actually outlining a flower-petal, you can make it stand out by lighting it differently than the background.

That way you get an integrated design and not just a flower or piece of fruit painted on the porcelain.

There are two different approaches to this technique:

• The "traditional" or Soft Painting method. This gives agreeably understated designs and I believe it to be the original technique. The design is created by accumulating layers of diluted paint, with a firing between each. This method calls for time and real precision, but it allows you to create pastel-shade designs with an "olde worlde" look to them.

• The "impressionist" method. Here the design is produced in only one or two stages. As a way of working it somewhat resembles oil painting and gives a much greater, more modern level of contrast than the "traditional" approach. It allows you to work fast, but requires a certain level of skill if you are to avoid kid-type daubs.

I recently met up with an ex-student from one of my American Technique classes. She had been workingly regularly and had all her pieces fired - and the improvement was staggering! So don't give up if you don't get the results you want first time round; perserverance will get you there in the end.

Jug: Christmas Roses and Holly (1995)
Impressionist method.

1. *Basic material*

For your work you'll need certain everyday materials and others specific to this technique. The first list covers the necessities, then come the optional items (which can make the business of painting much easier and more agreeable).

Essential Items

Powder paints

Use your normal porcelain paints.
For further information see the color chart on p. 9. You can also consult *Porcelain Painting: The Latest Techniques* by Catherine Bergoin (Ango).

Open medium

This product has a double function, as it is used for preparing the paint and also for keeping the bristles of your brushes in good condition. It has the characteristic of not drying out until it is fired: a thin coat painted on porcelain will still be moist six months later. Some people opt for more everyday products such as "3 in 1" oil or even sewing-machine oil, but it should be remembered that these lubricants are not made to be used in this way: they all contain detergents which can reduce the lifespan of your brushes and give off dangerous gases during firing. You may also come across slow-drying water-based mediums

allegedly recommended for this technique but in fact completely unsuitable: whatever their drying speed, the water evaporates - either out of the paint or off the brush. After evaporation the oily components of the medium stay on the brush and make cleaning that much more difficult.

Orange oil

This is a natural essence that is easily identified by its marked orange color - not to mention its unmistakable odor!
It is a highly effective cleaning agent and the oil it contains leaves a light coating on the bristles that will protect your brushes from the ravages of insects.
Here again, an important word of warning: you must beware of synthesized products such as citronella or light yellow citrus oils with a grapefruit smell; not only do they not protect your brushes, some of them actually eat into the bristles!

Square-tipped squirrel-hair brushes

Raphael 16240. Brush no. 20 is the the one you will use the most, but nos. 12, 8 and 6 can also come in handy. Using a size 20 brush for porcelain work may seem highly unusual, but let me assure you that if you use it as indicated, even highly detailed work presents no problems.

Painting materials.

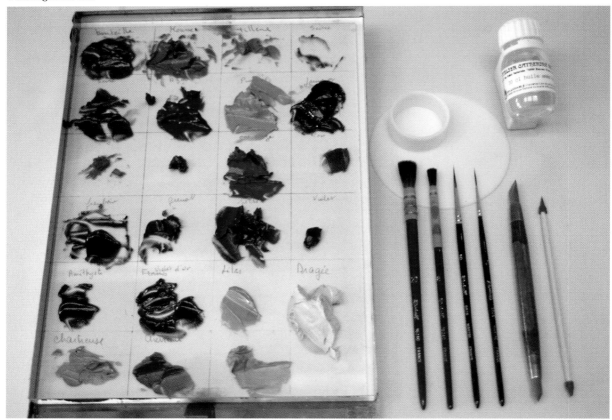

Sable brushes
Raphael 8826, nos. 2 and 6, for such details as branches.

Clean, non-fluffy cloth
A non-woven cloth can also be used. You'll need several different thicknesses. Your cloths are used for removing excess oil from the brush.

Mixing palette
- or a white bathroom tile around 20 x 20 cm (8 x 8 ins) square. I don't use glass for mixing on, for two reasons: it's transparent and so you can't see your colors clearly; and because glass is softer than a glazed tile, the surface gradually becomes worn.

Wipe-out tool
This is used for removing paint, pushing it around, cutting back a design and drawing in such details as a small branch crossing in front

PORCELAIN TABLEWARE COLORS — Minimum firing temperature 850° C

aubergine	Venice Purple	raspberry	candy	pink 17	tea rose	pale candy	skin tone	salmon	peach
magenta	antique pink	lilac	heather	burgundy	amethyst	gold violet	campanula	lavender blue	Sèvres blue
China blue	midnight blue	Delft blue	mineral blue	cornflower	royal blue	azure	thistle	pigeon blue	soft blue
sky blue	seaweed	peacock blue	jay blue	Hermes blue	denim	kingfisher	turquoise blue	sea green	pistachio
emerald	deep green	Russian blue	black green	empire green	forest green	olive-tree green	algae green	bronze green	chrome green
moss green	lime	almond green	chartreuse	ivory	eggshell	yellow	golden yellow	egg-yolk	old gold
mustard	curry	yellow ocher	café au-lait	rosewood	roebuck	Siena	chestnut	iron red	red ocher
rust	pomegranate	chocolate brown	wild mushroom	black	graphite	charcoal gray	mist gray	blue-gray	steel gray
silver-gray	gray for flowers	celadon gray			under-gold yellow	gold base	outline brown	outline black	

DECOR COLORS — FIRE AT 800° C
deep purple
gentian
saxon green
honey orange
saffron
deep black

CADMIUM TABLEWARE COLORS — FIRE AT 850° C
ruby
carmine
vermilion
orange
apricot
lemon
white
kiwi
field green
peridot
caramel
cinnamon

CATHERINE BERGOIN STUDIO

The color chart.

---

of a leaf. It comes in two sizes: the larger one, made of flexible rubber, is the most commonly used. Some people use a plastic stylus, which is more rigid, doesn't really follow the contours of the piece, gives a less precise line - and splits very quickly.

Fine "wet & dry" sandpaper
This sandpaper can be used with water and is used to smooth down a painted design after firing. After each firing, let the piece cool then hold it under the tap - without overdoing the water-pressure - and rub gently. If you don't take this precaution you run the risk of localized paint build-up that will give an uneven, patchy look to your designs.

Optional items

Oil-dish
This purpose-made container doesn't slide about on the work-table and allows you to dip your brush as necessary. This means you don't take medium directly from the bottle and thus avoid the risk of discoloring your entire supply.

Palette
For storing your paints you'll need a shallow metal or plastic box with a lid to keep dust at bay. Correctly used, this kind of inexpensive, homemade palette will enable you to keep your paint just about as long as you like. As in the photo on p. 8, line the bottom of the box with a squared sheet of white paper marked with the names of the colors, then cover with the piece of glass or Plexiglass that will be your actual storage surface. A word of warning: the box should be dustproof *but not airtight* - without air the mixed paint "slumps" and spreads.

Dust Remover
This is a kind of pencil with a soft "lead" made of wax; it is extremely useful for removing those annoying specks of dust that just love to float down on to your fresh paint.

Breton Fantasy (1997)
Impressionist method.

COLORS

Colors are divided into three main groups
the primary colors:
CYAN - MAGENTA - YELLOW
the secondary colors, which are mixtures of the three primary colors:
ORANGE
(MAGENTA + YELLOW)
GREEN
(CYAN + YELLOW)
VIOLET
(CYAN + MAGENTA)
the complementary colors, which are opposite one another on the color wheel:
RED and GREEN
ORANGE and BLUE
For a warm atmosphere, use these colors together.

There also exist two color subgroups which, properly used, can add to the atmosphere of your designs:
the "warm" colors:
BROWN, RED, ORANGE
the "cool" colors:
YELLOW, BLUE, GREEN, VIOLET
The character of these colors can vary according to the color or colors placed next to them.

2. *Mixing paint, choosing brushes*

For the classical china painting method, it is usual to mix the paint using the following ingredients:
Powdered paint + mixing oil
For the modern or "stippling" approach, we use:
Powdered paint + medium
When it comes to actually applying the paint, we dilute - either with turpentine or spike oil. The problem with these approaches is that once the paint is put on both mixes dry fast; this pretty much means you're stuck with your first attempt, as retouching is an extremely tricky business.

Now for the good news. If you opt for the American technique, you combine your powdered paint with open medium - and this mix never dries except when fired. This means limitless possibilities for reworking what's already been done. *Never* use solvents - turpentine, spike oil, etc - for this method: the open medium is all you need to mix your paint and grease your brushes. For cleaning the piece of china and your palette knife, use only alcohol-based cleansers such as methylated spirit; once again, *no solvents!* For cleaning your brushes, use orange oil or open medium.

Choosing your paints
It's not out of patriotism that I stick exclusively to the French brand Degussa; for me that's where the best quality is - not to mention the least color-variation between batches. Naturally it's up to you to find the brand that is best suited to your way of working, but try to avoid "doing things on the cheap". One important factor here is that the paint should always fire well at the temperature indicated: there's nothing more annoying than not knowing what's going to come out of the kiln.

Color charts
In all my workshops, the first piece of advice I give my students is to prepare a personal color-chart: a range of frequently-used colors fired on a ceramic tile or a plate. In my opinion, this is absolutely vital: in powder form the paint is not at all the same color as after firing, and what's more colors fired on porcelain don't necessarily come out the same on earthenware.

As the American technique calls for a lot of color-mixing to get a good range of shades, it's really important to make yourself up the type of palette shown on pages 8 and 13. Otherwise you'll have to mix up each color as you go along, which can be frustrating timewise. There's also the added advantage that the palette protects your paints against dust.

11

In case you're interested, for the classical techniques I have another little trick of the trade: I mix up my paints in advance and store them in glass pillboxes. This means I can use them whenever I like, without loss of time, and I know exactly what colors I have. I can easily harmonize my different shades by putting the pillboxes side by side until I get the tint I want. Since the paint is premixed, taking a tiny quantity for a detail presents no problem.

When the work session is finished, I can put the leftover paint back into its pillbox - as long as it hasn't been mixed with another color. On the other hand, I store my leftover "mixes" (more than one color) together in "trash cans" according to their dominant color: yellow, blue, green, etc. This means I almost never throw paint away - and sometimes my trash cans come up with really fantastic new colors!

Preparing the paint
To get the right consistency, take your tile and palette knife and mix the powder with open medium until you get a "toothpaste" mix with a slightly satiny look to it. Your pile of paint should be thick enough not to spread over the palette - and it should most certainly not be runny! If it flows off the knife,

the mix is too oily and you will have to add powder. When mixing with the palette knife, really grind the powder hard to get a smooth consistency. Then place your colors one by one on your homemade palette, without forgetting to note the name of each on the piece of paper under the glass.

Exercises
The aim here is to learn how to use the brush. For these initial exercises, you should prepare three colors: it's best to use fairly strong colors here - cornflower, deep green or yellow ocher, for example; the paint is applied very thinly and the overall effect is one of pastel shades, so paler colors are best avoided for the moment. It's also a good idea not to jump straight into the purples and pinks at this stage: they are much more expensive and you're

probably going to erase these exercises. Also avoid iron and cadmium colors, which are used or fired differently than the other types.

Heaps of paint
In the course of your work, you'll be shifting and spreading heaps of paint on the palette; so from time to time, use your spatula to push them back into their original shape.

A. *The slightly granular look means the mixture is not oily enough.*
B. *A good mix has a smooth, satiny look.*
C. *A shiny mix means there is too much open medium.*

The work-table

To avoid those pesky problems with dust, I don't work directly from my storage palette. Instead, I take out the various colors I intend using and place them on a ceramic tile.

It's important to do this the right way: pick up some paint with the palette knife and place it towards the top of the tile, then pull the knife towards you so as to get a progressively thinner layer of paint. Do this for your three colors - and don't forget to put the lid right back on your palette!

Once your three piles of paint are ready on the tile, arrange your work-table with the tile to the right and the clean cloth partially underneath it, as in the photo below. If you're lefthanded, reverse the arrangement.

The brushes

I know, I know, the main brush looks absolutely gigantic - especially if you've gotten used to doing detailed work in other methods with brushes whose heads have maybe three solitary bristles to their name. The head of the Raphael 16240 size 20 is 2 cm (.8 ins) long and all of 1 cm wide - you could practically hang wallpaper with it! But don't worry, everything will work out fine as long as you take great care never to use your American technique brushes for other methods; this inevitably causes problems related to solvents and mediums.

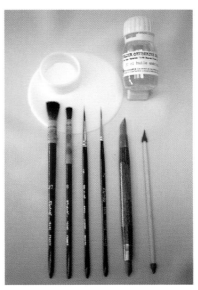

Upper part of the photo, left to right:
- oil-dish, for dipping the brushes
- bottle of open medium.

Lower part of the photo, left to right:
- 2 Raphael squirrel-hair brushes, series 16240, nos. 20 and 8
- 2 Raphael sable brushes, series 8826, nos. 6 and 2
- 2 rubber wipe-out tools.

The equipment laid out on the work-table; everything should be within easy reach.

Drying out the brush
Press with your finger to get rid of the excess oil.

Just right: a fan-shaped head.

My teacher used to say that a new brush is a wild animal that has to be tamed to make it behave the way you want it to. The taming process is as follows: pour some open medium into your oil-dish (or some other container) and dip your brush long enough for it to have a good "drink". Repeat the operation several times, to make sure the medium gets right into the head of the brush, then drain off by rubbing the brush gently on the edge of the oil-dish. Next, hold the brush like a pencil and press the head down against the cloth; this will get rid of the excess medium and give the head a fan-shape.

But how to know if the quantity of medium on the brush is just right? Simple: the bristles should be uniformly shiny from top to bottom and should stay stuck together. If they separate during painting, there's too little medium on your brush; too much medium, on the other hand, makes painting easier - but also causes runs during firing and then you can kiss your design goodbye. You need just the right amount of medium all through the painting process, otherwise your design will come out uneven; so as soon as you see the bristles begin to separate, repeat the soaking operation as before.

During the "taming" process, don't be surprised if your brush loses a few bristles - better it should happen now than half-way through a painting!
After all this, the tip should be fine and flat; if not, it's time to start taming again.

Improvisation in Blue
Impressionist method.

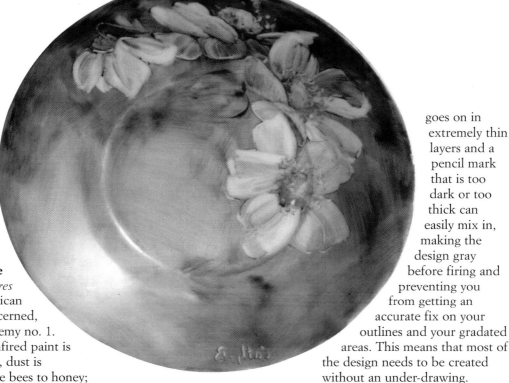

goes on in extremely thin layers and a pencil mark that is too dark or too thick can easily mix in, making the design gray before firing and preventing you from getting an accurate fix on your outlines and your gradated areas. This means that most of the design needs to be created without an under-drawing.

Important advice
Protective measures
Where the American technique is concerned, dust is public enemy no. 1. And since the unfired paint is permanently wet, dust is attracted to it like bees to honey; this means the piece being worked on has to be protected at all times - including during the coffee break!

When a design is finished - and if the piece happens to be a plate whose rim is not painted - you can cover it with clingwrap, which gives total protection. Bulkier or more complex pieces should go into a dust-proof box: a clear plastic cake-container does the job perfectly, but you can also put the piece in your kiln, where you can be pretty sure there's no dust!

Another enemy to watch out for is the friend who drops in to see how the work is coming along, says "No kidding, it really *never* dries?" - and checks with his fingertip, sending hours of painstaking work down the drain and leaving his fingerprints as a souvenir.

So be on your guard: since prevention is always better than cure, store your unfired work out of reach of the curious. That way you stay on good terms with your friends, too.

Warning!
Turpentine, mixing oil, universal medium and spike oil should never be used for the American technique, whether for cleaning china pieces or brushes, or for making up the paint: their presence makes the mix dry out fast and once dry, your design is there for good and all. Make only sparing use of the greasy Stabilo pencils nos. 8008 and 8046 in laying out your designs: the paint

Brushes
It's very rare that I pause to clean a brush while I'm actually working, except when changing from a dark color to a light one. When you do clean, use orange oil, which is good and greasy. It's a much better cleaning agent than turpentine, it smells good and it leaves a protective coating on the bristles that protects them from a whole range of absolutely voracious insects. Before you put your brushes away, grease them (with open medium), dry them out as explained on p. 14 and press them down into a fan-shape on your cloth.

A Savoy Mountain Scene
Enamelled metal sheet, 25 x 35 cm (10 x 14 ins)
For the technique, see Chapter 7.

3. *Starting work*

Loading the brush

For these exercises, use a white ceramic tile placed on the worktable. Working flat makes learning to handle the brush easier.

Pour some open medium into your oil-dish, soak your brush, then flatten the head into a fan-shape as shown on p. 14. Load *one side only* of the brush with paint: to do this, don't plunge the brush into the paint, but rather run it along the edge of the pile. First time round you'll have to do this maybe a dozen times to get the brush well loaded: aim to pick up just a very small amount of paint each time.

Brushstrokes

Throughout this book I'll be referring to specific brushstrokes in the context of specific tasks and effects, so I advise you to read the following sections carefully before moving on.

Loading the brush.

The side-load straight stroke
Load your brush on one side, hold it flat to the tile and bring it towards you along a broad straight line. The finished stroke is a rectangle with a color gradation.

Straight stroke, brush side-loaded to the left, then to the right. Work from top to bottom.

The full-load straight stroke
To get a straight stroke of a uniform color, I load my brush by running it along both sides of the pile of paint. If I actually dip into the paint, the result will be a straight stroke with a lot of paint in the middle, giving an area that cannot be reworked. The full-load straight stroke is useful for putting in backgrounds.

Striaght stroke, full load.

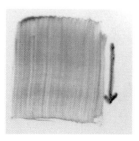

17

The two-color straight stroke
Working as before, load the left side of your brush with one color, then the right side with a different color. If you're careful, you'll obtain a rectangle with a different top-to-bottom color gradation on each side. This stroke is particularly useful for flowers and fruit.

Two-color straight stroke .

The angle stroke
Load your brush as for a straight stroke - side-loaded, fully-loaded or two-color - and draw it obliquely across the tile. You can tilt the stroke to the right or the left, so practice in both directions.

Double angle stroke.

The double angle stroke
Begin as for an angle stroke then, without lifting your brush, send it off in the other direction. Before starting, make sure the brush is sufficiently loaded to allow you to finish both parts of the stroke.

The C
The exercise is basically the same, but this time you're going to produce a curve. Load, then draw the curve without turning the brush: that way the beginning and the end of the stroke will be parallel.

The C, side-loaded to the left.

Angle stroke, side-loaded to the left.

Lines
To make lines, your brush should be flat and straight like the blade of a knife.
Hold it vertically so that the end is barely touching the tile, then

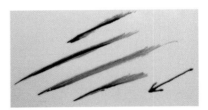

Unbroken lines.

move it from right to left to get a straight line.

To get a more irregular line, try holding your brush vertically and touching it two or three times on the surface of the tile, as in the photo below.

Uneven lines, made by joining dashes.

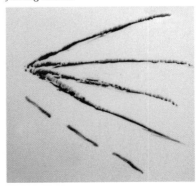

18

The whale tail
Make an S-shaped angle stroke then, without lifting your brush, the same stroke in the opposite direction - and you've got yourself a whale's tail! If you repeat the tail in staggered rows, you get the outer shape of a flower catching the light against a dark background. For an example see the chapter on the rose, p. 65.

The whale tail.

The curved comma
This brushstroke is made up of three movements in the following order:
- I place the tip of the brush straight down on the tile;
- I draw a slightly curved downwards angle stroke, keeping my brush in line with its point of departure;
- I finish with a sideways movement tailing off into a line.

The straight comma
This is exactly the same stroke as the preceding one, except that the angle is straight instead of curved.

The S
Draw an S with the flat of the brush, working from top to bottom without turning the brush.

The grape
This consists of two C strokes, one turned towards the other as in the photo below. Brought together they form a circle; I add a touch of paint to the centre to fill in and unify the color.

Handy Hint

Don't hesitate to really work hard at these exercises; that way you'll get a good grip of how your brush behaves and when it needs reloading. If you run out of space on your tile, clean it with spirit and start again.

19

1. Leaf strokes, at the base
*Left: the brushstrokes in order
Right: combining the strokes.*

2. Leaf strokes, at the tip.

3. A finished leaf
Combine the strokes shown in the first two photos.

2

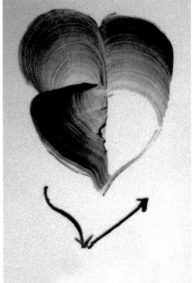

Leaves

To create leaves, we're going to combine the strokes illustrated above.

The leaf, near the base
- load your brush on one side and make a C;
- draw an unbroken line that touches the base of the C;
- under this line, make another C. You have just created the lower end of a leaf. Note that that brush should be sufficiently loaded to allow for the three brushstrokes, and that the darkest area should be towards the base of the leaf. So remember to load your brush on one side only.

The leaf, near the tip
- load your brush on one side;
- lay the brush flat and pull it towards you, gradually raising it vertically ;
- without lifting the brush, turn it

on the left-hand corner so as to get a point;
- still without lifting the brush, leave it on the left corner and make an upwards angle stroke, as in photo no. 2.

The finished leaf
If we combine the two preceding exercises, we can make a complete leaf.
- draw the lower end of the leaf

(two C strokes with a dash in between);
- *turn your tile through 90°* so as to have the base of the leaf uppermost;

3

1

- place your brush near the points of the left-hand C and make the stroke for the tip, as before. Remember to align the straight side of the stroke along the main vein. The other angle stroke should rise to meet the outer edge of the right-hand C.

So now you've roughed out your first leaf using the American technique. We're going to move on to another way of creating leaves, but since you already know the basic principles, I won't keep reminding you to load your brush.

Winter Landscape (1996)
Impressionist method.

A different leaf
Near the base
- begin with a right-to-left angle stroke;
- then a line at the base of this stroke;
- then a left-to-right angle stroke, but with your brush turning slightly to get a rising outer edge.

Near the point
- make a "straight comma" (see p. 19) then, without lifting your brush, run a line from the tip to the outer edge of the right-hand angle stroke.

A pointed leaf, near the base.
Left: the brushstrokes.
Right: combining the strokes.

A pointed leaf, showing both ends.

Wild Roses (1997)
Traditional method.

4. Creating a design

The leaves

The leaves in American technique mostly have the same shape and don't pay much heed to realism. On the other hand, the flowers are given much closer attention. You'll find that the leaves of fruit trees are generally shown as concave, while those of flowers are convex. One exception worth noting is the rose leaf, which can be either concave or convex. This is the theory; in practise, the shape of my leaves can vary according to the inspiration of the moment and the type of design I'm looking to create.

The convex leaf is constructed in exactly the same way as the "different leaf" on p. 21. The concave leaf is created using the same brushstrokes as the finished leaf on p. 20.

To get longer fruit tree leaves, I use the same brushstrokes as for the "different leaf". To the top and bottom of the main vein I add two or three angles strokes of diminishing size, according to the overall length I want for the leaf. When I reach this length, I add in the point of the "different leaf", remembering to turn the tile through 90°.

Rose leaves

These are always shown in groups of three or five. According to the kind of rose, they are the same size or progressively diminishing. They should be laid out as follows: one leaf at the end of the branch and two or four side leaves on each side of the stem. If they are different sizes, the largest should always be at the end

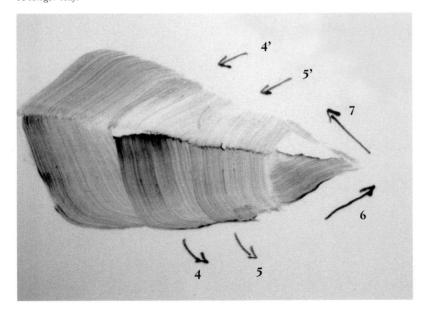

A longer leaf.

Serrated leaf.

of the branch, with the side leaves being smaller.

To portray a leaf turned back or folded over on itself (photo below), I make two open C strokes side by side but of decreasing size, then I turn the tile through 90° and add in a curved comma. To finish off, I take my series 8826 brush and draw the main vein along the bottom; I choose the size 2 or size 6 brush depending on the size of the leaf.

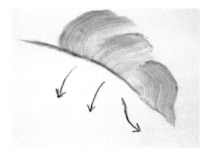

To show leaves with serrated edges - for poppies, thistles or daisies, for example (photo above right) - I proceed in two different ways according to the shape I'm aiming for:
• I begin with the main vein, using an unbroken line (1). Next, I add in lines of dots and dashes on either side of the vein (2), bringing the brush more and more vertical as I reach the end of each series. When the shape of the leaf is established, I

emphasize the serrations by drawing out extra points (3).

• If I want a less symmetrical leaf, I begin with an unbroken line for the vein (photo below), then I add a C on each side, followed by other C's as

Left: folded leaf.

Unsymmetrical serrated leaf.

necessary. I finish by drawing out the points and feathering to get even coverage.

Leaves to fill in a background
When I put in background leaves (see the photo below), their shape is more suggested than described. So I use straight commas for the middle leaf of a group and toned-down curved commas for the others. I bring them all together with the 8826 brush, using a line that represents a branch or a stem. Work on unsymmetrical leaves here - and don't go for the same shape every time!

Background leaves.

Blurred dark veins.

Leaf veins

These can be executed in three different ways:

• *Using darker colors*
I work here with the series 8862 brush, size 2 or 6, dipping it first of all in open medium, then drying it out a little by just touching it on the cloth. Next, I load it with plenty of paint. I hold the piece of china tilted back in front of me, with the stem end of the leaf uppermost, and pull the brush towards me. This way I draw the main vein, but without finishing it - I usually stop about two-thirds of the way along the leaf. The finishing touch is two or three secondary veins, preferably towards the stem end.

• *Using an unbroken line*
Here I use the 16240.20 brush, first pressing down hard to get a pronounced knife-shape. Holding it vertically as I load, I aim to concentrate the paint in the tip; then I place the brush on the design just where I want the vein, but without moving it. If I want a longer vein, I do the same thing a little further along, to get two dashes end to end. If necessary, I can complete the vein by using only a part of the tip, holding the brush on an angle.

The overall arrangement of the veins remains the same: a good, clear main vein down towards the stem, with two or three secondary veins.

Darker, more distinct veins.

25

Using the wipe-out tool to lighten the veins (also see the candy box, p. 38).

• *Using the wipe-out tool*
In this way I "cut back" to the white of the porcelain surface (photo above), using the conical end of the tool - not the slanted end.

Branches
Usually, when I place the brush on the painting surface then move it along so as to draw a line, the beginning of that line is "fatter" than the end. This is the technique we're now going to use to get realistic branches and tree-trunks.
For a tree-trunk, I always begin down near the roots, gradually moving upwards to the top of the tree and/or outwards towards the ends of the branches. As it is easier to pull the brush towards yourself than to push it in the other direction, I turn the piece around so as to work "upside down". The size of the brush will depend on the the size of the branch: I usually opt for the series 8826 brush, size 2 or 6.

If the branch is wide, I hold my brush perpendicular to it, pressing down until I get the width I'm after.

If the branch is relatively small, I draw my brush along parallel to its main axis.

Not all branches are straight or "in one piece". To change the direction of a branch, I stop the movement of the brush - but without lifting it off the surface - and move it backwards and forwards on the spot, holding it perpendicular. Then - still

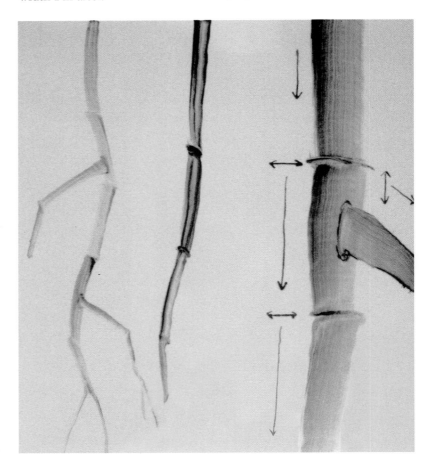

Branches

without lifting the brush - I continue its movement in the desired direction. When my branch is painted in and I want to add another one running off it, I put the brush on the branch at the desired spot, move it back and forth, then send it off in the direction of the new branch.

To add thorns to a stem or branch, I use the same method, but finishing with a pointed brushstroke. As it is always best to paint a branch with a single stroke of the brush, make sure

Thorns.

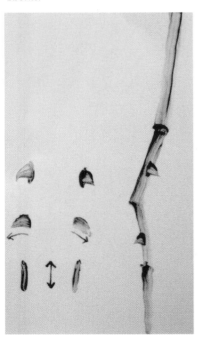

you load enough paint into your brush before starting.

Backgrounds

For putting in a background I load my brush carefully and uniformly by running it along both sides of the pile of paint (see p. 17). It is important to realize that you must never load the brush on both surfaces of the head - you always work using only one surface. I'm going to put my paint down in irregular, staggered strokes, making sure to choose a color that fits with the design I have in mind.

Once the colors are laid in, I set about feathering them to get uniform coverage and remove the brushmarks. Feathering is one of those basic techniques that is simple enough when you know how - but you'll need to practice

in order to get systematically good results.

So I take my brush, holding it some three centimeters (1.5 ins) from the end of the handle: the aim is to spread the paint with a regular but almost pressure-free backwards and forwards movement resembling that of a pendulum. *This movement must come from your fingers* - not from the arm, wrist or hand. When

Feathering: how to hold the brush.

Laying in the background.

you begin, remember to hold your brush perpendicular to the painting surface.

With practise, you'll find that you can also feather holding the brush at an angle. Whichever way you work, the tip of the brush should barely touch the paint: if there's too much pressure the white of the porcelain will reappear and you'll have to repaint. The movement of the brush should be sweeping and fluid, and the tip should make contact with the paint in the middle of each to-and-fro. Begin by feathering the entire area in the same direction, then turn the piece through 90° and work crossways.

• Once you've got a feathered background, practice the following exercises again:
- the brushstrokes (Ch. 3)
- leaves
- branches.
Take care here: a painted surface requires a different touch from an unpainted one.

Feathering: how to hold the brush

To get into the habit of holding your brush by the end of the handle, place a rubber band about 3 cm (1.5 ins) from the end, as a reminder.

Before and after feathering.

28

5. The traditional
american technique

Make no mistake, this method is the toughest, the most time-consuming and the one that demands the most attention to detail. Whether your design involves flowers, fruit, a face or whatever, you need:
- a sound grasp of your subject;
- an equally sound grasp of the rules of perspective;
- paint-mixing and color-matching know-how;
- a clear mental picture of the finished design, so as to be able to work freehand. Avoid using the china pencil unless absolutely necessary - and even then your lines should be almost invisible.

Before launching into my design, I have to find the right place for it in terms of the shape of the plate. To do this I simply apply the "golden section", which provides a specific size relationship and allows you to:
- fix the points of balance of a drawing;
- modify the size of a design without altering its proportions. All the main lines of the design should pass through or intersect at these points.

For a round plate the system is very simple:
- I draw a circle whose side is equal to the diameter of the plate (see the diagram p. 30);
- inside the square I draw a circle representing the plate;
- I divide the sides of the square into eight equal parts;
- I run two perpendiculars through the square as shown in

Worth Remembering

As some pieces require repeated firings, having your own kiln makes the work much simpler and minimises the risks inherent in handling and transporting. In addition, if you have to wait a week between firings you are going to "lose the thread" each time and probably end up losing interest as well. If you don't have a kiln, at least find a suitable container for transporting your pieces safely.

A balanced design

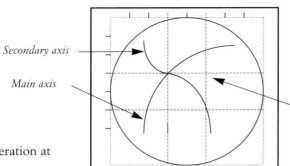

Secondary axis

Main axis

Focal point: all the main lines of the design should cross here.

the diagram;
- I repeat this last operation at right angles.

This is the theory as explained in most basic introductions to painting and personally I find that it works extremely well.

First stage
Unlike the impressionist method (see Chapter 6), "traditional" designs are created via successive, extremely light applications of paint. You have to fire between each application in order to create a good, solid "paint base" and to get your colors right. As you continue, you can add different colors so as to obtain all the subtle, soft-edged blends you want.
My approach is to always begin with a very detailed foreground and to put the background in last. The background calls for very delicate, accurate treatment - after all, it's there to set off your design to the best advantage.
For this method I use nothing but open medium, both for mixing up the paints and for oiling and cleaning my brushes. For this design - using a plate 15-18 cm (6-7 ins) in diameter, I'll use the series 16240 size 10 brush, with a size 6 from the same series for the fine work. For the stems

and other linear-style details, an 8826 size 6 will do just fine.

Wild roses
First off, I thoroughly clean my brush with methylated spirit. Then I have the choice between two ways of working:
• I much prefer to start by using the 8826 brush to draw in the

basic design, using a color that will figure in the composition. Beginning this way also allows me to give my design the right balance.
• The other method involves drawing the design with the china pencil. The line has to be as light as possible, since the graphite in the pencil mixes with the paint and can give a misleading idea of the final color. Personally, I don't like this method.

Wild roses: *flowers and leaves.*

For this exercise, I outline the flower in amethyst on one of the points of balance, using the 8826.6 brush.

Wild rose: the first painting.

My aim is to get a very pale flower, so once the outline is finished I oil and dry the brush, then begin to spread the paint used for the contours.

Even though I'm only using a tiny quantity of paint here, I immediately get a light/shade contrast. For the very light areas - turned-back petals, for example - I use the wipe-out tool. Note that the difference between the two photos above is that I've moved paint - no paint has been added.

The outline is brushed in.

The background is laid in.

The next step is to open up the center with the wipe-out tool, then paint it in, leaving a paler spot to indicate where the light is coming from and to provide contrast. Then I use the conical end of the wipe-out tool to put in the stamens.

So now our flower is ready and I'm going to move on to the first part of the background. I load my brush on one side - to the right for righthanders, to the left for lefthanders - with forest green and chocolate brown and set it moving in little circles (1 or 2 mm/.1 ins), bringing it steadily towards me. This movement allows me to re-draw the petals at the same time as I surround them with a color gradation that makes them stand out: the darkest part is up against the petals and the lightest part is the furthest away, on the outer edge of the shaded area.

Feathering the background.

Now it's time to feather the dark background color around the flowers (see p. 27). You don't need any extra paint for this: just clean your brush with open medium and go to work. Once the feathering is done, I rough in the background flowers or leaves.

I put in the background.

I move some paint on to the petals.

Now I clean the brush again with open medium, dry it and set about turning the first painting into fully-fledged flowers or leaves. With practise you'll fond that you can skip the roughing-in stage and work directly, using a very lightly loaded brush.

First painting of the second flower seen from underneath, using the 8826 brush.

As we're working with a turned-back flower, I emphasize the stem that appeared in the preceding photo. Working this way means you can find the right place for the flower before you begin to paint it: in the event of a mistake, it's always easier to retouch a brushstroke than to rework an entire flower.

Lastly, I add in the sepals and the stalk, using a mix of lime green and forest green.

The backdrop for this flower is painted in the same way as for the preceding one. I use the same colors - forest green and chocolate brown - but I add some lime green to lighten the design. *Note that here "add" does not mean adding on the brush!* Lime green is lighter than the other greens used: this is because this flower is set in the upper part of the design and therefore is catching the light. Once these colors are all in place, I feather to get rid of the brushstrokes and to tone down the differences between the various shades.

Color Mixes

Don't forget to make a note of the mixes used - colors and proportions - as you'll need them for the second stage.

Laying in the sepals and the stalk.

The other flowers are painted in the same way, paying attention to their arrangement. The wild rose's shape means you can arrange it just about any way you like.

Adding in flowers.

If I want the background leaves and stems to come out nice and sharp, I get to work on them before the first firing. On the other hand, if my aim is a more blurry look, I'll wait until the second firing - or maybe even the third.

Important: if I want very soft or pastel shades for the stalks, I should use the wipe-out tool to define their position before the first firing. The paint we use being highly transparent, a much more pronounced color is needed to make them stand out against the background and this kind of color can easily clash with the rest of the design. To introduce flowers that are still at the bud stage, I begin by drawing them in using the base color for this design - amethyst - then I finish off with forest green and lime green to get the overall color harmony right. Since buds are usually more brightly colored than the actual flowers, I use more amethyst for painting them.

A balanced design

Bearing in mind the advice given concerning harmony and balance in your compositions (p. 29-30), I add in the lines defining the positions of the flowers and leaves and maybe also of the trompe-l'oeil elements.
Take careful note of the lines of balance in relation to the preceding photo: you'll see at once that even though it's only a matter of a simple brushstroke, the design suddenly takes up more space on the plate and is better-proportioned. To cover up the balance lines, I add in flowers or leaves over the top.
The first phase of the work is now finished. I check to make sure I haven't let any unwanted spots of paint slip in, then I do the first firing.

Trompe-l'oeil

A style of painting intended to deceive the eye.

With the guidelines hidden by the details, we proceed to the first firing.

Second step: retouching

Before starting to retouch - and even though the plate has come out of the kiln apparently quite clean - I run it under the tap and rub it down with the fine wet & dry sandpaper (see p. 9) to get rid of any rough patches due to dust or the insulation inside the kiln. What happens is that with each rise in temperature the kiln insulation expands, tiny particles fall onto the articles being fired - and stick there. It's important to remove them so as to avoid paint build-ups on the design.

Once the cleaning is finished, I can move on to the retouching. First off, I wipe the piece down with methylated spirit - just to be sure there are no greasy spots. Now I take a good look at the design: it's really vital to do this and to weigh up which parts need adding to, which need to be given extra emphasis and which

need to be toned down.

What you have to remember here is that *here's no point retouching for retouching's sake*. The aim is to work towards the best possible design, enriching it as you go along with details and subtleties of shading.

As an example: on the design I've just fired, I'm going to add flowers in the background for extra depth. Inevitably the colors of these flowers are going to be less bright, since they are being painted over other colors and not directly on to the white of the porcelain. I work in the same way as for the first stage, using the series 16240 size 20 brush. The stalk low down on the design crosses in front of the flower, but as it does not really catch the light, I concentrate on lighting the flower.

Next I retouch the main flowers, beginning with those surrounding

the central flower and where the lines of balance intersect. For the flower seen from underneath - on the top part of the plate - I reinforce the color to emphasize the shadow created by the folded-back petals.

This shadow is darker because the curve of the petal is more pronounced: this is how you really add depth and solidity to a design. I also retouch the sepals and outline them lightly to accentuate their place as part of the whole.

Additions to the background.

Retouching the turned-back flower.

The two flowers under the main one have been retouched.

Retouching the main flower, adding in the stamens.

I've deliberately kept the traditional method to two firings here - enough to give a clear idea of the process as a whole. Once you get some practise, you'll be able to increase the number of firings at will and come up with real masterpieces. This way of working is more time-consuming than the impressionist method (see Chapter 6), but I think you'll agree that the results justify the work involved.

As for the two flowers "underneath" and to the left of the main one, I decide to deepen the shadow: the flower to the far left is partially masked by the two others.

Since the middle flower of the three is seen from the side, its near part needs no retouching; but its interior, beyond the center and the stamens, should be shaded. I also take care to emphasize the divisions between the petals.

As I've accentuated the contrast between the flowers, I do the same for the leaves, where I also add in such details as veins and stems.

I come to the main flower last of all. Given that the light hits it directly, the emphasis should be on the light itself. This means that certain details of the flower should not appear, so I carefully shade the curls of the petals and the spaces between them; but at the same time I take care to leave plenty of white or pastel pink on the turned-back areas.

Next I finish the stamens, using gold-violet for the highlights. I place the paint with the 8826.2 brush, then press the conical end of the wipe-out tool into the center of the paint: the center of the stamen will come out light and its edges a strong yellow, as the wipe-out tool pushes the paint outwards.

And now: the second firing.

For the finished piece, see p. 22.

A selection of violets.

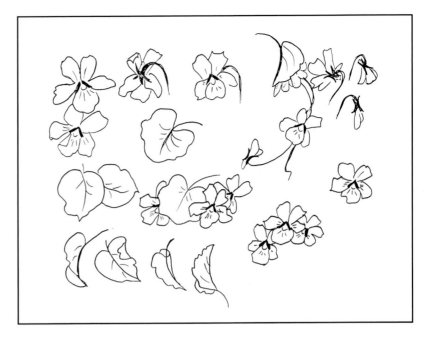

Violets

The method is the same as for the wild roses. I outline the flower using gold-violet and my 8826.2 brush, then use the same color for the petals, using the 16240.6 brush; I load it with plenty of paint, since this is a strongly-colored flower.

Violets have five petals: two on top, one on each side and a larger one at the bottom (see the drawings this page). The leaves are rounded and almost heart-shaped.

I begin by painting several flowers in shades of gold-violet, lilac or lavender, grouping them so as to get a bouquet at the spot where the lines of balance intersect. I then add a few leaves to the bouquet, using deep green and forest green, to which I add just a trace of gold-violet.

As the design takes shape, I add in the backdrop using the same colors. The backdrop is always darkest in close to the bouquet and gradually lightens as you move outwards. To get this lighter color I gradually add in more and more sky blue.

In the interests of overall balance, I sketch in a few more flowers and buds in the background.

Inside the flowers I place a speck of yellow ocher to mark the center and to bring the flower as a whole into focus.

Lastly, I complete the balance of the design with stems that work as links - just as I did with the wild roses. Then it's into the kiln for the first firing.

Bouquet of violets: background and first painting.

Balancing out the design (see the diagram p. 30).

Violets:
he finished plate.

After the first firing, don't forget to rinse your piece under the tap, rubbing it down gently with wet & dry sandpaper to get a good clean surface.

Next, I highlight both the backdrop in the center of the bouquet and the violets that I want to make into focal points. You'll note that the foreground flowers are highly colored, whereas those in the background are much more loosely treated and emerge in pastel tones. When all this is finished, it's time for the final firing.

White Roses (1990)
Traditional method.

Convulvulus Plate (1996)
Impressionist method.

The convulvulus
The way of working remains unchanged. First off, a painted line to define the overall shape of the flower, then for the petals I load my 16240.20 brush consecutively with sky blue,

turquoise blue, peacock blue, lavender and lime green. For the leaves and stems I use algae green, then I place a speck of golden yellow in the center.
I also wanted to show you here that it's possible to create designs

that have no background. This Gien earthenware dish has had a single firing at 750° C/1380° F.

Remember that the more often porcelain is fired, the tougher it becomes; but that for earthenware it's the opposite, so two firings should be the absolute maximum.

Showcase:
Flowers

All the pieces in this showcase were created using the impressionist method. For a detailed explanation of how to handle flowers, see Chapters 5 and 6.

Candy Box Lid (1997).

A realistic approach for the flowers, a freer treatment for the leaves.

Blue rose on Gien earthenware (1995).

Plate (1996).

Bowl (detail).

Lampstand and bowl (1996).

A riot of color.

Shapes and colors: a combination of spontaneity and realism.

Close-up.

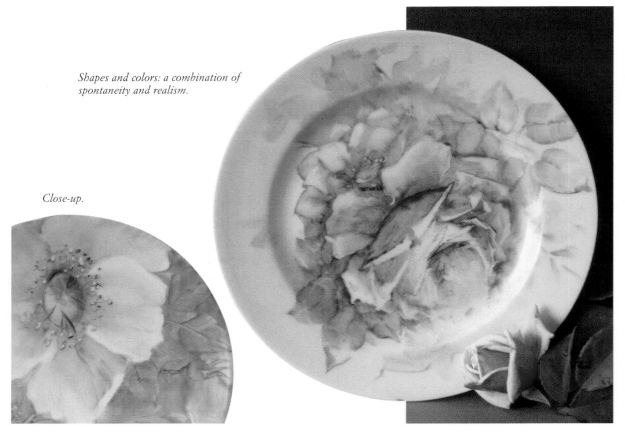

**Convulvulus Breakfast
Setting (1995)**
*Impressionist method
When the piece was finished, I
coated it with flux and did a fast
firing at 950° C (see p. 77).*

White Roses (1990)
Traditional method.

Daisies (1996)
Impressionist method.

6. *The impressionist*
American technique

There are two ways of painting flowers using the impressionist technique:
• I begin with a background, then bring out the flowers - daisies or pansies, for example - by moving or removing paint.
• I paint the flower and add in the background afterwards, as for roses or wild roses.

First technique

The background
Since you've read all about backgrounds on p. 27, you already know that the brush to use is the 16240.20. The background doesn't necessarily cover the entire piece, but it should be big enough for the design you have in mind - it's always easier to reduce a background than enlarge it. Balance it out against the piece as a whole; this means knowing what the design is going to be, so I sometimes make myself a rough sketch on paper first.
Since the choice of colors has a real influence on the feel of the design, note down the colors used for your sketch.
When you start working on backgrounds, don't mix too many colors: two or three will do for a start, then you can add more as you gradually master the technique.
I begin by laying in patches of the initial color (Delft blue) on different parts of the piece. There

Laying in the first color: Delft blue.

43

should be an uneven number of patches and their sizes should be different. Then comes the second color (azure), using the same approach. If you're a beginner, make the feathering easier for yourself by having the patches of color touch or overlap.

Then comes the third color: algae green.

When all your colors are in place, you can start feathering. The aim here is more or less to get rid of the brushmarks and blend the colors into each other.

Feathering.

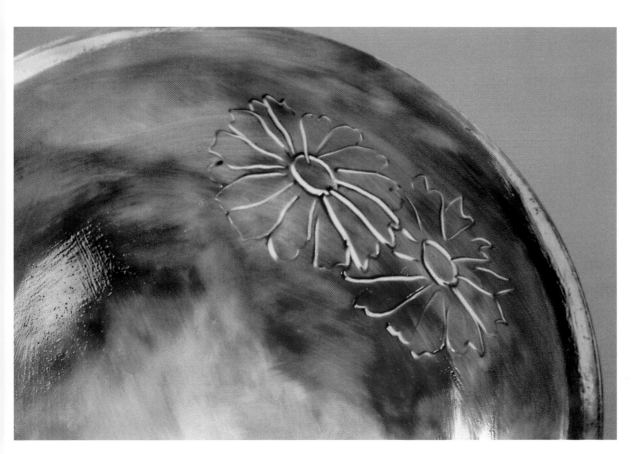

Once the background is ready, I draw in the flowers with the slanted end of the wipe-out tool. The drawings in this chapter will give you some ideas.

Flowers drawn with the wipe-out tool.

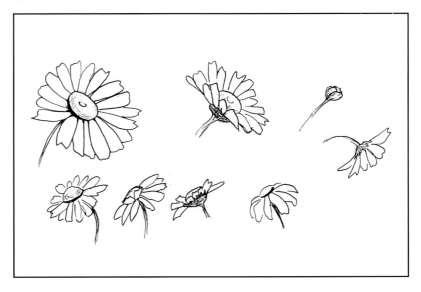

Daisies.

Flowers

Daisies

One of my rules is never to show flowers from above, but rather on an angle. This means that the flowers and their centers look oval. Be very careful in this regard: if your flowers are too symmetrical the whole design will finish up out of kilter.

I always work pulling the brush towards me; daisy petals are arranged like the spokes of a wheel, so as I work I gradually turn my piece through a full circle.

Another thing is that I always create a foreground and a background for my flower groups, as this approach gives the design more depth. For the foreground I work with the brush and orange oil, so as to take out more color. For the background I replace the orange oil with open medium, since the aim is just to lighten the colors slightly.

Remember too that the brushstrokes used for the petals should not be too regular: some should be rounded, some should taper off into a point and some should give a square end. They should also be of different lengths.

The petals.

Now let's get down to our daisies. Each petal is composed of two parallel brushstrokes going from the outside of the flower towards the center. The actual brushstroke is a little different here, so read carefully: after dipping the 16240.8 brush in orange oil, I dry it a little then lay it on the surface tilted at an angle and move it along slowly so as to really lift off the background color. After doing a third of the petal, I make the brush move faster: this way I lift off less color and give volume to my petal by creating the illusion of a lit area and a shaded one. To finish this first petal I go straight to the second brushstroke, parallel to the first and right up against it.

I then move on to the second petal, turning the piece slightly so that the brushstroke can be aimed directly at the center of the flower. In this way I gradually work my way around the entire daisy.

When all the petals are in place, I clear away the heart of the flower with the slanted end of the wipe-out tool. Here you really have to lift the paint off - if you just push it aside you'll get a paint build-up that could easily flake off during firing. Each time I lift paint off, I wipe the tool with a cloth.

Next I fill in the centre using two or three colors that blend into each other and make one side darker than the other.

I draw the center with the wipe-out tool, then paint it.

To show a daisy seen from the side, first of all I draw in the back petals using the 16240.8 brush and open medium. Then I move to the foreground and create the petals using the same brush and orange oil. I clear away the center of the flower with the wipe-out tool, then paint it in.

Closely observing the angle of the flower, put the base in last, along with the stem. To do this I use the 8826.2 or 8826.6 brush, depending on the size of the stem.

When all the daisies are finished, I sometimes add stalks to give the impression of a real bouquet. If you feel like adding serrated leaves, take a look at the instructions on p. 24.

To round the design off I need to finish the background. I have three choices here:

Adding in other daisies balances my design.

- a color gradation leading back to the white of the porcelain;
- using the wipe-out tool to make a clean break;
- using the wipe-out tool to suggest leaves. In this case I add veins using either the 8826 brush (size 2 or 6) or the wipe-out tool again.

Then I proceed to the firing. See Chapter 8 for details of temperatures and other advice on firing.

Geraniums

Hortensias (1995)
Impressionist method.

Hortensias

This flower is created in the same way as the daisy, so even if you're making an urgent present for a member of the family, at least take the time to read pages 46-48 before starting.

The hortensia is in fact a ball made up of many small flowers with four petals. Most times I do the petals the same way as for the daisy: I begin with the ends and work in towards the center of the flower, leaving more color near the center to suggest the curve of the petal.

Each petal is made up of two brushstrokes, with the tip of the brush tilted in the opposite direction for each. The inner ends of the petals are straighter than for the daisy, but should not be regular.

The flowers all overlap to a greater or lesser extent. This is why I draw in the foreground flowers with the brush and the orange oil, while for the background ones I use the open medium. This overlap means that you rarely see all the petals of any given flower, except of course the foreground ones.

I begin with the background - see the hints above - then draw in the outline of the flower with the slanted end of the wipe-out tool. In all I draw three or four flowers to make up the foreground. As with the daisy, don't forget to flatten each flower into a slightly oval shape to get the perspective right.

Using the wipe-out tool, I draw the main flowers on the background colors (pomegranate, antique pink, curry).

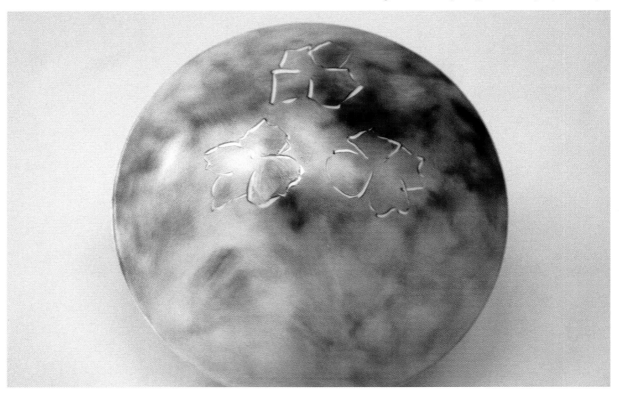

Next, using the 16240.20 brush, I remove paint from the outer area of the petals. I leave the inner area darker for the same reason as when I was painting the daisies: to bring out the curve of each petal. Here too the petals are arranged like the spokes of a wheel, so to get the flower right I have to turn the piece a little as each new petal comes up.

Note however that as the hortensia petals actually touch, you don't have to indicate a space between them.
When the foreground flowers are finished, I move to the mid-ground ones: these should be less well-defined and darker in color. Here I use the 16240.20 brush with open medium.
When the "ball" or head of the hortensia is finished, I mark in

the centers of the individual blooms: for each one I put in several dots using the pointed end of the wipe-out tool. These dots represent the stamens; you can leave them white if you want, or paint them using the 8826.2 brush.

The head of the hortensia and the stamens.

51

Once the first head of flowers is finished, I add in others in the background; but I make them much less sharp and gradually blur the details down: for the last flowers only the silhouette remains. When you've got the hang of feathering, try it on this type of background: that way you'll get a much more regular effect.

The finishing touches.

**Hortensias
seen from below**
To bring in a head of hortensia seen from underneath, I begin with the flowers that are in shadow, using the 16240.20 brush and my open medium to get very low definition.

Close-up: the stem meets the flower.

The head of the hortensia.

Over the top I add very sharply-defined flowers, with the same brush but this time using the orange oil. To finish I add the main stem and the little branches running off under the shadowed flowers. For this part I change to the 8826.6 brush to create thick, knotty stems. If you want leaves, they should be big and just slightly serrated.

It's not for nothing that this technique is called "impressionist": there's no obligation to put stems in - and even if you do they don't necessarily have to be attached to the flowers. It's preferable to bring out the flower via its shape, color and lighting than by a purely "photographic" approach. Last of all - since the flower-balls are quite sizeable - pay close attention to the overall balance of your design and to the direction the light is coming from. This calls for a consistent approach to your creation of flowers and individual petals.

The finishing touches are the same as for the daisies.

Hortensias (1994)
Impressionist method, on glass.

Painting on glass

The dish used for this design is made of glass; this calls for another type of powdered paint, but I still use open medium for mixing. I use the same kinds and sizes of brushes, but I have *a second set which is used exclusively for glass paints.*
Firing is done at 580° C (1075° F), holding it at that temperature for 20 minutes at the end.

Hortensias (1994)
Detail.

Geraniums (1996)
Impressionist method.

Geraniums

The technique here is the same as for the hortensias, with three exceptions:
- the flowers have five petals instead of four;
- the clusters are smaller and often contain buds among fully opened flowers;
- the leaves are much more rounded.

Pansies.

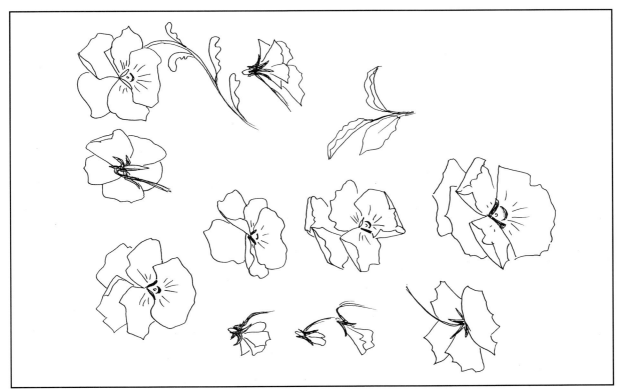

Pansies

The pansy is not only beautiful and easy to paint, it also never fails to hit the spot with the viewer!

You can create your pansies just like the other flowers in this chapter - at least in a general way. I always start with a background of several carefully feathered colors, then I draw in the outlines of the flowers with the wipe-out tool. As the petals are substantially larger than those of the other flowers, I hold my 16240.20 brush down flat and repeat the stroke two or three times to really get the color off.

Pansies: the petals outlined on the background.

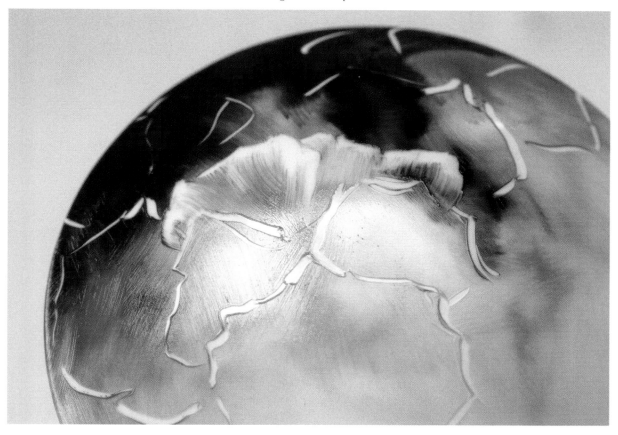

The pansy is composed of five overlapping petals. The two background ones are almost symmetrical and, as a rule, smaller than the others. The two mid-ground petals are symmetrically placed in relation to the center. The fifth petal is in the foreground and by far the largest. Pansies can be of any and every color, often with very marked contrasts - so don't have any misgivings about letting yourself go.

Once I've drawn in the overall outline, I use my 16240.20 brush to bring out the two back petals, starting in a corner of each and working my way across with successive strokes. One of these petals always overlaps the other; to show the difference, I lighten the edge of the one in front and darken the edge of the one behind. Take the trouble to clearly define the beginning and end of each petal: that way you get a real flower and not just a

pansy-shaped blob.
Here I choose between open medium and orange oil, according to how much color I want to take off. Your petals should not be too evenly colored: a gradual shading-off from light to dark will give them a good rounded surface.

57

For the two mid-ground petals I turn the piece as the work advances. The central third of the petals should be highly colored. The main petal is treated in the same way.

Now I take my wipe-out tool and draw an inverted V at the base of the main petal. Using a 8826 brush size 6 or 8, I tint the sides of the V with a color close to that of the petals; the inside of the V is filled in with a color gradation whose dark area is at the point. To finish off, I add unbroken lines to the three lower petals.

Adding a pansy.

The finished pansy.

Once the first flower is done, I can add others to the background using my brush and open medium. Pansy leaves are so small that I leave them out - which is what I also do for the stems.

Pansies: the finished candy-box lid.

Pansy Plate (1995)
Impressionist method.

Jewel Box (1992)
The flower is painted using the American technique, with matt gold for the box.

For the outside, I mainly use colors like golden yellow and lime green. For the middle of the leaves I use yellow ocher with iron red or aubergine, which gives warmth to the design. Using the 16240.20 brush dipped in open medium, I rework the colors to unify them. As usual, I work from light to dark. I have to go confidently here, since there's no turning back: if I do, the light colors are darkened by the dark ones and the flower loses its variations of shading.

Tulips
For this exercise I'm going to use a brightly colored hybrid tulip whose distinctive appearance means it can be painted on directly, without a background. In addition, its strong tones and serrated edges provide good practise in handling colors and tools.

Since the china pencil can make it hard to get the colors exactly right, I don't use it. Instead, I work as follows: I take a 8826 brush, load it with a light color mixed up with this flower in mind and quickly draw the outline of the tulip. Then I do the leaves in the same way. Note that if the leaves are going to touch the flowers, I paint them in first.

Then I move on to the light colors mixed for the inner part of the flower, putting them in with little staggered brushstrokes.

Tulips.

Tulip Plate (1995)
Impressionist method.

As to the petals, I start with the background ones and do the foreground ones last. To get real separation between each petal, I lighten their edges with a brush dipped in orange oil then squeeze-dried. Once the petals are finished, I clear away the centre area with the wipe-out tool and - if the position of the flower leaves them visible - draw in the pistils.

Referring back to my model, I then set about serrating the edges of the leaves with the wipe-out tool.

When I've finished the flower, I move on to the stem. This needs to be thick, so I use the 8826.6 brush again, loading it with various greens in sufficient quantity to be able to do the entire stem in a single brushstroke.

Now it's the turn of the leaves. I use the same brush, taking care - for once - to leave in the parallel lines of the brushmarks; as it happens the leaves of this kind of tulip are heavily lined.

So here's a flower you can paint fast and without any real

difficulty. The design has to be fired, of course, but before doing so I check that there are no unwanted spots of paint elsewhere on the piece. Following the same basic principles I can also use this method for painting irises and poppies.

Roses.

Roses

This subject is different than the others in that I paint the flower first and add in the background afterwards. The rose itself is in three parts for painting purposes: the center, the corolla and the petals. The wild rose is divided up in the same way.

To get an interesting perspective effect - rather than just a flower seen from above - use the circle system as shown in the box

below. The more concentric your circles are, the more your view of the flower will be vertical. For this rose I paint the center, the corolla and the petals in that order, then do the details in reverse: petals, corolla, center.

For the center of the rose, I load the left side of my 16240.20 brush with antique pink and lay in little staggered anticlockwise strokes that follow the center circle.

Flowers: getting the balance right

Work on the basis of three circles of 2, 4 and 6 cm (.8, 1.5 and 2.5 ins) in diameter: for the center, the surrounding area and the petals respectively.

The center.

The corolla.

For the corolla, I load the left side of my brush with the same color; using the same strokes as before and working in the same anticlockwise direction, I follow the circle.

For the outer petals, I repeat the process, but this time I work clockwise. This change of direction allows me to emphasize the difference between the corolla and the outer petals; this is important here, since the entire flower is painted with antique pink. With a little experience you'll soon be able to paint multi-shaded roses.

Laying in the outer petals.

The colors are lightly feathered.

Next I do some light feathering to get rid of the brushstrokes. I don't add any color here - I just redistribute the paint already in place.

Adding in "whale tails".

Using "whale tails" (see p. 19), I position my petals around the flower. The choice of colors is important here: if, for example, the curved commas are painted algae green, I can use the color to put in background leaves; if I use antique pink, as I have done for this rose, I can use it to paint other flowers.

Now I move on to the background, using staggered brushstrokes: green for foliage or pink for other flowers. The background should cover quite a large area: for the moment I don't know what the exact size of the overall design will be, but as it's easier to remove paint than to add it, I "spread myself". To finish, I quickly feather the background; I'll come back to it later on.

In order to get a geometrically harmonious design, I put in a white spot to mark the spot where the (hidden) stem would meet the flower. This spot is also where the petals converge, so I put it beside the center of the flower. To put in the petals I begin with the underneath ones, using the 16240.20 brush. As usual, if I want light, almost white petals, I use orange oil; but to get a darker, more blurry effect I opt for open medium.

The background is feathered, then we move on to the outer petals. Note the white spot beside the center: it shows where the petals converge.

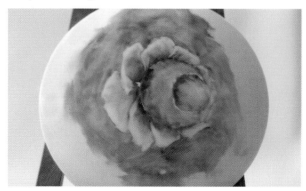

When the outer petals are finished, I move on to the corolla. Using the wipe-out tool I first outline the inner petals, then take my 16240.20 brush and orange oil to lighten the upper turned-back part, which is well-lit and so has to show up white.

Detailing the petals.

Detailing the center petals.

Lastly I use the brush and open medium to create all the petals of the corolla, bearing in mind the direction of the light and the that of the petals as well. I finish off the details of the center by working in the same way with a 16240.8 brush.

For the background I use the method already shown earlier in this chapter; according to the kind of overall design I want, I add either leaves or extra flowers. Then I round off with some careful feathering.

I check to be sure there are no unwanted specks of paint on the porcelain. If necessary I clean the surface, then it's time for firing.

The feathered background.

Rose (1997)
Finished and fired.

Grapes

First off I lay in a fairly dark background using China blue, bottle green and gold-violet. I then draw the grapes and leaves into the background with my 16240.20 brush.

The line of the bunch of grapes is essentially vertical: the bunch contains a number of grapes in a heavy, hanging mass, with the larger ones at the top and the smaller ones below. The overall shape is triangular. When I include grapes in a still life, I show a complete bunch; but if they are still on the vine, I only show a few individual grapes - the others are hidden by the leaves.

The grape is basically made up of two C strokes facing each other (see p. 19). I fill in the area between them with chartreuse and Sèvres blue. In all cases the colors are laid in using staggered strokes, then lightly feathered. My color scheme also takes account of the lighting, with the dark colors to one side and the light colors to the other. I add a few stalks with the 8826 brush, using wild mushroom or bottle green.

Grape Vase (1994)
Detail.

Vine leaves
Vine leaves are serrated and five-pointed. The central point is always the largest, with the four others being uniformly smaller.

The leaf also has five main veins, running from the stem to each of the five points.
To create my vine leaf, I begin with five rose leaves.

A vine leaf has five main veins.

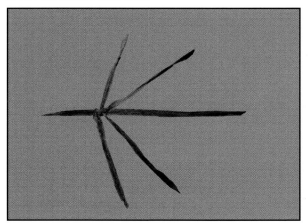

Begin with five rose leaves.

69

Opposite page: Fruit Bowl (1997)
*Impressionist method on white glass.
Two firings at 580° C.
Painted in the same way as the
hortensias, p. 54.*

Feathering, creation of the serrated edges, making the veins sharper.

Next I feather to even out the color of the five leaves and turn them into one single leaf. I bring out the serrations with the corner of the 16240.20 brush: for each serration I turn the piece slightly so as to be able to pull the brush towards me. I finish off the leaf by putting in the five veins.

Vine leaves have to be big and serrated. Paying close attention to all the details, I paint several of them, using - for example - moss green, lime green and yellow ocher (see the Grape Vase, p. 68). I round off the design by linking several leaves together with the 8826 brush, then add in branches with mushroom - as I did for the rose plant, but using straighter lines.

An Exception

The bunch of grapes is an exception in terms of the impressionist method. If you want your design to have real depth and solidity, you have to use several consecutive layers of paint, firing between each layer. As you work on each layer, bear in mind the direction of the light and don't forget that the bunch is triangular.

Mountains in Savoy (1997)
On enamelled metal sheet, fired at 780° C.

7. *Having fun*
A Mountain Landscape

To finish on a light note, let's try having fun with *a piece of enamelled metal sheet.* You can buy this in craft shops, usually in two sizes: 10 x 15 cm (4 x 6 ins) and 25 x 35 cm (10 x 14 ins). The painting is done with the standard paints before being fired at 780° C (1436° F). Once finished the picture can be framed. If you want to make a number plate for your house, buy a plaque with holes in it; after firing the painting is completely frost-resistant.

This little landscape was painted in less than an hour and fired only once. If necessary it could be retouched, then fired again. The brushes used were a 16240.20 and a 16240.10.

To start, I clean down a large-size plaque with methylated spirit and sketch in my design with a china pencil. I place the two foreground fir trees with the

The outline drawing.

73

I begin the actual painting with staggered brushstrokes for the sky. On my brush are peacock blue, soft blue and lilac.

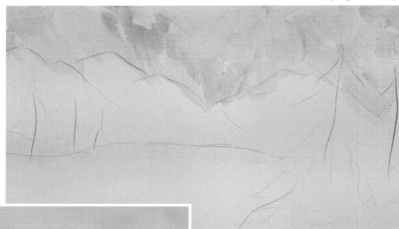

Feathering.

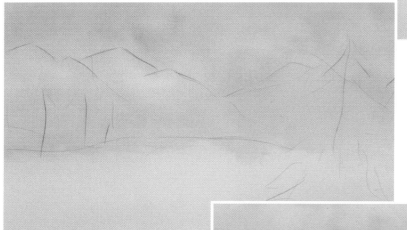

Once these colors are laid in, I feather, carefully drawing the paint down towards the far edge of the lake to create background color on the mountains.

To pull paint from the mountain peaks on to the sky, I turned the piece upside down.

For the mountains I make a mix of China blue and chocolate brown. *I turn the plaque upside down* so that I can paint the mountain peaks and draw the paint on to the sky.

Detailing the mountains.

I turn the plaque right side up again and clear the snow-covered areas away with the wipe-out tool, leaving just a fine line of paint to provide the silhouette. Lastly I feather the mountains. For the snow I use the 16240.10 brush and open medium - but no extra paint!

The lake.

For the lake I lay in peacock blue along the banks, with China blue and black green for the middle area. The light area is done with peacock blue spread very thin to give a pastel effect. For the land area between the mountains and the lake, I mix peacock blue, forest green and a hint of raspberry.

With my 16240.10 brush I draw in the trunks of the larches at the foot of the mountains, using black green and peacock blue. The foliage is then added in with the same colors.
For the foreground grass, I apply moss green and chocolate brown with the 16240.20 brush.
Then I feather.

The larches in the background, the grass in the foreground.

75

The first fir-tree is added to the foreground.

16240.20 brush, using black green, moss green and China blue. To distinguish the two trees from each other, I vary the proportions of my colors.

As for the foxgloves in the foreground, they're done with

moss green for the stems (8826.2 brush) and raspberry for the flowers (using the corner of the 16240.4 brush).

The rocks are painted in using

the same brush held at an angle: for this I mix wild mushroom and black green. The white areas are brought out using the wipe-out tool.

The second fir-tree is added and detailed; shadow is added at the base of the trees; details all round; then the finishing touches.

8. *Firing and retouching*

Firing probably holds no secrets for you, but we're going to go back over a few simple rules you really can't afford to forget.

The powdered paints we use are made by fusing various components at a temperature of around 1400° C (2550° F). The resultant material is then ground up and mixed with a certain proportion of flux to give ready-to-use paint powder. Since the flux has the effect of lowering the melting point of the glaze on the porcelain, it helps the color to penetrate.

I often hear it said that firing should be done at 750° or 800° C (1382° or 1472° F); but since this does not melt the glaze sufficiently, the color stays on the surface and lacks sheen. This also means that the design is not resistant to acids - lemon juice, vinegar, etc - nor to being put through the dishwasher. This is not really a problem in the case of purely decorative pieces such as vases, but for items such as plates a design fired in this way does not meet today's health protection standards. If you fire tableware colors at over 850° C (1562° F), the glaze will melt as it should, the paint will penetrate the glaze and the finish will be shiny. There will also be no danger to health.

To get an even more sparkling finish, you can fire at 950° C (1742° F). This is my normal practise, except for iron red and the cadmium colors. I have also long since given up beginning with a low-temperature firing and holding a mid-range temperature for a certain time: in my opinion this way of working is strictly for potters. Your firings should

Color Type	Firing Temperature	Firing Time
decor colors	780°-800° C 1435°-1470° F	max. 5 hours
iron colors	800° à 820°C 1470°-1508° F	''
cadmium colors	850° à 900°C 1562°-1652° F	''
tableware colors	Min. 850° C/1562° F	''
tableware colors	950°C/1742° F	max. 2 hours

follow the indications in the box on this page.

By "firing time" I mean mean the total time it takes to go from zero up to the desired temperature. These times apply to fiber-insulated kilns. If you're using a fire-brick kiln, do your best to adapt your firings to the parameters I suggest.

Note that for my blues and purples I fire at 1000° C (1832° F), as this brings out the full potential of these colors. When I work this way I fire for around 30 minutes - but I'm fortunate in that I have a very powerful kiln that gives rapid rises in temperature.

There you have a quick summary of the basic firing rules. If in doubt, check with someone who has the necessary experience or give me a call. It would be a shame to spoil a piece that has taken a lot of time and hard work.
The American technique for

porcelain usually means very fine layers of paint. Irregular coverage can pose real problems, for you can end up with some areas of your design very shiny, while others have a satin or even matt finish. The reason for this is that the less shiny areas have less paint - which means less flux - on them, so the color stays on the surface.

The solution is to repaint the defectively finished piece with a coat of flux. Mix the powdered flux with open medium until you get a smooth texture, then dilute with spike oil, adding a little more than is used for diluting porcelain colors in the classical techniques. I spread this mix all over the design with an 8274.6 brush, then stipple with a foam stick, working fast so as to get uniform coverage before the mix dries. Note that iron red and cadmium colors should never be re-coated with this mix: the result is an absolute disaster! The most effective means of avoiding this problem is to protect the areas in question with masking fluid before applying the flux.

When the flux has dried, fire at 850° or 950° C (1562° or 1742° F) - but don't forget to remove the masking fluid first!

Of course, a uniformly shiny finish is not absolutely necessary.

Personally, I enjoy playing with these accidental variations, as the different reflections they give can sometimes reinforce the impression of foreground and background.

Between firings

If you want to retouch your design after firing, or add a coat of flux, remember to take off the rough patches first. These are due to dust or tiny fragments of insulation material that fall on to the piece during firing. The cleaning is done by holding the piece under the tap and gently rubbing with very fine wet & dry sandpaper.
If you omit this step before moving on, you'll get a build-up of paint on the rough parts and these thicker areas will emerge from the next firing much more brightly-colored than their surroundings. As you rub down, take care not to damage the sheen of the porcelain itself: after all, it's the glaze and not the paint that provides the shine.

Runs

These are always the result of using too much open medium. It's much easier to paint with a nice oily mix, but if you overdo it you'll get runs even on a horizontal surface. During firing the medium will sizzle like oil in a frypan and this will make the paint run. The solution is to make sure there's just the right amount of medium on your brush when mixing (see Ch. 2).

Retouching after firing

If a design needs retouching after firing, I proceed as follows. I put on the paint as I would for a background - but much more lightly, since the aim is not to block out the design out but to modify and enrich it. In addition, retouching is usually aimed at specific areas; you rarely need to rework the entire design.

Let's take a head of hortensia as an example: maybe you want to give it a more pronounced spherical look. Remember that in painting generally, red tends to bring the subject closer and blue tends to make it seem more distant. With this principle in mind, begin by feathering all around the edge of the sphere with predominantly blue colors; then for the head itself, use paints with pink or purple as the dominant color. The paint is put on very lightly with the 16240.20 brush, then feathered to get rid of the brushmarks. When you've finished your retouching should show up not as added color, but quite simply as "atmosphere".

BOOKS ALREADY PUBLISHED OR SOON TO APPEAR

● PAINTING ON PORCELAIN
Composition and technique
Dony Alexiev

● PORCELAIN PAINTING
Catherine Bergoin

● THE ART OF FURNITURE
DECORATION
Paule & J-Claude Roussel

● MODELING IN CLAY
Patricia Liversain

● DECORATING PORCELAIN
The american technique
Catherine Bergoin

● THE PORCELAIN
PAINTER'S HANDBOOK
Aude Creuzé & Véronique Habègre

● ART EMBROIDERY
Liz Maidment

● AGATEWARE: POTTERY MAGIC
Mireille de Reilhan